LIFE ON THE TYNE

Life on the Tyne

Water Trades on the Lower River Tyne in the Seventeenth and Eighteenth Centuries, a Reappraisal

PETER D. WRIGHT
Newcastle University, UK

ASHGATE

© Peter D. Wright 2014

All rights reserved. No part of this publication may be reproduced, stored in a retrieval system or transmitted in any form or by any means, electronic, mechanical, photocopying, recording or otherwise without the prior permission of the publisher.

Peter D. Wright has asserted his right under the Copyright, Designs and Patents Act, 1988, to be identified as the author of this work.

Published by
Ashgate Publishing Limited
Wey Court East
Union Road
Farnham
Surrey, GU9 7PT
England

Ashgate Publishing Company
110 Cherry Street
Suite 3-1
Burlington, VT 05401-3818
USA

www.ashgate.com

British Library Cataloguing in Publication Data
A catalogue record for this book is available from the British Library

The Library of Congress has cataloged the printed edition as follows:
Wright, Peter D., 1960–
Life on the Tyne : water trades on the lower River Tyne in the seventeenth and eighteenth centuries, a reappraisal / by Peter D. Wright.
   pages cm
   Includes bibliographical references and index.
   ISBN 978-1-4724-2633-8 (hardcover : alk. paper) – ISBN 978-1-4724-2634-5 (ebook) – ISBN 978-1-4724-2635-2 (epub) 1. Shipping–England–Tyne River–History. 2. Inland water transportation–England–History. 3. Tyne River (England)–History. I. Title.
   HE664.Z7T969 2014
   386'.35409428709033--dc23
                                                                                2014008230

ISBN 9781472426338 (hbk)
ISBN 9781472426345 (ebk – PDF)
ISBN 9781472426352 (ebk – ePUB)

Printed in the United Kingdom by Henry Ling Limited,
at the Dorset Press, Dorchester, DT1 1HD

Contents

List of Figures	*vii*
List of Tables	*ix*
Glossary	*xi*
Preface	*xvii*

Introduction		1
1	Newcastle upon Tyne, the Coal Trade and the Local Economy	7
2	The River Tyne, its Navigability and the Problem of Ballast	23
3	The Water Trades Community of Tyneside	43
4	All Saints: The Growth of a Riverside Parish	63
5	Who Were the Owners? Networks of Working Boat and Ship Ownership	81
6	The Shipping Trade on the River Tyne	107
7	Ralph Jackson on Tyneside, 1749–1756: A Contemporary Perspective	133
8	Conclusions	161
Appendix: Ships 'Fixed' by Newcastle Hostman Jefferson between March and December 1756 as described in the Ralph Jackson Diaries		173
Bibliography		*177*
Index		*193*

List of Figures

2.1	Map of the River Tyne, 1650. 1650. By permission Tyne and Wear Archives and Museums	25
2.2	Captain Greenvile Collins's Chart of Tyne and Approaches, 1693. By permission Tyne and Wear Archives and Museums	29
2.3	Chart of the Tyne, 1700–1750. By permission Tyne and Wear Archives and Museums	31
2.4	Buck Brothers' engraving of Newcastle upon Tyne, 1745. © National Maritime Museum, Greenwich, London	34
2.5	Map of Newcastle upon Tyne by Corbridge, in Rev. Henry Bourne, *The History of Newcastle Upon Tyne* (1736). By permission Tyne and Wear Archives and Museums	35
3.1	The bond used by hostman Anthony Hood to bind his keelmen. By permission Newcastle City Libraries	52
3.2	Handbill listing keelmen employed by hostmen in 1750. By permission Newcastle City Libraries	59
4.1	Anglican parishes around the lower River Tyne, 1600–1800	64
5.1	Boat ownership on the River Tyne by decade	85
5.2	Types of working boat on the River Tyne, 1600–1750	86
5.3	Keels off Newcastle Quay. Detail from Buck Brothers' engraving of Newcastle upon Tyne, 1745. © National Maritime Museum, Greenwich, London	88
5.4	Ship ownership on the River Tyne by decade	93

List of Tables

1.1	Urban population in England (in thousands)	8
1.2	Total coal shipments from Newcastle upon Tyne 1600–1800 (five year averages)	13
2.1	Ballast shores listed in Newcastle Chamberlains' Accounts	42
3.1	Population of Newcastle between 1560 and 1831	44
3.2	Estimated populations of Newcastle keels and keelmen from coal exports	57
4.1	Water tradesmens' occupations from parish burial register	67
4.2	Marriages from All Saints parish registers, 1600–1800	70
5.1	Distribution of probate inventories showing boat or ship ownership among parishes surrounding the lower River Tyne	84
5.2	Estimated ship valuations from probate inventories, by decade	93
5.3	Henry Maddison's probate inventory, ships and boats 1634	102
6.1	Shipments in 1702–03 coastal outwards port book	116
6.2	Number of shipments of commodities other than coal or salt carried coastal outwards, 1702–03	118
6.3	Newcastle outward coastal destination ports used other than London, 1702–03	119
6.4	Newcastle inward coastal shipments, 1702–03	119
6.5	Ports of origin of inward coastal shipments to Newcastle, 1702–03	120
6.6	Imports listed from London into Newcastle, 1702–03	120
6.7	Shipments in 1702–03 coastal and 1698–99 overseas outward port books	122
6.8	Newcastle overseas outwards foreign destinations, 1698–99	123
6.9	Most common cargoes overseas outwards, 1698–99	123

6.10	Shipments in 1702–03 coastal and 1698–99 overseas inward port books	124
6.11	Ports of origin of overseas inwards shipments into Newcastle, 1698–99	125
6.12	Main commodities imported into the Tyne from overseas, 1698–99	126
6.13	Coastal outwards port book, 1756	127
6.14	Monthly shipments in coastal outwards port book, 1703 and 1756	127
6.15	Non-coal commodities coastal outwards, 1756	128
6.16	Coastal destinations other than London, 1756	128
6.17	Comparative levels of shipments to and from Newcastle upon Tyne and Bristol	131

Glossary

Ballast	Dense heavy material carried in ships to maintain stability when not carrying cargo. In this context usually sand or gravel.
Barque	Sailing ship of three or more masts with the fore and main masts square rigged and the mizzen(aft) mast rigged fore and aft.
Brig	Two-masted sailing ship square rigged on the fore mast and fore and aft rigged on the main mast.
Can-house	The house where the keelmen met to receive their orders and get paid by their hostman, the hostman also providing 'cans' of beer as part of their wages.
Can-woman	A woman employed by a hostman to manage the Can-house.
Carvel	A form of timber boat construction where the planks are placed edge to edge to give a smooth sided hull.
Chalder	An alternative word for Chaldron.
Chalder boat	A description of a small cargo (usually coal) carrying boat with its capacity being described by the number of chaldrons it can carry, i.e. a two- or three-chalder boat.
Chaldron	A measure of coal. One Newcastle chaldron weighed 52½ hundredweight, equivalent to just over two and a half tons. A London chaldron was smaller, being almost half the weight with a ratio to a Newcastle chaldron of 217:136.

Clinker	A form of timber boat construction where the planks of timber overlap one another, giving a characteristic appearance to the hull. Derived from ancient Scandinavian boat-building techniques.
Coal boat	A description of a coal-carrying river craft, which shares many of the characteristics of a keel, and is probably an alternative name for the keel.
Collier	A coal-carrying seagoing ship.
Fathom	A measure of the depth of water, being equivalent to six imperial feet.
Fittage	A term used to describe the process of arranging with the master of a collier to obtain a shipload of coal, have it loaded, often by keelmen from a keel, and manage the payment and customs clearance of the ship
Fitter	The person who arranges the fittage of a ship with coal.
Fore and aft	An arrangement of sails in which the sails are rigged along the centre line of a boat, with one sail in front of the mast and another behind.
Gaff sail	A sail rigged aft of the mast which has a timber boom at its base and an upwards tilted timber gaff along the top.
Harbour Bar	A shallow area of sand or gravel that occurs at the mouth of a river or entrance to a harbour, sometimes referred to as a Barr.
Hostman	A member of the Company of Hostmen of Newcastle upon Tyne who acted as agents for the sale of coal and grindstones.
Key	Another spelling of Quay.
Keel	A timber built, carvel-constructed coal-carrying river craft with a capacity of eight Newcastle Chaldrons, (21½ tons) of coal. Usually propelled with a large oar and steered with

	another, and often carrying a square sail on a mast, which could be lowered to pass under a bridge.
Keel-bullies	Another name for keelmen, or those who worked on the keels.
Keel-deeters	Women, usually wives and daughters of keelmen who swept the keels clear of coal residues, keeping them for their own use.
Keelman	A water tradesman who worked on the keels.
Keelroom	A place on the river bank where a keel could be moored. A rental fee of around 20s per year was charged by the Common Council of Newcastle for the use of each keelroom.
Lighter	A general term for a cargo-carrying river craft.
Master Mariner	The captain of a sea going ship.
Mizzen Mast	The rear most mast in a ship or boat with more than one mast.
Neap tides	The tides with the smallest range between high and low tides, usually occurring midway between spring high tides.
Norway boat	A type of clinker built rowing boat, similar in design to Scandinavian craft.
Pann Keels	A type of keel that was used to ferry poor quality coal to the salt panns, and to carry salt and other cargo.
Salt Panns	Salt-making works where water was evaporated from seawater, often using coal, to obtain salt.
Sculler	An open river craft propelled by a single oar over the stern, often used as a ferry.
Shipwright	A ship or boat builder or ship repairer.
Skipper	The person who was in command of and steered a keel.

Snow rig	Three-masted sailing ship with square sails on the fore and main mast and a loose footed gaff mizzen sail set from a small mizzen mast.
Spring tides	The monthly high tides when the tidal range between high and low tides is at its greatest.
Sprit sail	A rectangular sail usually mounted on a piece of timber projecting over the bow of a boat called a bowsprit.
Square rigged	A sailing ship rigged with transverse square sails hanging from timber beams called yards attached to the mast.
Staith	A timber or stone structure built on the shore of a river with relatively deep water alongside to allow the mooring and loading of ships or boats.
Staithman	A person of some significance in the coal trade who managed the use of the coal staiths and controlled the loading of coal and unloading of ballast.
Staithroom	The piece of riverbank where the Common Council of Newcastle gave permission for the building of a staith, often associated with a way-leave for a wagon way, charging annual rent of around £10 for the staith and its associated keelrooms.
Stay sail	A triangular sail rigged in front of a mast.
Swape	A term used to describe the large oar used to propel a keel.
Top sail	A sail rigged at the top of a mast, which may be a square sail or a fore and aft sail above a gaff.
Trow	A sailing barge that worked on the river Severn, with either a square sail or fore and aft rig.
Vend	The amount of coal sold by an individual hostman or group over a period of time, chaldrons per week, month or year.

Wagon-way	The timber and later iron track ways that carried the coal-carrying wagons from the collieries to the river-side coal staiths.
Waterman	A water tradesman, the term often being interchangeable with the terms keelman and wherryman.
Way-leave	Permit to build a coal-carrying wagon-way across private land, for which the land owner charged a rent.
Wharf	An alternative term for a quayside or staith.
Wherry	A cargo-carrying river craft, that did not carry coal, and was often used for carrying people. Usually of timber clinker construction with a fore and aft rig.
Wherryman	A waterman who worked on a wherry.

Sources: For the words and terms used in relation to the keels and coal industry during the eighteenth century: J. Brand, *The History and Antiquities of the Town of Newcastle upon Tyne*, (London, 1789). For other nautical, boating and shipping terms: A. Osler and T. Barrow, *Tall Ships Two Rivers* (Newcastle upon Tyne: Keepdate, 1993); M. Stammers, *Sailing Barges of the British Isles* (Stroud: The History Press, 2008).

Preface

This book is the ultimate outcome of a lifetime of recreational boating, mainly on the Northeast coast of England, during which my frequent voyages up the River Tyne from its mouth to the Tyne bridges led to a fascination with the changing environment, as over 50 years the heavy industrial scenery progressively disappeared to reveal once more the green riverbanks that must have existed hundreds of years ago. The landscape along the river remains littered with many of the scars left by over 400 years of industrial development, though they have been softened by the passage of time and the return of trees and grassy banks. These changes stimulated my interest in the evolution of the industries that had originally existed along the lower Tyne and particularly the water trades communities that supported them, culminating in a period of detailed academic study and a doctoral thesis from which this book has evolved.

None of this would have been possible without a great deal of help and support. I must first express my appreciation to the School of History, Classics and Archaeology at Newcastle University, and in particular to the Head of School at the time, Professor Jeremy Boulton, for enabling me, upon my retirement from a career in the National Health Service and Newcastle University as an Academic Surgeon, to pursue this lifetime interest in boats, the city where I have spent most of my life, Newcastle upon Tyne, and its history and development. When I approached Jeremy about the prospect of further developing my interest in water trades on the river Tyne within the more structured discipline of a postgraduate degree, I found nothing but enthusiastic and constructive support from him and from the entire department. The support I received from both Jeremy and Professor Helen Berry cannot be underestimated and were essential to the completion of the initial studies, which led to the doctoral thesis. Their subsequent help and advice as the work evolved has been invaluable and a significant contribution towards the preparation of this book. In addition, I am also particularly grateful to Dr Joan Allan, Dr Graham Butler, Dr Fred Milton and Professor Keith Wrightson for their helpful comments and wise advice, which has been much appreciated. I should also like to express my appreciation to the staff of the Newcastle University Library, and particularly those who work in Special Collections for their unstinting support. The staffs in the search room at Tyne and Wear Archives and Museums, at the Discovery Museum, and also Sarah Mulligan and her staff in the Local Studies section of Newcastle City Libraries, were also most helpful in their diligent searches for an ever increasing range of documents. Particular mention must be made of Jonathan Bush in the Search Room in Durham University Library at Castle Green for his assistance in reviewing numerous probate inventories and also to Francis Gotto from the North East Inheritance project for his assistance with collating the data from the probate inventories. I should also like to thank Jenny Parker and Teeside Archives for their kindness and assistance with access to the Ralph Jackson Diaries. The staff at the Borthwick Institute in York University were also most helpful in their provision of information about northeast wills and inventories, and I must also acknowledge the efficiency and helpfulness of The National Archives at Kew, without whose assistance the work on reviewing the Newcastle Port Books would not have been possible. There are a number of other individuals who merit special mention, in particular Dr Adrian Osler, formerly maritime historian at Tyne Wear Archives and Museums service, who provided much support and advice throughout the project. I am indebted to Sir Leonard Fenwick CBE, chairman of the Incorporated Companies of the City of Newcastle upon Tyne, whose unsolicited gift of a private publication of the diaries of Ralph Jackson opened the way to the seventh chapter of this book. I am also indebted to Dr Leigh Shaw-Taylor and to Professor Robin Pearson for their kindness in providing advice and access to their data.

Last, but by no means least, I am deeply indebted to my wife Ilva, and the rest of my family for their patience and encouragement over the years that this project has taken to complete. Without their support none of this would have been possible.

Peter Wright,
February 2014

Introduction

Newcastle upon Tyne and the other communities surrounding the lower part of the River Tyne underwent a period of rapid economic and social change between 1600 and 1800, and, as with any community, the way in which trade developed with any commodity was of necessity a reflection of the geography and physical environment prevailing at the time. Newcastle was the commercial centre of the coal trade, and, being positioned on the lower river Tyne about eight miles from the sea, it was at the centre of those mining communities which surrounded that part of the river. This was largely that lower section affected by the tides extending from the mouth of the river in the East to the upper limits of the tidal Tyne between Newburn and Wylam in the West. The tidal nature of the river, with its consequent daily variations in depth, made it difficult for heavily laden ships to move freely at all states of the tide, and a process thus evolved of moving heavy and bulky cargoes such as coal from the staiths on the river bank to waiting ships anchored closer to the mouth of the river and the sea. Traditional boats called keels were used move the coal, and these were operated by a particular group of tradesmen known as keelmen. These water tradesmen were an important group of people in the community, conveying freight and people to the collier brigs, waiting close to the mouth of the river. The collier brigs would carry their cargo either to other parts of England, particularly London, or to continental Europe. The nature of the river, with its variable depth and winding course, and the presence of a low bridge in Newcastle, meant that the key to its economic success in providing vast quantities of coal for London and other towns was this ability to transport coal in boats from the riverbank to the waiting colliers close to the mouth of the river. Consequently, those who operated these boats and made the transport system work were essential in ensuring the success of the trade, and it cannot be stressed enough that the efforts of these river tradespeople were largely responsible for sustaining the extraordinary growth in the North-East coal trade during the seventeenth and eighteenth centuries. This burgeoning coal trade, mainly with the rapidly developing metropolis of London, made Newcastle and the growing coal fields surrounding the lower river Tyne a uniquely important part of England in this period.¹ Most of the historical literature describes the work of the coal-carrying keelmen, but does not indicate whether they or other types of watermen carried other significant exports, or the large quantities of incoming trade, although Hatcher implies that they did, but provides little supporting evidence.² It remains unclear whether the coal owners or their agents, the hostmen, were involved in the trade in other commodities, or whether their keels were used to provide intermediate transport for any commodities other than coal. There is a reference in the Orders and Minutes of the Company of Hostmen to pann keels or pann boats that were not measured in the same way as the keels. Pann keels were probably used to carry pan coals which were small coals destined for local industrial use, or salt from the salt-pans, most of which were close to the mouth of the river at North and South Shields. On occasion these pann keels were used illicitly for transporting coal to colliers as a way of evading coal duties, and the Company attempted to impose significant penalties upon those who misused these boats for carrying coal destined for shipment.³

Despite its crucial importance, the history, size and nature of the whole community of water tradespeople on the Tyne has been largely under-explored. This is surprising, considering their key economic role, and still more so given their known political activity and identity. It is apparent from the available documents that there were a number of different cargo-carrying river craft – there are references to lighters and wherrys in addition to keels, indeed Brand notes that there was an attempt to create a fraternity of watermen and wherrymen, distinct and separate from the keelmen, in 1656. The details of these aspects of trade have been obscured in the literature by the overwhelming quantity of information relating to the coal trade, the keelmen and the politics surrounding

---

[1] H. Bourne, *The History of Newcastle upon Tyne* (Newcastle upon Tyne: John White, 1736; rep., Newcastle upon Tyne: Frank Graham, 1980); J. Brand, *The History and Antiquities of the Town of Newcastle upon Tyne*, 2 vols (London, 1789); J. Baillie, *An Impartial History of the Town and County of Newcastle upon Tyne and its Vicinity* (Newcastle upon Tyne: Vint and Anderson, 1801); E. Mackenzie, *Descriptive and Historical Account of the Town and County of Newcastle upon Tyne* (Newcastle upon Tyne: Mackenzie and Dent, 1827); R.J. Charleton, *Newcastle Town* (London: Walter Scott, 1885; rep., 1978); J.U. Nef, *The Rise of the British Coal Industry*, 2 vols (London: George Routledge & Sons, 1932), Vol. 2; S. Middlebrook, *Newcastle upon Tyne: Its Growth and Achievement*. (Newcastle upon Tyne: Newcastle Journal, 1950); J. Hatcher, *The History of the British Coal Industry*, Vol. 1, *Before 1700: Towards the Age of Coal* (Oxford: Clarendon Press, 1993).

[2] Hatcher, *The History of the British Coal Industry*, p. 467.

[3] F.W. Dendy, *Extracts from the Records of the Company of Hostmen of Newcastle Upon Tyne*, Surtees Society, 105 (Durham: Published for the Society, 1901), p. 93 with note.

them.[4] A wide range of material has been published about elements of the history of the coal trade on the River Tyne and containing references to keels, keelmen and hostmen; this literature dates back to *Chorographia* in the mid seventeenth century.[5] Most of the earlier publications were a series of broad-based accounts of the history of Newcastle and the surrounding area appearing in the latter half of the eighteenth century and at intervals throughout the nineteenth century.[6] During the later part of the nineteenth century and into the twentieth century study of the history of the trades union movement was in vogue, and the keelmen, with their history of strike action, were studied frequently as proto-trades unionists.[7] Later in the twentieth century a number of very detailed studies of the evolution of the British coal industry were published.[8] Each of these included accounts of the contribution of hostmen, keelmen and keels on the River Tyne to the development of the coal industry over several centuries up to 1850, when they disappeared as a meaningful part of the coal trade. Throughout all of these publications, from the earliest to the latest, the primary sources of information about the trade on the Tyne were very limited. Many of the more recent texts simply refer to the earlier texts as their source; however, some of these early sources, such as Brand, are particularly well referenced.[9] The main source for all of Brand's references to the water trades, keels, hostmen and keelmen were the records of the Company of Hostmen. There are one or two references to minutes of the Common Council of Newcastle upon Tyne,

---

[4] Brand, *History and Antiquities*, p. 361.

[5] William Gray, *Chorographia, or a Survey of Newcastle Upon Tyne* (Newcastle upon Tyne: Frank Graham, 1970. Originally published 1649).

[6] Bourne, *History of Newcastle upon Tyne*; Brand, *The History and Antiquities*; Mackenzie, *Descriptive and Historical Account*; J. Guthrie, *The River Tyne, its History and Resources* (Newcastle upon Tyne: Andrew Reid, 1880); Charleton, *Newcastle Town*; Welford, *History of Newcastle and Gateshead*, 5 vols (London: Walter Scott, 1885), Vol. 3.

[7] S. Middlebrook *Newcastle upon Tyne*; J.M. Fewster, 'The Keelmen of Tyneside in the Eighteenth Century', *Durham University Journal*, 50 (1957) Pt. 1 pp. 24–33, Pt. 2 pp. 66–75, Pt. 3 pp. 111–23; D.J. Rowe, 'The Decline of the Keelmen in the Nineteenth Century', *Northern History*, 4 (1969), pp. 111–31. J.M. Fewster, *The Keelmen of Tyneside: Labour Organisation and Conflict in the North-East Coal Industry, 1600–1830* (Woodbridge: Boydell & Brewer, 2011).

[8] Nef, *The Rise of the British Coal Industry*; T.S. Ashton and J. Sykes, *The Coal Industry in the Eighteenth Century* (Manchester: Manchester University Press, 1929); W.S. Mitcalfe, 'The History of the Keelmen and Their Strike in 1822', *Archaeologia Aeliana*, 4th ser., 14 (1937), pp. 1–17; M.W. Flinn, *The History of the British Coal Industry*, Vol. 2, *1700–1830: The Industrial Revolution* (Oxford: Oxford University Press, 1984); Hatcher, *The History of the British Coal Industry*.

[9] Brand, *History and Antiquities*.

which often concerned disputes involving hostmen, together with references to petitions made to parliament over disputes about the management of the keelmen's hospital charity. There were a number of cases of disputes referred by the hostmen to magistrates for settlement. Most of the other authors have used the same sources, quoted either from earlier publications, from the extracts of the records of the Company of Hostmen, published by Dendy in 1901,[10] or directly from the records themselves. The most recent contribution is that of J.M. Fewster, whose review of the keelmen and their role in the coal trade explores in greater depth many of the local and national documentary sources used by earlier authors, and focuses mainly on their contribution to labour organization and industrial conflict in the coal industry.[11] Fewster gives a vivid picture of the keelmen and the part they played in labour history and the evolution of the trades union movement, but does not explore in such detail the wider aspects of the water trades communities on the river.

During the seventeenth and eighteenth centuries the hostmen and coal owners held a monopoly of power in Newcastle. Not only were they controlling the coal trade, but they also formed a majority of the Aldermen and Common Council. In addition, most of the Magistrates were members of the Hostmen's Company. Common to all of these historical bodies is the influence on them of one interest group in the town, the Company of Hostmen. A consistent feature of the history of Newcastle was the power of the hostmen, magistrates and council over the running of the town and its trade, their strategy being based almost entirely on self-interest and profit rather than the benefit of the wider community. This philosophy extended beyond the coal trade and the hostmen to other guilds, notably the monopoly imposed by the Company of Shipwrights, as exemplified by the papers relating to Thomas Cliffe and Ralph Gardner, who had a prolonged battle with the Burgesses of Newcastle between 1650 and 1658.[12] With their history of a consistently self-interested approach to economic life, the records of the Company of Hostmen and any other organization with which they were involved, including the Common Council and the Magistrates, were likely to be significantly lacking in objectivity, and to 'spin' events in a way that worked to their own advantage. With this in mind, their accounts may not have been the most accurate basis upon which to write a history of Newcastle and the trade of the River Tyne. Notwithstanding the dominance of coal, the range of

---

[10] Dendy, *Company of Hostmen*.
[11] J.M. Fewster, *The Keelmen of Tyneside*.
[12] R. Howell, ed., *Monopoly on the Tyne, 1650–58: Papers relating to Ralph Gardner* (Newcastle upon Tyne: Society of Antiquaries of Newcastle upon Tyne, 1978); Papers Relating to Ralph Gardner, TWAM.

trading activities on the river Tyne extended far beyond the coal industry and into a wide range of other imports and exports that supported the flourishing communities that developed in Newcastle and along the river in the seventeenth and eighteenth centuries, and was reflected in the nature and composition of the water trades community that supported them.

Two secondary sources are of particular value in any study of Newcastle during the early modern period. First in their seminal work *The Making of an Industrial Society: Whickham 1560-1765*, David Levine and Keith Wrightson provide a detailed insight into the development of an industrial community in North East England which, together with their earlier related work, 'Death in Whickham', has enormous relevance to the study of the water trades on the lower Tyne.[13] This work provides a perceptive analysis of the changes that occurred as the industrial community developed in Whickham, a parish bordering the lower River Tyne intimately involved in the coal trade. Similarly, the important works of Joyce Ellis, elaborating upon the social and industrial development of Newcastle during the seventeenth and eighteenth centuries, forms a substantial basis of literature.[14]

In the light of the relatively restricted range of sources used by many earlier historians of Newcastle a reappraisal of many wider aspects of the historiography of the town in the seventeenth and eighteenth centuries is long overdue. This book explores in depth the water trades community during this period using a number of previously underused primary sources including parish registers, probate inventories and exchequer port books.[15] These sources have allowed a deeper insight into the nature of the growth and development of the wider water trades community that occurred in the town in response to the coal driven economic stimulus. Of particular interest was that part of the town's population that worked in the water-related trades along the River Tyne and underpinned

---

[13] D. Levine and K. Wrightson, *The Making of an Industrial Society: Whickham 1560-1765* (Oxford: Clarendon Press, 1991); K. Wrightson and D. Levine, 'Death in Whickham', in *Famine, Disease and the Social Order in Early Modern Society*, ed. J. Walter and R. Schofield (Cambridge: Cambridge University Press, 1989), pp. 129-65.

[14] J. Ellis, 'A Bold Adventurer: The Business Fortunes of William Cotesworth, c. 1668-1726', *Northern History*, 17 (1981), pp. 117-32; J. Ellis, 'The Decline and Fall of the Tyneside Salt Industry, 1660-1790: A Re-Examination', *Economic History Review*, 2nd ser., 33 (1980), pp. 45-58; J. Ellis, *The Georgian Town 1680-1840* (New York: Palgrave, 2001); J. Ellis, 'The "Black Indies": The Economic Development of Newcastle, c. 1700-1840', in *Newcastle Upon Tyne: a Modern History*, ed. R. Lancaster and B. Colls (Chichester: Phillimore, 2001), pp. 1-26.

[15] P.D. Wright, 'Water Trades on the Lower River Tyne in the Seventeenth and Eighteenth Centuries' (PhD diss., Newcastle University, 2011).

the successful coal trade. We are fortunate that many of the parish registers relating to the riverside communities contain details of occupation throughout the seventeenth and eighteenth centuries, enabling some aspects of the demography of the water trades communities to be explored. The probate inventories provide us with a clearer understanding of the patterns of ownership of both the working river craft and shipping using the river; they also reveal the development of associated business networks. These illustrate the impact of the economic growth that was driven by the coal trade. This growth fostered a growing middle class with an attendant rise in consumer demand for more luxurious foods and household goods in the town and its hinterland; and this in turn created growth in the non-coal import trade from home and abroad. This is clearly shown by the very wide range of commodities imported into Newcastle that can be found in the exchequer port books of the time. It was fortunate that the previously unpublished diaries of an apprentice hostmen, Ralph Jackson, became available. These diaries seem to have been almost unknown to modern historians and have not been mentioned even in recent studies of the period. They provide a detailed insight into the life of an apprentice living among people of the 'middling sort' in Newcastle during the mid eighteenth century. In addition, they provide an illuminating account of the details of the work of a hostman in his management of the coal trade along the river and the circumstances under which it was undertaken. These diaries draw together many of the threads that have emerged in this re-appraisal of a critical period in the history of Newcastle upon Tyne, a time when it was arguably one of the most important providers of the energy required to underpin the rapid growth of London and England as a whole.

Chapter 1
Newcastle upon Tyne, the Coal Trade and the Local Economy

In 1726 Daniel Defoe, in a description of his tour through Great Britain, wrote of his first impressions when approaching Newcastle from County Durham:

> From hence the road to Newcastle gives a View of the inexhausted Store of Coal and Coal Pits, from whence not London only, but all of the South Part of England is continually supplied: ... Newcastle is a spacious, extended, infinitely populous Place; 'tis seated upon the River Tyne, which here is a noble, large and deep River, and Ships of any reasonable Burthen may come up safely to the very Town. ... the wall of the Town runs parallel ... with the River leaving a spacious Piece of Ground before it between the Water and the Wall, that Ground, being well Wharf'd up, and fac'd with Free-Stone, makes the longest and largest Key for landing and lading Goods that is to be seen in England.[1]

This view of Newcastle upon Tyne in the eighteenth century epitomized the bustling centre of trade and commerce that the town had become as a consequence of the burgeoning coal trade and its impact upon the town and its surroundings. Newcastle and the other communities surrounding the lower part of the River underwent a period of rapid economic and social change between 1600 and 1800, and even by Elizabethan times Newcastle had become a significant town that boasted a population of around 10,000; by 1700 it was one of the largest in the country (Table 1.1).[2] This development was underpinned by the large reserves of coal in the hinterland of the lower Tyne, which were being mined and exported

---

[1] Daniel Defoe, *A Tour Thro' the Whole Island of Great Britain* (London, 1726, London: Frank Cass & Co., 1968), p. 659.

[2] E.A Wrigley, 'Urban Growth and Agricultural Change: England and the Continent in the Early Modern Period', *Journal of Interdisciplinary History*, 15: 4 (1985), pp. 683–728; T.S, Willan, *The Inland Trade* (Manchester: Manchester University Press, 1976), p. 32; P. Corfield, 'Urban Development in England and Wales in the Sixteenth and Seventeenth Centuries', in *The Tudor and Stuart Town, 1530–1688: A Reader in English Urban History*, ed. J. Barry (London: Longman, 1990), p. 46; C.W. Chalklin, *The Provincial Towns of*

Table 1.1   Urban population in England (in thousands)

c. 1600	c. 1670	c. 1700	c. 1750	c. 1801
London 200	London 475	London 575	London 675	London 959
Norwich 15	Norwich 20	Norwich 30	Bristol 50	Manchester 89
York 12	Bristol 20	Bristol 21	Norwich 36	Liverpool 83
Bristol 12	York 12	*Newcastle 16*	*Newcastle 29*	Birmingham 74
Newcastle 10	*Newcastle 12*	Exeter 14	Birmingham 24	Bristol 60
Exeter 9	Colchester 9	York 12	Liverpool 22	Leeds 53
Plymouth 8	Exeter 9	Gt Yarmouth 10	Manchester 18	Sheffield 46
Salisbury 6	Chester 8	Birmingham 9	Leeds 16	Plymouth 43
Kings Lynn 6	Ipswich 8	Chester 8	Exeter 16	*Newcastle 42*

Source: Wrigley, 'Urban Growth and Agricultural Change', pp. 686–7. The data in this table is taken from Wrigley's published table to highlight the relative size of the population of Newcastle between 1600 and 1800.

at an increasing rate, the majority of the coal being transported coastwise to London and other towns throughout the East and South of England.[3] These changes in Newcastle and its surrounding communities occurred in the context of Britain's flourishing trade with the rest of Europe and colonies throughout the world. From the late seventeenth century to the end of the eighteenth Britain was in the process of an evolution that combined an increasing population (from 6.5 million in 1680 to 8.7 million in 1801) with developing urbanization.[4] With the increasing size and concentration of population, Britain became a highly developed commercialized economy, associated with a growing proportion of the working population being involved in non-agricultural activities – all part of the progression that became known as the Industrial Revolution.[5] Concurrent with this process, the role of Britain in the world changed to a role of dominance, both in world trade and militarily. Throughout the seventeenth and eighteenth centuries the development of the coal industry was taking place against the

---

Georgian England, A Study of the Building Process, 1740–1820 (London: Edward Arnold, 1974), p. 14.

[3] Hatcher, *The History of the British Coal Industry*, p. 465.

[4] T.S. Willan, *River Navigation in England 1600–1750* (London: Frank Cass & Co., 1964), p. 1; E.A. Wrigley, 'British Population During the Long Eighteenth Century', in *The Cambridge Economic History of Modern Britain*, Vol. 1, ed. R. Floud and P. Johnson (Cambridge: Cambridge University Press, 2004), p. 57.

[5] J. Mokyr, 'Accounting for the Industrial Revolution', in *The Cambridge Economic History of Modern Britain*, Vol. 1. p. 2.

background of a national economy that was being stimulated by the increasing flow of raw materials and manufactured goods to and from the American, Asian and African outposts of Empire.[6]

Britain's internal markets at this time were well developed, and its infrastructure was rapidly improving, providing a healthy environment for would-be entrepreneurs who were willing to take risks and work hard. By 1688 it was already a wealthy and sophisticated country by many standards,[7] and this increased activity was reflected in the rapidly growing coal industry and export from the North East coast of England. It was towards the second half of our period that the process known as the Industrial Revolution began. The reasons it occurred in Europe, and in Britain in particular, were partly the availability of coal and other energy resources, but also the 'ghost acreage' of colonies abroad. In addition to being a source of raw materials, these colonies provided a demand for manufactured goods, which in itself stimulated growth and development; but though consumption increased, investment nationally remained relatively low.[8] One of the reasons Britain was particularly well placed to take advantage of these changes, argues Joel Mokyr, was that it had the benefit of a social elite with an unusual interest in technical improvement and an ability and willingness to absorb and apply useful ideas generated elsewhere. In addition Britain had the makings of a well-functioning transport system favoured by nature and improved by investment, and the propitious location of some key resources, especially coal.[9]

These progressive changes emphasized the need for improved communication between centres that would enable trade and the movement of goods and people. Transport patterns within England were evolving during this period, largely driven by internal trade in a wide variety of commodities. Particularly during the later part of this period, technological innovation and change enabled a rapid evolution in the methods and quantity of production, which, together with rationalization of production, led to the development of larger units forming

---

[6]   S.L. Engerman and P.K. O'Brien, 'The Industrial Revolution in Global Perspective', in *The Cambridge Economic History of Modern Britain*, Vol. 1, p. 458.

[7]   Mokyr, 'Accounting for the Industrial Revolution', p. 27.

[8]   Mokyr, 'Accounting for the Industrial Revolution', p. 15. 'Whereas spectacular inventions were made and developed in the second half of the eighteenth century, the true miracle of the industrial revolution was that it did not peter out, but was followed after 1820 by a series of secondary inventions which although less spectacular, provided the "muscle" to drive the downward trend in production costs and the spread of applications that maintained the momentum of the Industrial Revolution'; N.F.R. Crafts, *British Economic Growth During the Industrial Revolution* (Oxford: Clarendon Press, 1985), p. 90.

[9]   Mokyr, 'Accounting for the Industrial Revolution', p. 17.

factories in many of the major centres. This meant that the need for improved transport between centres became more pressing. These internal forces, together with an increasing external demand for raw materials and manufactured goods from the wider Empire, stimulated the development of more sophisticated means of transport between the centres of production and consumption and the port cities for export. J.A. Chartres observed that:

> The history of transport in the sixteenth century remains largely unwritten and apart from Willan's work on water carriage, little of substance exists for the seventeenth century. The linkages between farm and market, between coal staith and consumer and between weaver and clothier were all largely by road. Developments in the road transport industry and costs of carriage underpinned the development of the home market.[10]

Overland communication between centres remained difficult during the seventeenth century, most routes were suitable only for foot or packhorse carriers, the movement of larger loads carried by cart were limited by the poor road system.[11] David Hey, in his description of the evolution of overland transport, emphasizes the poor state of roads in the seventeenth century, which only began to improve with the development of increasing numbers of turnpike roads in the eighteenth century.[12] The growth in demands made upon the road system had led to the introduction in 1662 of the first Acts to take responsibility for the repair of roads out of the local parish community and into the realm of turnpike toll finance; and by the 1750s England's trunk roads were largely turnpiked. This included the Great North Road, which was turnpiked north beyond Newcastle by 1747, and additionally from Newcastle to Durham, Sunderland and North Shields by 1749.[13] These changes extended the potential markets for goods and allowed the faster and cheaper transport of people and posts – and consequently the movement of news and information.[14] The introduction of the longer wheel-based wagon in the mid sixteenth century spread quickly over the next 50 years,

---

[10] J.A. Chartres, *Internal Trade in England 1500–1700* (London: Macmillan, 1977), p. 39.

[11] M. Spufford, *The Great Reclothing of Rural England: Petty Chapmen and their wares in the Seventeenth Century* (London: The Hambledon Press, 1984), pp. 18–22; T.C. Barker and D. Gerhold, *The Rise and Rise of Road Transport, 1700–1900*, Economic History Society Series (Basingstoke: Macmillan, 1993), pp. 34–6.

[12] D. Hey, *Packmen, Carriers and Packhorse Roads* (Leicester: Leicester University Press, 1980), p. 86.

[13] W. Albert, *The Turnpike Road System in England 1663–1840* (Cambridge: Cambridge University Press, 1972), p. 48.

[14] Chartres, *Internal Trade*, p. 41.

improving transport by road. Growth continued during the seventeenth century, with the development of the larger stage wagon with a swivelling front axle, as a result of which there was a further increase in road traffic; Chartres estimates a doubling of scheduled services between 1637 and 1715.[15]

The key role of river and coastal transport was emphasized by T.S. Willan, who noted that trade in all the major river basins in England tended to gravitate towards the river, then downstream, with the most effective route of communication between many regions proving to be the coastal route.[16] The synergy between overland and water-based transport is perhaps best illustrated by Hey's account of the significant role of Bawtry as an inland port fed by a variety of pathways from its surrounding Yorkshire and Derbyshire hinterland; the city provided a route for import and export of commodities to and from both the rest of England and abroad.[17] The construction of a network of canals in the eighteenth century enhanced the ability to transport large quantities of freight at acceptable cost between many centres of population in the southern two thirds of England. This did not become an option in the northern one third of England, where trade tended to gravitate to the main rivers, exemplified by the Tyne, where the vast majority of trade with the rest of the country was conducted by water. Carriage of goods on rivers and waterways had very considerable cost advantages in terms of cost per ton for each mile carried, resulting in the continued development and improvement of river navigations and the building of canals. In the seventeenth century people tended to regard the coasting trade as an extension of the river system. However, the balance between the two is difficult to estimate because of the existence of statistical resources for the coasting trade that are not available for the inland trades, thus leading to a possible exaggeration of the former's role in the totality of transport provision.[18] Available evidence suggests that the amount of coastal shipping increased substantially, over threefold, in the seventeenth century, with tonnage of coal-related shipping increasing from 28,223 in 1609 to 78,212 in 1702, with consequent reductions in freight charges creating further potential expansion of market share.[19]

The trade of the North East coast of England was dominated by coal, which because of its bulk tended to be transported by sea. Newcastle upon Tyne was the greatest coal port in the country during this period, and by the late 1590s

---

[15] Chartres, *Internal Trade*, p. 40.
[16] Willan, *River Navigation in England*, p. 3.
[17] Hey, *Packmen, Carriers and Packhorse Roads*, p. 105.
[18] Chartres, *Internal Trade*, p. 42.
[19] Chartres, *Internal Trade*, pp. 39–44.

it was exporting 26,277 tons of coal to Europe, and shipping 186,454 tons coastwise.[20] A number of attempts have been made to estimate the annual tonnage of coal exported in both the coastal and overseas trade from Newcastle in the seventeenth and eighteenth centuries; first attempts were made by Dendy in an appendix to his *Records of the Company of Hostmen of Newcastle upon Tyne* of 1901, and these were included by Nef in his *Rise of the British Coal Industry* published in 1932. The most authoritative account of exports for the seventeenth century comes from Hatcher, in his critical re-analysis of the figures from Nef and Dendy, particularly those for the earlier part of the seventeenth century, which he published in *The History of the British Coal Industry* in 1993. The figures collected by Dendy for the years between 1700 and 1800 appear to be authentic.[21] A combination of these figures has been used to construct Table 1.2, which shows that Newcastle progressively increased its exports of coal between 1600 and 1800, by which time it was exporting over one million tons each year. In addition, Newcastle became an active centre of general trade, exporting other commodities such as glass and salt in addition to coal, and importing grain and other consumables. In 1726, Defoe referred to Newcastle as:

> a spacious, extended infinitely populous place, 'tis seated upon the River Tyne, ... The Situation of the Town to Landward is exceeding unpleasant, and the Buildings very close and old ... which, together with the Smoke of the Coals, makes it not the pleasantest Place in the World to live in.[22]

The hinterland of Newcastle was quite unusual, in that it was relatively isolated from the rest of England, particularly with respect to the long distance transport of heavy materials in large volumes, by virtue of the inadequacy of the road system. The most effective mode of communication was by local road, and latterly wagon-way, to the river and down to its mouth, and then by sea, either abroad or to other parts of the country. The destination for most of the coal exported from the Tyne was London, which had rapidly increased in size and activity, and had become the driving force behind the development of the

---

[20] T.S. Willan, *Studies in Elizabethan Foreign Trade* (Manchester: Manchester University Press, 1959), p. 67; Wrigley, 'Urban Growth and Agricultural Change', p. 32; Hatcher, *The History of the British Coal Industry*, p. 488.

[21] F.W. Dendy, *Extracts from the Records of the Company of Hostmen of Newcastle Upon Tyne*' Surtees Society, 105 (Durham, Published for the Society, 1901), pp. 260–61; J.U. Nef, *The Rise of the British Coal Industry*, 2 vols (London: George Routledge & Sons Ltd., 1932), Appendix B; Hatcher, *The History of the British Coal Industry*, p. 497.

[22] Defoe, *A Tour Thro' the Whole Island of Great Britain*, p. 660.

Table 1.2 Total coal shipments from Newcastle upon Tyne 1600–1800 (five year averages)

Period	Chaldrons	Tons
1606–1610	113,295 (2)	300,232
1611–1615	108,078 (4)	286,407
1616–1620	111,938 (3)	296,636
1621–1625	143,207 (5)	379,499
1626–1630	132,051 (2)	349,935
1656–1660	173,289 (3)	459,216
1661–1665	182,810 (5)	484,447
1666–1670	151,411 (5)	401,239
1671–1675	165,873 (5)	439,563
1676–1680	215,365 (5)	570,717
1681–1685	226,283 (5)	599,650
1686–1690	192,514 (5)	510,162
1691–1695	172,559 (5)	457,281
1696–1700	195,654 (5)	518,483
1701–1705	189,804 (5)	502,980
1706–1710	177,358 (5)	469,989
1721–1725	260,324 (3)	673,190
1726–1730	275,972 (5)	732,295
1731–1735	285,632 (5)	756,924
1736–1740	290,571 (5)	770,012
1741–1745	279,806 (5)	741,867
1746–1750	284,048 (5)	752,727
1751–1755	310,245 (5)	822,148
1756–1760	282,516 (5)	748,667
1761–1765	322,546 (5)	844,746
1766–1770	353,000 (1)	935,450
1781–1785	453,500 (2)	1,204,275
1786–1790	434,000 (1)	1,150,350

Sources: Figures in brackets indicate the number of observations upon which the annual average tonnage over a 5-year period are based; Figures for 1600–1700 derived from: Hatcher, *The History of the British Coal Industry*, 497; Figures from 1701–1790 based on Dendy, 'Company of Hostmen', p. 260, Dendy derived the figures from the Hornsby Manuscript and included them in this publication. Gaps in the columns indicate lack of data for the relevant years.

coal industry and its associated economy in Newcastle and along the river Tyne. Not only did the London coal trade stimulate a rapid increase in the volume of coastal shipping to carry the coal to the metropolis, but the stimulation of the local economy led to increasing demand for consumer goods, much of which used the same coastal route to bring such goods back to Newcastle on the return trips, carrying north many of the benefits of London's international shipping trade.[23]

Any student of the history of Newcastle will be indebted to F.W. Dendy, who in 1901 published a detailed history of the hostmen together with copious extracts from the records of the Company of Hostmen of Newcastle upon Tyne.[24] The hostmen of Newcastle played a key role in the development of trade on the River Tyne and its hinterland. In the Middle Ages, hostmen were those free inhabitant householders to whom were assigned the duties of entertaining merchant strangers and supervising the sales and purchase of any of their wares and merchandise that were not already monopolized by an already established trade or guild. Coal and grindstones were the particular products of Newcastle that were not already controlled by a trade or guild, and it was these commodities that became the particular preserve of the Newcastle hostmen.[25] Coal had been identified as a source of income by the Crown as early as the fifteenth century, and a form of small cargo-carrying boat, the keel, had been used to carry coal on the river from the coal staiths to the colliers anchored near the mouth of the river. Taxes had been levied on each keel load of coal, however the capacity of the keels was illicitly increased thus avoiding excise duty, and as a result an Act was passed in 1421 to enforce the measurement and marking of keels to fix their capacity at 8 Newcastle chaldrons.[26] The first references to hostmen in Newcastle occur in the fourteenth century, with no further references until the sixteenth century, by which time they were exercising a monopoly over coal

---

[23] B. Dietz, 'Overseas Trade and Metropolitan Growth', in *London 1500–1700: The Making of the Metropolis*, ed. A.L. Beier and R.A.P. Finlay (London: Longman, 1986), pp. 115–40; M.J. Kitch, 'Capital and Kingdom: Migration to Later Stuart London', in ibid., pp. 115–223; E.A. Wrigley, 'A Simple Model of London's Importance in Changing English Society and Economy, 1650–1750', *Past and Present*, 37 (1967), pp. 44–70.

[24] Dendy, *Company of Hostmen*.

[25] Dendy, *Company of Hostmen*, p. xxxvii: J. Brand, *The History and Antiquities of the Town of Newcastle Upon Tyne*, 2 vols (London, 1789), pp. 261–311; R.J. Charleton, *Newcastle Town*, 4th ed. (London: Walter Scott, 1885, rep., 1978), p. 256; Nef, *Rise of the British Coal Industry*, pp. 302, 405; Middlebrook, *Newcastle upon Tyne: Its Growth and Achievement* (Newcastle upon Tyne: Newcastle Journal, 1950), pp. 41–2.

[26] Charleton, *Newcastle Town*, 254; H. Bourne, *The History of Newcastle upon Tyne* (Newcastle upon Tyne: John White, 1736; rep, Newcastle upon Tyne: Frank Graham, 1980), p. 158.

exports both to the continent and to London and other parts of England. Dendy quotes from Harrison's description of England (prefaced to the *Hollingshead's Chronicle,* edited in 1577), referring to a rapid increase in the use of coal as a domestic fuel being reported, noting that the reduced availability of wood as a fuel was resulting in increased use of coal, and observing that 'the home trade was beginning to grow from the forge into the kitchen and hall in most towns and cities that lay about the coast'.[27] It was in London where this increased need for coal as a domestic fuel was most significant, increasing demand from all producing areas, most prominently the North East of England and Newcastle in particular.[28] In *Chorographia,* printed in 1649, William Gray observed that 'trade of coale began not past fourscore yeares since ... and many great ships of burthen were built, so that there were more coales vented in one yeare, then was in seven yeares, forty yeares by-past'.[29]

The hostmen, who were often also the Burgesses of Newcastle and the coal owners, exploited a custom often used in other cities of 'foreign bought and foreign sold'. This custom provided that any goods brought into the town by a foreigner (either an Englishman or an alien) who was not a freeman, could be bought only by a freeman, and similarly any goods purchased must be bought from a freeman. Thus, in every case of a purchase or a sale, one of the parties must be a freeman. The value of this custom had been greatly enhanced by a statute passed in 1529 designed to protect the Crown, and for easier collection of customs duties by the hostmen on behalf of the Crown, which stated 'that no person should ship, load, or unload any goods to be sold into or from any ship, at any place within the river of Tyne within tidal limits, except at the town of Newcastle'.[30] The effect of this statute was that any coal owners in Northumberland or Durham who wished to ship coal from the Tyne had to take their cargo to Newcastle, and then, on the basis of the custom of 'foreign bought and foreign sold', they had to sell the cargo to the freemen of Newcastle to be subsequently re-sold to the buyers.

---

[27] Dendy, *Company of Hostmen,* p. xxix.

[28] Hatcher *The History of the British Coal Industry,* p. 474; B. Dietz, 'The North East Coal Trade, 1550–1750: Measures, Markets and the Metropolis', *Northern History* 22 (1986), pp. 280–94; Deitz, 'Overseas Trade and Metropolitan Growth', pp. 114–40; W.J. Hausman, 'Market Power in the London Coal Trade: The Limitation of the Vend, 1770–1845', *Explorations in Economic History,* 21 (1984), pp. 383–405.

[29] William Gray, *Chorographia, or a Survey of Newcastle Upon Tyne* (Newcastle upon Tyne: Frank Graham, 1970. Originally published 1649), p. 90.

[30] Dendy, *Company of Hostmen,* p. xxxi.

Trade in Newcastle and on the Tyne had a number of other characteristics that differentiated it from trade in other parts of England. As described by Roger Howell, in his accounts of politics in Newcastle during the seventeenth century, the town had always been run by a small and exclusive 'inner ring' of powerful merchants – mainly coal merchants including the hostmen and mercers often known as the 'Lords of Coal' – whose power had in large part been legitimized by a series of charters from the crown towards the end of the sixteenth century.[31] The key to this power was the granting of what came to be known as the Grand Lease. In 1578 Elizabeth I obtained from the Bishop of Durham the lease of some very productive coal mines in the manors of Whickham and Gateshead. The Queen passed her rights to Thomas Sutton, the Master for the Ordnance for the North. Sutton's intentions had been to work the mines for himself, but persistent opposition from the merchants of Newcastle prevented him gaining the freedom of the town, which was necessary for him to conduct trade in his own right. Sutton eventually gave in, and in 1583 he agreed to pass the rights to the Burgesses of Newcastle. Unfortunately, because Newcastle had not received a charter of incorporation, the town was unable to receive the rights to the Grand Lease, but it provided much of the money to allow the mayor Henry Anderson and an alderman William Selby to purchase the rights on the town's behalf, pending the granting of a charter.[32] In 1589 a charter was granted to Newcastle, but Anderson and Selby refused to transfer the extremely profitable Grand Lease to the town. The effect of this was that a small group of merchants who had a share in the Grand Lease held a monopoly over the trade in coal, and were maximizing their profits by raising the prices. Eventually, following protests from all of the guilds in Newcastle and the Mayor of London, the Privy Council instituted an enquiry, which resulted in a new charter granted to Newcastle in 1600. In this charter the coal merchants, or hostmen, who were members of the Newcastle Company of Merchant Venturers, were formally incorporated as a separate company, the Company of Hostmen, with exclusive rights to trade in

---

[31] R. Howell, 'Newcastle and the Nation: The Seventeenth Century Experience', in *The Tudor and Stuart Town, 1530–1688: A Reader in English Urban History*, ed. J. Barry (London: Longman, 1990), pp. 274–96. This article gives a detailed account of the political conflicts between the Crown and national government on one hand and local government on the other using Newcastle as a case study; R. Howell, *Newcastle upon Tyne and the Puritan Revolution* (Oxford: Oxford University Press, 1967), pp. 35–62.

[32] Examination of the Durham Probate Indexes reveals an Inventory for a Henry Anderson, Merchant and Hostman dated 1637, which is valued at only £188, but does include a Mill (DUL, DPRI/1 Inv1637). Presumably this refers to the Henry Anderson named above, although there were a number of Andersons with other forenames listed who had significantly greater wealth. Sadly, there was no surviving Inventory for a William Selby.

coal provided that they did not excessively increase its price; they levied a tax on behalf of the Crown of 1s. per chalder on all coals shipped to English ports and 5s. on coals shipped abroad.[33] This group had been opposed throughout by a reform group within the town, which sought to preserve the rights of the general body of freemen. An additional issue was the conflict between the Burgesses of Newcastle, based mainly on the north bank of the river, and the Church, as manifested by the Bishopric of Durham, which owned much of the land south of the Tyne and influenced key areas such as Tynemouth Priory. By virtue of its position on the north bank, at the mouth of the river, the Priory exerted a degree of control over trading ships entering the river. Notwithstanding the ownership of the riverbed resting with the Crown, agreement was reached that control over the water of the river would be exercised in thirds, the northern third by the Burgesses of Newcastle, the southern third by the Bishopric of Durham and the central third shared.[34] However, the Burgesses of Newcastle continued to exercise an effective monopoly over trade on the river Tyne, particularly in coal, by implementing the taxation measures on behalf of the Crown, and imposing trading rules ensuring that any trade in coal could only be conducted through agents in Newcastle, the hostmen.

In the seventeenth century the situation was further complicated by Charles I making an agreement with the hostmen that he alone was to have a monopoly of the sale of coals. The agreement contracted the hostmen to sell coals only to the King at a fixed price; the price at which he was to sell them was at his discretion. These arrangements lapsed on the establishment of the Commonwealth, when the Commissioners of the Parliament of England ordained that a free and fair trade should be held in Newcastle for coals.[35] Fortunately for the hostmen, on the Restoration of Charles II in 1660 the monopolies were re-instituted, and trade flourished. However, there were several attempts by 'unfreemen' to sell coals directly to ship owners, bypassing hostmen and freemen and resulting in frequent legal disputes and attempts by freemen to impose fines upon the 'offenders'. At the beginning of the eighteenth century, the monopoly rights of the hostmen came under more intense legal challenge; and by the end of that

---

[33] D. Levine and K. Wrightson, *The Making of an Industrial Society: Whickham 1560–1765* (Oxford: Clarendon Press, 1991), pp. 17–25.

[34] Brand, *The History and Antiquities*, Vol. 2, p. 5: Levine and Wrightson, *The Making of an Industrial Society*, pp. 1–10.

[35] Dendy, *Company of Hostmen*, pp. xxxiii, 77n. Charles I even recognized the concept of gift coal in 1637 in an Order in Council, R. Welford, *History of Newcastle and Gateshead*, 5 vols (London: Walter Scott, 1885), Vol. 3, p. 346.

century the hostmen had ceased to assert their alleged privileges.[36] During the latter half of the seventeenth century there were a number of occasions when the demand for coal, and hence its price, fell significantly. This took place partly when demand fell because of the Dutch wars at that time, when blockades were interfering with the coastal trade, and also because the coal mines were producing much more coal than was required by the buyers. Several attempts were made by the coal owners and hostmen, who were frequently one and the same, to form a combination to regulate the vend of coal and artificially maintain high prices. Many attempts were made to undermine this process by some coal owners providing 'gift-coal', giving 25 chaldrons to the score rather than 20, thus effectively undercutting the competition.[37] In 1710 an Act of Parliament was passed making such combinations and undercutting contracts illegal, although this did not completely eliminate the practice.[38]

At the beginning of the seventeenth century most of the hostmen were coal owners, and the fitters were apparently their paid servants or agents, appointed individually or as a group to fix cargoes with buyers for them from a distance, and to get the coal delivered by keels from the colliery staiths to the ship.[39] As time passed a greater proportion of the hostmen were no longer coal-owners, and were using their position as hostmen to act as agents (or fitters) for the sale of coal from both freemen and unfree coal-owners. This changed the nature of the hostmen to a fraternity of chartered fitters; indeed the role was so-defined in 1703, in a case referred to the Attorney General:

> There are at Newcastle-upon-Tyne, men called hostmen or fitters. The Business they take upon them is to take care of the loading of coals brought from the adjacent collieries into keels or boats and conveying them in such keels or boats to the ships that bring them from Newcastle. And it is now become a practice for these hostmen to buy coals at certain prices of the owner of the collieries and to carry them in keels and sell them to the ship masters.[40]

By 1800 the Hostman's Company's claim to a monopoly of dealings with coal had become extinct, and the position of the fitters was less dominant; indeed Dendy

---

[36] Dendy, *Company of Hostmen*, p. xlix.
[37] Dendy, *Company of Hostmen*, pp. xlv–xlvii; Nef, *The Rise of the British Coal Industry*, Vol. 2, pp. 110–19.
[38] Dendy, *Company of Hostmen*, p. xlv.
[39] Dendy, *Company of Hostmen*, p. xlvii; J. Hatcher, *The History of the British Coal Industry*, pp. 466–8.
[40] Dendy, *Company of Hostmen*, p. xlviii.

quotes Nathaniel Clayton in evidence to the House of Commons Committee as saying: 'The price is fixed by the coal-owners and the fitter is not at liberty to sell at more or less than that price'.[41] During the course of the eighteenth century the work of the hostmen continued to be regulated strictly. The records of the company in 1735 listed the main rules under which they worked:

1. That the several Fitters' vends be proportioned each month.
2. That no Fitter load a ship where a Brother or his coal owner is an adventurer.
3. Every Brother to contribute his proportion of the costs of the trade.
4. No Fitter to make any allowance, abatement or gift to any merchant. Ship owner or ship's master ... for use in money coals or any other respect.
5. That every Brother shall give in every month a full and true account of all the ships he has loaded and with what sort of coals.
6. Each fitter who has exceeded his vend to make up the vends of those fitters who were short.
7. No brother to load a ship that has not delivered regularly until 10 days after the ship that delivered in London before her is loaded.[42]

Included in these records were comments from a number of dissenting Brothers, who made it very clear that they were not prepared to co-operate with these rules; but there are few entries subsequently to indicate whether either party followed up these refusals. It is notable that priority was being given to both the London trade and those ships which were regulars in the trade; indeed there are further directions which indicate that a ship which was not a regular in the Newcastle coal trade with London could load with two keels of coal on arrival, but could not complete loading until the 10 day rule was fulfilled.[43]

There is a theme in much of the literature of portraying the coal-owners as being unscrupulous profiteers, forever striving to increase profits from the sale of coal, if necessary by forming combinations and cartels to increase prices artificially. However, in *Chorographia*, Gray suggested that there were considerable risks to coal owning, and that very few were making large profits: 'One coale merchant imployeth five hundred or a thousand in his works of coal; yet for all his labour, care, and cost can scarce live of his trade; nay many of them had consumed and spent great estates and dyed beggers'.[44] Similarly, Ellis argued

---

[41] Dendy, *Company of Hostmen*, p. xlix.
[42] Dendy, *Company of Hostmen*, pp. 194–5.
[43] Dendy, *Company of Hostmen*, pp. 196–7.
[44] Gray, *Chorographia*, p. 84.

that it was entirely plausible that the primary aim of cartels among the Newcastle coal-owners was defensive, designed to protect the huge sums of capital involved from what was an unparalleled risk in contemporary enterprise. Where the proportion of fixed capital costs were so high, productivity and profitability had to be guaranteed at a high level to maintain the viability of a colliery.[45] Although most literature referring to trade on the River Tyne relates to coal and the complex trading processes involved, there was a wide variety of other water-borne trade, both leaving and arriving in the river and the Port of Newcastle. Willan perhaps best illustrates the overall character of trade on the Tyne in the seventeenth century when he writes: 'Newcastle was the centre of three important industries, coal-mining, glass-making and salt-making. Of these three coal-mining was the most important both in itself and the fact that the other two depended on it'.[46] In addition to coal, there were significant exports of salt and glass, both in the form of windowpane glass and also glass bottles. Over the subsequent hundred years the same pattern of trade continued, with the addition of butter as a significant export by 1731, during which year 10,952 firkins were exported to London.[47] Imports included consumables, particularly grain and increasing quantities of household goods, particularly from London, together with significant amounts of wine, sherry and port. Local newspaper advertisements of around 1720 invariably contained extensive adverts for port wine.[48]

The social and economic background to Newcastle and the communities along the lower river Tyne during the seventeenth and eighteenth centuries were a reflection of the growing size of the population, that paralleled the progressive growth in the coal trade, as the demand from London and elsewhere stimulated the market in Newcastle and its hinterland. The consequence of the position of the town, close to the North East coast, was the development of a trading community that was focussed on the seaborne transport of coal to the rest of England, northern Europe and elsewhere. This community had a number of features unique to the Tyne, largely due to the limited navigability of the river, which fostered a community devoted to both managing and undertaking the

---

[45] J. Ellis, 'Cartels in the Coal Industry on Tyneside 1699–1750', *Northern History*, 34 (1998), pp. 134–48.

[46] T.S. Willan, *The English Coasting Trade, 1600–1750* (Manchester: Manchester University Press 1938), p. 115.

[47] Willan, *The English Coasting Trade*, 116; J. Ellis, 'The "Black Indies": The Economic Development of Newcastle, c1700–1840', in *Newcastle Upon Tyne: a Modern History*, ed. R. Lancaster and B. Colls (Chichester: Phillimore, 2001)', pp. 1–26.

[48] *Newcastle Courant*, April, 1725, Newcastle Libraries and Information Service, Local Studies Section. (NCL/LS).

transport of coal from riverside staiths to collier ships waiting close to the mouth of the Tyne. To understand better the work of this community, a clearer understanding of the geographical constraints to the coastal trade from the Tyne is necessary.

Chapter 2
The River Tyne, its Navigability and the Problem of Ballast

Notwithstanding the vast amounts of income earned by the town of Newcastle over hundreds of years of trading, very little was spent on maintaining the navigability of the river itself. This was in stark contrast to many port cities around the English coast, including Sunderland, which spent large sums deepening the rivers and improving access and navigability. Little such investment was made on the Tyne, and even by 1860 the river remained in a poor state. Guthrie observed that ships had to be partly unloaded at North or South Shields in order to reduce draught sufficiently to reach Newcastle Quay, or were unable to depart until the highest tides when fully loaded: 'Vessels of moderate size and draught were detained for weeks after loading, unable to get to sea at the top of high water'.[1] Many loaded ships were running aground at the Tyne bar, and trade was rapidly being lost to Sunderland where the depth of water in the port was several feet deeper. The reason for the deterioration of the Tyne was twofold. In addition to neglect by the Burgesses of Newcastle it was also caused by uninhibited deposition of ballast in and around the river, as evidenced by the numerous ballast hills along the river banks, and Henry Bourne records a John Phillips being fined in 1616 for illegally 'casting ballast' between Souter and Hartley.[2] It was this limited navigability of the river that led to the necessity of transporting cargoes from Newcastle and the surrounding areas by boats and keels to the larger cargo-bearing ships moored close to the mouth of the Tyne at North and South Shields. It could legitimately be argued that the whole community of river-based water tradesmen, in particular the keelmen, was created as a result of this strategy of relative neglect of the need for improvement to maintain the navigability of the river by the town of Newcastle. Without some form of

---

[1] J. Guthrie, *The River Tyne, its History and Resources* (Newcastle upon Tyne: Andrew Reid, 1880), p. 122; J. Ellis, '"Black Indies": The Economic Development of Newcastle, c1700–1840', in *Newcastle Upon Tyne: a Modern History*, ed. R. Lancaster and B. Colls (Chichester: Phillimore, 2001), p. 20.

[2] H. Bourne, *The History of Newcastle Upon Tyne* (Newcastle upon Tyne: John White, 1736; rep, Newcastle upon Tyne: Frank Graham, 1980), p. 160.

intermediary transport, it would not have been possible for the coal industry in and around Tyneside to develop in the way that it did. The coal-carrying keels became an integral part of the trade in coal and the implementation of coal-related excise duties. This service was provided on the basis of private finance by the traders themselves, rather than the town maintaining the navigability of the river by clearing and deepening the channel.

To appreciate fully the evolution of trade on the Tyne it is important to understand the geography of the area – in particular the topographical relationships between Newcastle, the River Tyne and the coast at Tynemouth – and the impact of the coal trade and the consequent deposition of ballast from incoming ships on the character of the river banks and the navigability of the River itself. A number of surviving maps and prints show Newcastle upon Tyne and the River Tyne during the seventeenth and eighteenth centuries, and viewed together these various sources provide an illuminating picture of the development of Newcastle and its surrounding communities along the river. They include examples of the finest contemporary chart and print making, together with some relatively crude hand-drawn maps that, in spite of their simplicity, yield some very valuable information about the evolution of the river as a trading waterway. As was noted by Robinson, in his history of British chart making, up to the middle of the seventeenth century English sailors were dependent on the Dutch for charts, as only they had both the cartographic and copper engraving skills.[3] Even when John Seller published *The English Pilot*, a compilation of charts of the English coast, in 1671, he was dependent on refurbished Dutch copper-plate engravings that had been bought as scrap. It was not until 1681, when Captain Greenvile Collins (d. 1694) began a detailed survey of the coast, that quality English charts were produced.[4] Four surviving charts of the River Tyne, a Map of Newcastle upon Tyne and a contemporary engraving of Newcastle help to understand the geographical background of Newcastle's river traffic and the individuals who took part in it.

The earliest of these maps (Figure 2.1) is dated 1650[5] and has been ascribed to the well-known mapmaker Herman Moll (?1654–1732), but the attribution is doubtful. At best, Moll could only have been the maker of a later copy of a map of that date, as he was not born until 1654, in Bremen, and did not arrive in England until about 1675[6] Indeed, it is doubtful whether Moll made

---

[3] A.W.H. Robinson, *Marine Cartography in Britain: A History of the Sea Chart to 1855* (Leicester: Leicester University Press 1962), pp. 38–42.
[4] Robinson, *Marine Cartography in Britain*, pp. 38–42.
[5] River Tyne Map 1650, TWAM dx.275.4.
[6] D. Reinhartz, 'Moll, Herman (1654?–1732), *Oxford Dictionary of National Biography* (Oxford, Oxford University Press, 2004; online edn, 2008), www.oxforddnb.com. Moll arrived

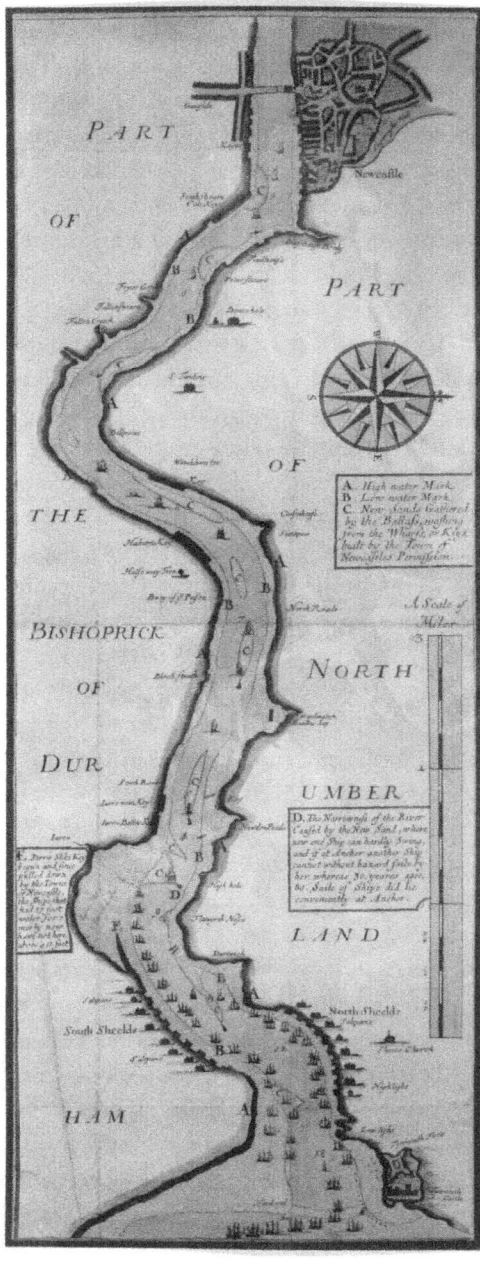

Figure 2.1 Map of the River Tyne, 1650. By permission Tyne and Wear Archives and Museums

any contribution at all to this map, as there is no evidence of his characteristic signature 'H. Moll sculph'. If there is doubt about the attribution, then can we trust the date? This question is helped by the city plan of Newcastle and Gateshead that appears at the top of the map. A comparison of this city plan, with a map of Newcastle upon Tyne, prepared by Corbridge in 1736 (Figure 2.5), is informative. In the 1736 map, both Newcastle and Gateshead are shown as much more extensive towns, with Newcastle showing significant spread beyond the city walls. This tends to indicate that the more modest size of Newcastle in Figure 2.1, with little or no extension outside the city walls, is likely to represent the true size of the city some 70 years earlier, supporting the dating of around 1650. Notwithstanding the questions around its attribution, the 1650 map provides us with useful information about the geography of the River Tyne and its immediate surroundings, and how they might have influenced trade.

The range of the 1650 map extends from Newcastle and the Tyne Bridge in the West to the mouth of the Tyne and the harbour sand bar at its entrance. It is provided with a compass rose to demonstrate its orientation and a detailed descriptive legend that identifies the high and low water marks (A and B) together with the various sand banks and obstructions due to 'New Sands Gathered by the Ballast washing from the Wharfs or Keys built by the Town of Newcastle's Permission' (C). These features are found throughout the length of the river. Many of the sand banks caused by excess ballast deposition were of sufficient navigational significance to warrant marking with beacons and buoys, and four of them were large enough to form islands in the middle of the river; further difficulties were caused by significant narrowing of the river by deposits at the inner banks on a number of bends in the river. Two additional features are identified closer to the river mouth. On the north bank, at Howdon Ponds opposite Jarrow, a further obstruction 'D' is noted: 'The Narrowness of the River Caused by the New Sand, where now one Ship can hardly Swing, and if at Anchor another Ship cannot without hazard sail by her whereas 30 yeares ago 80 Sail of Ships did lie conveniently at Anchor'. A short distance further towards the sea there is another annotation, 'E', at the place now known as Jarrow Slake: 'Jarrow Slike Key begun and since pulled down by the Town of Newcastle, the Ships that had 17 foot water formerly now have not here above 11 foot'.

Throughout the length of the river, the map displays depths expressed in feet, which by convention were almost certainly depths at low tide. From the readings it

---

in England in about 1675, living in London and becoming known as an engraver on copper and a prominent member of coffee house society with a circle of friends, which included Daniel Defoe and the scientist Robert Hooke.

would appear that the depth at the mouth of the river between North and South Shields was 18 feet, shelving to 12 feet by one mile into the river, as taken from the distance scale on the right of the map. Further up the river towards Newcastle the depths shelved to between 9 and 11 feet. The deepest point was just off Bill Point, about one third of the way towards the mouth, where the river deepened to 21 feet, almost certainly as a result of scouring of the river bed as it turned the bend; this contrasted with some shallower points with depths falling as low as 6 feet. The volume of shipping trade using the Tyne is indicated by the very large number of ships shown on the map, particularly from the mouth up to Jarrow. The map also implies the size and type of ships using different parts of the river. Up to point 'E', at the Eastern end of Jarrow Slake, the ships are almost exclusively portrayed as being three-masted, with many of them displaying a fore and aft sail on the mizzen mast, the ships moored above this point were all two-masted, and by implication smaller. The larger ships were almost certainly Newcastle Colliers, often called 'Cat Barques', most of them being three-masted with a Gaff sail but no topsail on the mizzen mast.[7] The most famous example of this type of ship was James Cook's *Endeavour*, which was Whitby built, 97 feet (29.6 m) long and 368 tons burden.[8] As shown on the maps, the ships were usually moored close to the mouth of the river. The keels were brought alongside and the coal loaded by shovels through rectangular open ports cut into the collier's topside planking. Before departure for sea, the ports were closed and caulked to make them watertight.[9] Further up the river there appear to be a number of smaller boats, mainly single-masted which are likely to have been either sailing keels or other small trading craft with more complex rigs.

On either side of the river can be seen a number of smaller communities some of which still exist. Shortly after Newcastle, heading toward the coast, Glasshouse Bridge crossed the mouth of the Ouseburn, where a more modern bridge of the same name exists today in exactly the same place. Further East on the North side comes 'Petershore' – currently known as St Peters – just opposite

---

[7]   A. Osler and A. Barrow, *Tall Ships Two Rivers: Six Centuries of Sail on the Rivers Tyne and Wear* (Newcastle upon Tyne: Keepdate Publishing, 1993), pp. 18–24. This is a detailed historical review of the evolution of English coastal trading ships from their origins as Dutch trading ships called Fluyts and one of their close relatives the Katschips. At the end of the first Dutch War (1652–54), England gained between 1,200 and 1,500 fluyts and katschips as prizes, with a further 1,000 being gained from the subsequent Dutch Wars. These trading ships joined the English trading fleet and significantly reduced demand from English shipbuilders for many years; newly built ships retained the designation of a 'Cat Ship' or 'Cat Barque'.

[8]   Osler and Barrow, *Tall Ships, Two Rivers*, p. 19. The ship was launched in 1764 as the *Earl of Pembroke*, a collier. She was purchased by the Navy in 1768 for the scientific mission to the Pacific Ocean and commissioned as *HMS Endeavour*.

[9]   Osler and Barrow, *Tall Ships, Two Rivers*, p. 24.

Fryers Goose on the South shore which is also still there today, together with 'Fallenshore' (now Felling). Just East of St Peters is Dents Hole, once a very busy community where many keels were based, but no longer existing. The river makes a very sharp turn around Bill Point on the North shore, with the area known today as Bill Quay opposite on the South shore. Just East of Bill Point lies Winckhamlee, where there was a very important coal quay that was the base for many of the Newcastle hostmen to export their coal. Just over halfway from Newcastle to the sea lies 'Woolington Ballast Quay' on the North shore. This now exists as Willington Quay with many small boat moorings around the inlet. About two miles before the river meets the sea we reach the important community of Jarrow on the South shore, with Howdon opposite on the North shore. From Jarrow Eastwards on both banks of the river down to North and South Shields the map shows numerous salt-pans. Here the saltwater from the sea was heated in pans using coal to evaporate the water producing salt that was sold in large quantities both at home and abroad until alternative sources were discovered in the middle of the eighteenth century.[10]

The second map is the Navigational Chart of the River Tyne and its Approaches from 1693[11] (Figure 2.2), and it is one of the most important to appear in the seventeenth and eighteenth centuries. It is a navigational chart prepared by the Hydrographer to the King, Captain Greenvile Collins. A very important figure in cartography, he had travelled the world, including voyages to the South Seas; he had also been on an expedition to explore the North East Passage to China, where he was rescued from shipwreck near Novaya Zemlya. During these voyages he became known for the quality of his hydrographic skills and his maps. In 1681 he was commissioned to undertake the first comprehensive survey of the coasts of Britain. This work was supervised and financially supported by Trinity House, and Collins became a member of its governing body – an Elder Brother – in 1693. The work was completed in 1693, and about one third of the charts were engraved, a significant number of these engravings being prepared by Herman Moll at an early stage in his mapmaking career.[12] This chart of the Tyne is dedicated by Collins to the Master and Brethren of Trinity House, and it clearly originates from one of Herman Moll's engravings as it carries his mark 'H.Moll Sculph'. The map represents a navigational chart of the coast around the mouth of the Tyne from Sunderland up to Blyth, and provides a detailed outline

---

[10] Ellis, 'The Decline and Fall of the Tyneside Salt Industry, 1660–1790: A Re-Examination', *Economic History Review*, 33 (1980), pp. 45–58.

[11] Chart of Tyne Approaches 1693, TWAM D/NCP/5/1.

[12] E. Baigent, 'Collins, Greenvile (d. 1694)', *Oxford Dictionary of National Biography* (Oxford: Oxford University Press, 2004; online edn, Sept 2010), www.oxforddnb.com.

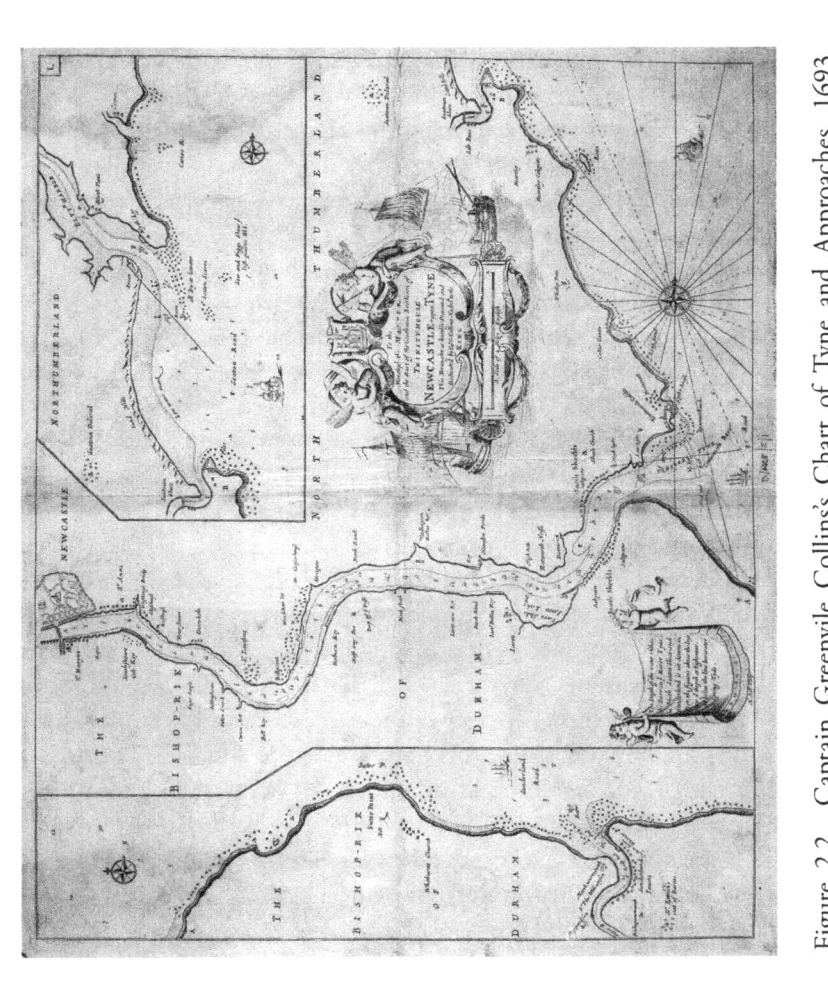

Figure 2.2 Captain Greenvile Collins's Chart of Tyne and Approaches, 1693. By permission Tyne and Wear Archives and Museums

of the coast and the navigable parts of the rivers Wear, Tyne, Seaton Sluice and Blyth. The detail is remarkable, showing depths in the rivers at both low water and high water spring tides at intervals of approximately 200 yards all the way up the rivers to the limits of navigation, which in the case of the Tyne is taken as the Tyne Bridge. The detail is clearly described on the chart: 'The Depth of the water within the Barr in the River Tyne, in Blyth Seaton Sluice and Sunderland is set down in Feet, the figures above the line show the depth at high water and below the line low water, both at Spring Tyd's'. Beyond the harbour bar, the depths in the sea are shown as fathoms. This chart is of the highest quality, and very similar in style and notation to the Admiralty Charts published today.[13] In addition to information about depth, the chart shows navigational hazards such as rocks, and also displays the leading marks for the Tyne entrance, the High Light and the Low Light, and the bearing on which they lie when in line to give ships a safe route into the river. The detail shown on the banks of the river and along the coastal strip is very similar to that shown in the 1650 map, although by 1693 Newcastle and Gateshead seem to have expanded beyond the boundaries shown in 1650. In addition, although all of the settlements and quays are shown, together with the salt-pans around North and South Shields, the chart does not include pictures of the ships anchored near the shore. It does indicate, however, the sites where ships might lie safely at anchor, by a small symbol of an anchor – a charting convention that is used to this day.

The chart indicates a tidal range between spring high and low tides of 13 feet falling to about eight feet at neap tides, which is very similar to the tidal range at spring tides of four metres that we might expect today, and this range would be about the same in Newcastle as at Tynemouth. This would mean that with a minimum depth in the river at about six feet, both near Newcastle Quayside and at a number of points between Newcastle and Tynemouth, the depth at spring high tide would be of the order of 19 feet, falling to 14 feet at neaps. However, there were some points where the river became extremely shallow, the chart indicating zero depth at lowest tides. From Chapman's data, modified by Osler, it is clear that in the mid-eighteenth century the draught of a 100-foot long English 'Cat', with a tonnage of between 150 and 200 tons, was about 15 feet.[14] This means that, with care, the river was navigable to quite large ships

---

[13] United Kingdom Hydrographic Office, International Chart Series, *England East Coast – River Tyne*, Chart no. 1934, 2009.

[14] A.G. Osler, Personal Communication regarding a table in F.H. Chapman, *Architectura Navalis Mercatoria* (Stockholm, 1768), showing dimensions of various cargo-carrying eighteenth-century sailing ships (draughts expressed in Swedish feet are corrected by Osler to English feet).

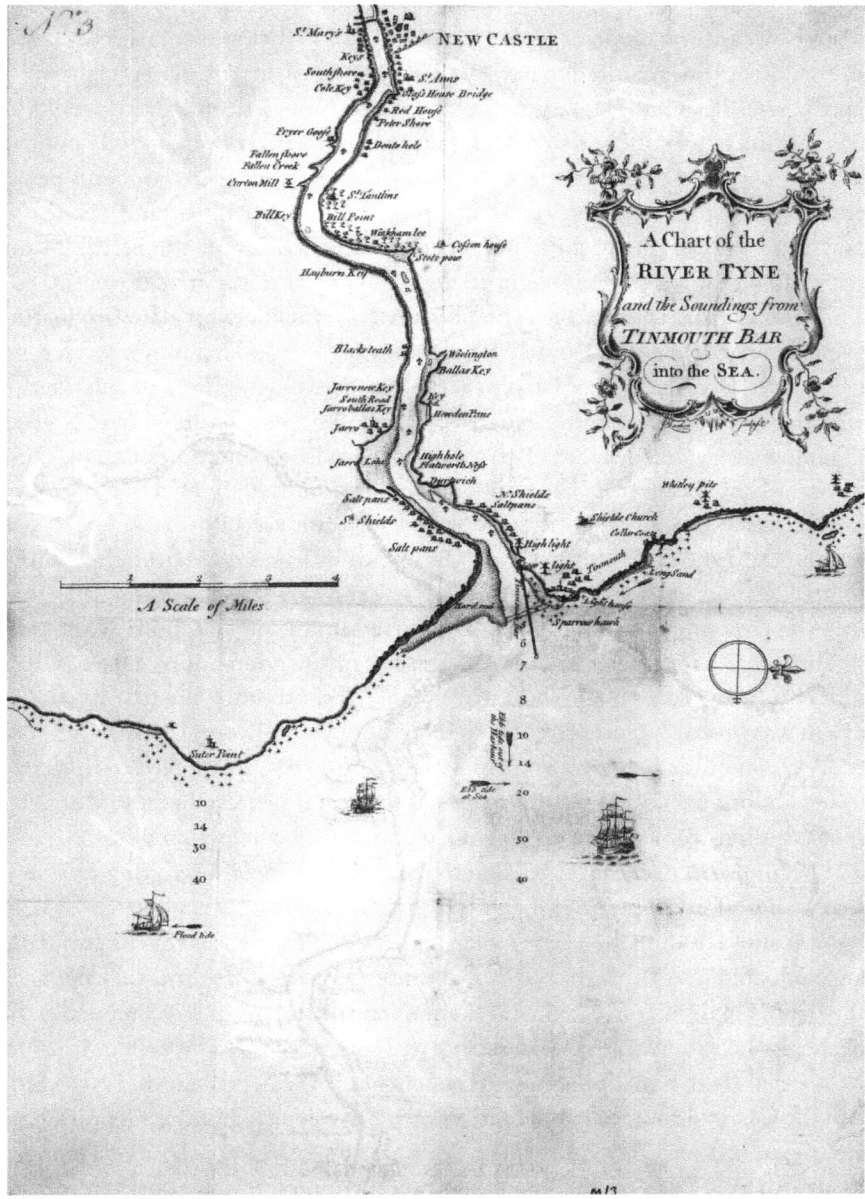

Figure 2.3 Chart of the Tyne, 1700–1750. By permission Tyne and Wear Archives and Museums

up to Newcastle quayside, as Defoe stated in 1720.[15] The problem faced by larger ships was the time required to navigate the distance of approximately eight miles up the river between the harbour entrance and Newcastle quay; this would be possible in a single tide with a favourable wind, but with contrary winds and low tides it may have been necessary to anchor and await deeper water and better conditions, rather than face the risk of running aground and stranding. This is one of the reasons many ships' masters chose to anchor near the mouth of the river and have their cargo brought to them in keels or other small boats.

Another chart of the River Tyne[16] (Figure 2.3) is of uncertain date, originating some time between 1700 and 1750; the only sign of an attribution is a legend below the title shield 'Jas Larken Sculphsit'. No biographical details of this engraver can be found, but the chart is very similar to the Collins chart of 1693 in almost every detail, apart from an absence of depth soundings and marking of hazards in the river. It has only one depth sounding, of 11 feet just east of Winkhamlee staith. Much more detailed navigational information is shown around the Tyne entrance, where depths in fathoms are shown from the Bar out to sea, together with the bearing of the High and Low lights to allow safe entry into the river. In addition, it provides illustrations of the directions of the tidal streams at different states of the tide. The size of the population centres is little different from those shown in the 1693 Collins chart, implying that its date of origin was probably closer to 1700 than 1750.

A rather crude hand-drawn map dating from 1765[17] is believed to be a copy of the Collins map of 1693. This map is of particular interest, because it updates the soundings provided in Collins map and shows where a number of buoys had been placed in the river to denote hazards. The most interesting feature is that at almost every point two depth readings are shown, a reading for 1752 in red ink and a reading for 1765 in black ink. When the depths for the two dates are compared they show that at many points there was little difference between the depths in 1752 and 1765, and if anything the depths in 1765 tended to be deeper. When comparing the soundings with those recorded by Collins in 1693, we see that there have been a number of changes. The depths around Newcastle and the Quayside are little different; however, the depths around Bill point have almost halved by 1765, and where there was an island just East of Hebburn Quay in 1693, by 1765 the island had become joined to the South shore with a sand spit shown as 23 paces wide. From Willington Quay to the mouth of

---

[15] D. Defoe, *A Tour thro' the Whole Island of Great Britain*, Vol. 2 (London: 1726; reprint London: Frank Cass & Co., 1927, 1968), p. 659.
[16] Chart of the River Tyne, 1700–1750, D/NCP/5/2.
[17] Map of the Tyne, 1765, Bell Collection, Vol. 1, NCL.LS. L942.8 T98.

the Tyne there had been little further change in depth apart from some silting up around the North Shields shore where the depths had been reduced from 18 feet to 13. These changes in depth seemed to confirm a degree of general silting up of the river, probably as a result of excessive ballast deposition. However, the degree of silting in tidal rivers is notoriously variable, being subject to scouring from the increased flows after intermittent storms and unusually high tides. The annotations along the river banks show an increasing number of staiths over the intervening time since the Collins chart was drawn; in particular, a number of docks have appeared, particularly at Howdon on the North bank and Jarrow on the South bank, as well as a dry dock at South Shields. Of particular significance, there was no sign of any salt-pans being marked, possibly indicating the demise of the earlier coastal salt industry.[18]

One of the most revealing pictures of Newcastle and the River Tyne in the eighteenth century is provided by the engraving *The South East Prospect of Newcastle upon Tyne*, made by Samuel and Nathaniel Buck in 1745.[19] This engraving (Figure 2.4) was one of a large series published by the Buck brothers. The brothers were born near Richmond in Yorkshire; Samuel (1696–1779) was the first to become an engraver, moving to London in the 1720s and becoming an active member of the Society of Antiquaries. His first series of engravings of 'Prospects' of a number of Northern towns were published between 1720 and 1725. Samuel's brother Nathaniel (d. 1759) was first mentioned in 1724, although the date of his birth is unknown. The two brothers worked together, producing a large number of engravings of many cities and castles across the country, until Nathaniel died in 1759, after which Samuel continued alone. They produced a number of collections of prints of their engravings, which they sold from their house in Garden Court, Middle Temple, London.[20] The picture of Newcastle upon Tyne shown in the Buck engraving gives a very clear outline of the city in the mid eighteenth century, particularly when viewed together with a contemporary map of the Town engraved by Corbridge for Henry Bourne's 1736 book (Figure 2.5).[21] Although the Buck engraving gives a rather stylized view of the city from the South East that is not entirely to scale, it manages to show most of the significant buildings, particularly the castle and the main churches, together with the most important civic buildings along

---

[18] Ellis, 'The Decline and Fall of the Tyneside Salt Industry', pp. 45–58.
[19] National Maritime Museum, Greenwich, London, Image ref. B2547.
[20] R. Hyde, 'Buck, Samuel (1696–1779)', *Oxford Dictionary of National Biography* (Oxford: Oxford University Press, 2004),www.oxforddnb.com, and 'Buck, Nathaniel (1724–1759)', *ibid*.
[21] Corbridge, Map of Newcastle upon Tyne, 1736, TWAM D/NCP/2/6.

Figure 2.4 Buck Brothers' engraving of Newcastle upon Tyne, 1745. © National Maritime Museum, Greenwich, London

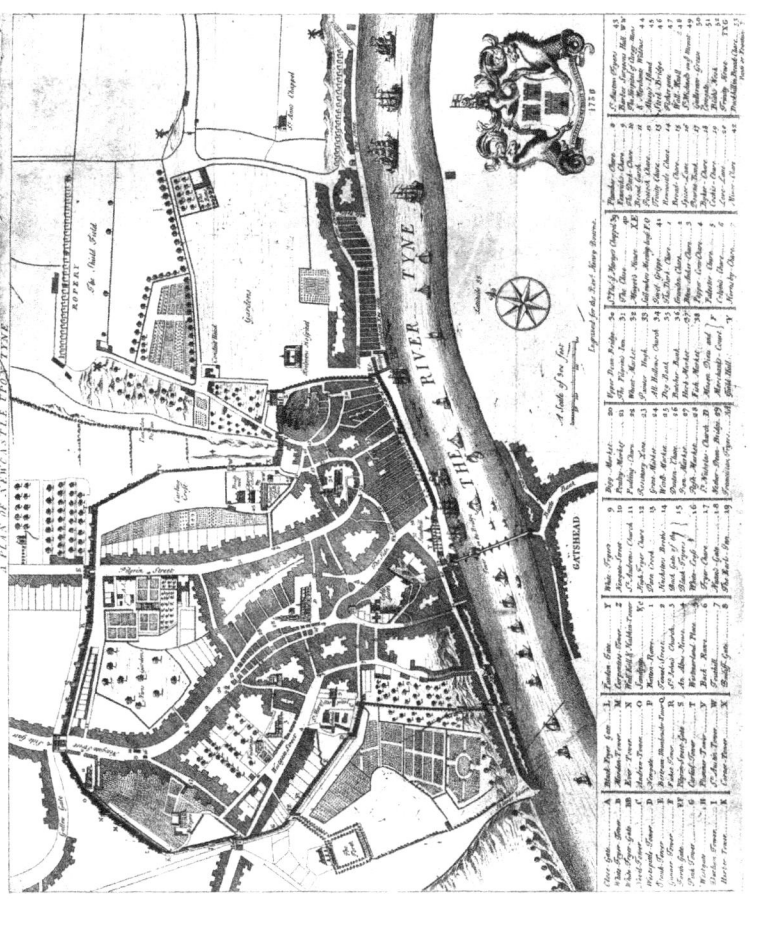

Figure 2.5 Map of Newcastle upon Tyne by Corbridge, in Rev. Henry Bourne, *The History of Newcastle Upon Tyne* (1736). By permission Tyne and Wear Archives and Museums

the waterfront. The picture clearly shows the extensive quayside between the city walls and the river together with the two cranes it was reputed to have. The scope of the picture extends from Elswick in the West across to the Keelmens' Hospital and the edges of the Ouseburn Valley in the East and North towards the edges of the Town Moor. There is relatively little to see of the south bank and Gateshead, other than some buildings adjacent to the south end of the Tyne Bridge. The picture is illuminating, as it provides clues not just to the quantity of river and seagoing craft but also their variety. Above the bridge four keels carrying coal are clearly seen, each having three crew rowing, and a helmsman, most probably the skipper. In the centre of each keel can be seen the coal piled high being taken down the river to awaiting collier ships. In the centre of the river above the bridge there is what appears to be the Newcastle Mayoral Barge, which has been well described elsewhere.[22] At the bridge itself we can see a single keel passing through the second arch from the Southern end. Below the bridge there is considerably more activity, including 11 keels loaded with coal being rowed and three keels with square sails similarly loaded, all travelling down river. In addition to these smaller craft there are three sailing ships of different sizes sailing on the river. Perhaps the most illuminating aspect of the picture is the view of the quayside, which appears to be bustling with activity, particularly around the cranes. There are no fewer than 18 ships tied up at the quay, in places three or four abreast; these were probably 'Cats', eight or nine of which appear to have three masts (Frigate rig), and the remainder two masts (Snow rig). They appear to vary in size, but are likely to have been between 80 and 110 feet in length 100 to 180 tons burden and drawing 12 to 15 feet. In addition to the sailing ships, there are also a number of small rowing boats tied up at the quay, almost certainly for local use. The picture probably represents a realistic view of Newcastle and its quayside in the mid-eighteenth century, as there is no plausible motivation for the Buck brothers to portray the city other than as they saw it, which would suggest that the number of boats and ships illustrated in the picture represented reality. The only feature that might cast doubt is that there is no evidence of any coal pits or other industrial activity anywhere in the picture, though we know that there were pits and other related industries all around Newcastle at the time. The aim of the Buck prints was mainly to illustrate towns and buildings, however, and it may be that they considered industrial detritus a distraction from the views they were attempting to convey.

---

[22] A. Osler, 'Newcastle's Last Mayoral Barge', *Archaeologia Aeliana*, 5th series, 16 (1988), pp. 239–43.

These different maps, charts and prints have provided us with very detailed information about the development of Newcastle and the River Tyne as a trading port during the seventeenth and eighteenth centuries. Not only do they tell us how the different communities were expanding during this period, they also indicate a change in the balance of trades, showing the reduction of the importance of salt production by the middle of the eighteenth century. The information provided on the changing navigability of the river over the years, as well as quite remarkable detail about the size and hence capacity of the shipping reaching as far as Newcastle quayside, tend to support the size and variety of both coal and general trade shown in the port books of the time, and emphasize the importance of Newcastle as a maritime trading centre. One of the key features shown in the charts is the impact of the deposition of ballast from collier ships arriving to load coal upon the banks of the river. We see an increasing number and size of ballast hills; and the illicit or accidental deposition of ballast in the river itself caused a significant and continuing limitation to the navigability of the river.

Little has been written about the ballast contained in ships coming to the River Tyne to load with coal during the seventeenth and eighteenth centuries, even though it is frequently mentioned in contemporary records as an issue of great concern to the Burgesses of Newcastle and all of those who used the Tyne. In 1734 Henry Bourne gave an account of two ships' masters being fined five pounds for ... 'casting ballast between Souter and Hartley to the Damage of the River'. This became such a problem that in 1760 a Mr Liddell proposed a plan for taking the ballast out to sea and dumping it offshore in positions where it would not wash back into the harbour. However, in spite of petitions from many ships' masters, the Council failed to act on the suggestion.[23] There is a very clear account in a letter preserved in the Bell Collection from a gentleman in Newcastle to a friend in London, dated 1765, in which he recounts the serious problems being encountered with ballast being improperly stored on the banks of the river, resulting in it being washed into the river at high tides and during storms. This often had the consequence of obstruction to the channel, causing serious problems to ships and keels attempting to navigate the river and load or unload their cargoes.[24] Almost three quarters of the ships that arrived in the Tyne were carrying ballast, which had to be unloaded before the ship could load its coal. Newcastle provided a number of 'ballast shores' where incoming ballast

---

[23] H. Bourne, *History of Newcastle upon Tyne* (Newcastle upon Tyne: John White, 1736; rep, Newcastle upon Tyne: Frank Graham, 1980), 160; Guthrie, *The River Tyne, Its History and Resources*, pp. 56–60; J. U. Nef, *The Rise of the British Coal Industry*, 2 vols (London: George Routledge & Sons, 1932), Vol. 1, p. 31.

[24] Bell Collection, Vol. 1. NCL/LS, L942.8 T987B.

could be deposited. These were a type of staith where a ship or keel could unload its ballast for storage in a mound near the river. The mounds often became quite large and were called ballast hills. This facility generated revenue for the town as ships' masters were charged a fee for this service. In an effort to avoid these fees, attempts were often made to evade the regulations by illicitly depositing ballast in the river, which would incur fines from the Newcastle Common Council.[25] This illicit deposition of ballast in the river, together with the erosion of pre-existing authorized ballast shores continued to cause the river to silt up and was a cause of frequent friction between the river users and the town, who they regarded as responsible for maintaining the navigability of the river. The impact of the ballast in further limiting the navigability of the tidal river to larger ships was sufficient to necessitate the maintenance of the intermediary river transport using keels to carry cargo to be loaded on larger ships moored nearer the mouth of the river. The ballast was usually of sand, which often came from the South East coast in ships working in the coal trade from London. This sand was not an entirely valueless cargo, as it was used as a raw material by the many glass manufacturers who sprang up near the banks of the Tyne around Newcastle.[26]

There are few sources of documentary information about ballast and its handling during the seventeenth and eighteenth centuries. Two very useful sets of documents survive. The Newcastle Common Council Minute Books record in some detail the proceedings of the Council concerning the management of ballast, giving a picture of how and by whom the ballast was dealt with, and the Newcastle Chamberlains' Account books list all of the ships that entered the river and deposited their ballast and loaded coal or salt. For each of these transactions the town charged a fee, and the entry listed all the fees paid by the ship's master, including dues for coal itself, a fee for the ship or boat and the amount of ballast and the fees charged for depositing it, including a record of the ballast shore where it was to be deposited. The Common Council books identify much of the process by which ballast was managed.[27] It appears that on arrival a ships' master would be allocated to a ballast shore or staith to unload the ballast. Although this may have been done by ballast being unloaded directly onto the staith, there

---

[25] TWAM, 589, 4–16, f 289. At a Newcastle Common Council meeting on 30 June 1735, a document was issued complaining about the chalk, chalk rubbish and manure that was being brought to the port as ballast. Instructions were issued to ballast assessors that if they accepted such ballast they would not be paid and any person who conveyed such ballast from a ship would be fined 20 shillings.

[26] Ridley, 'History of Glass Making on the Tyne and Wear', *Archaeologia Aeliana*, 4th series, 40 (1962), pp. 145–51.

[27] Newcastle Common Council Books (NCCB) TWAM 589, Vols 4–16.

are references to keelmen unloading ballast and taking it to the ballast shores in a keel – indeed there are references to keelmen being fined for not taking the ballast to the shore for which they had a warrant.[28] Some of the ballast shores used are listed in the Chamberlains' Accounts, often based on their geographical site. The Council minutes, however, imply a much wider range of ballast shores, referring to many of them by the name of the owner. There are some mentioned which appear to be owned by women, in particular shores owned by Lady Riddell and one owned by Lady Brandling are often mentioned in connection with complaints from the owners to the council over unpaid fees.[29] Once the ballast had been loaded onto the staith it was conveyed to nearby ballast hills by women, known as conveyors. There are Council minutes noting complaints from a Mrs Alney[30] that she had not been paid properly for conveying the ballast; these are followed by a Council resolution that she should be paid to 'convey her heaps of ballast'. Some months later there appears a further petition, complaining that because she had still not been fully paid she no longer had enough money to feed her children. The council responded by making her a grant of £50 payable in £10 monthly instalments to cover her costs.[31] The process of ballast management was overseen by a Ballast Office, with an assessor and a team of assistants who were appointed by the Council. In 1660 there is a record of the appointment of Francis Anderson, a merchant, to the post of Water Serjeant 'to aid the Water Bailiff to make out Ballast Bills and perform the other tasks pertinent to the office of Water Serjeant'. Another record shows a William Cutter being sworn in as Ballast Assessor in June 1657,[32] but he did not last very long in this role as in September 1660 he was discharged, with a minute recording the event as follows:

> Whereas William Cutter, wine cooper, was by act of Common Council of 24th September 1657, appointed to assess ballast cast on Jarrow shore, Haineing shore, Cattdeene shore, Hughworth shore, and Felling shore, at a salary of £40 a year and an allowance of £5 towards keeping a horse, whereas he was not well affected towards the present government and neglected orders for assessing ballast, he was discharged and Thomas Maddison, merchant, who had suffered great loss in the late times for his loyalty was appointed to the office during the pleasure of the

---

[28] NCCB, f. 246a, 1715. There was a complaint that keelmen were casting their ballast at a ballast shore other than the one for which they had a warrant. In future they would forfeit their dues plus an additional 10 shillings to the informer.
[29] NCCB, f. 361, 1649.
[30] NCCB, f. 94, 1646.
[31] NCCB, f. 141 1647.
[32] NCCB, f. 414, 1657.

Council, excluding however Jarrow shore He was to receive the same salary as William Cutter. Orders and Directions to be observed:

To diligently attend his work and so discharge his assessment that neither the town, nor the conveyor, nor the master have cause for complaint.

To take the advice of the conveyor, or his deputy, or masters of ships if need be, but to keep the whole power in his own hands; to certify his assessment promptly to the ballast office so that no master should lose time in his clearance.

To view the shores on his going down and send certificates if need be every morning before 10 o'clock from Lady Day to Michaelmas, before 2 o'clock in the afternoon from Felling, Heworth, Catt Deane, and Haineing shores, and shall send his certificate to the ballast office every day, summer and winter before 2 o'clock in the afternoon and if afterwards the times and hours did not serve for the dispatch and encouragement of trade he was to observe such directions as were appointed by this committee or the Common Council.[33]

This document not only gives some insight into the way local political changes were taking place after the Restoration, but also that those associated with the previous regime lost favour.[34] It also gives clear insights into how the town and its council managed the very large amounts of ballast that were arriving in the Tyne. Comparison with other ports in England is made difficult by the lack of literature about ballast and its management in the seventeenth and eighteenth centuries. Newcastle is one of the few ports for which there is any reference to ballast.[35] This may be because the port was unique in the nature of its main export, coal, which was exported in such large volumes – far exceeding any possible returning import cargo – that far more ballast was likely to be brought into the Tyne than any other port in the country. The Chamberlains' Accounts include the amount of ballast deposited by each ship cleared and the dues charged, and it is notable that the ballast weight was expressed in tons,

---

[33] NCCB, f. 42, 1660. It is possible that the Thomas Maddison referred to in this document was the son of that name of Henry Maddison, formerly mayor of Newcastle, who died in 1634. Details of Henry's probate inventory are discussed in Chapter 5.

[34] Members of the Maddison family were notable Puritans, and is very probable that the Thomas Maddison referred to in the above extract of the Common Council minutes was indeed the son of Henry Maddison whose case has been examined in some detail.

[35] E.M. Halcrow, 'Chamberlain's Accounts, Newcastle upon Tyne', *Journal of the Society of Archivists*, Vol. 1, Issue 10 (1955), pp. 289–91.

unlike the coal, which was measured in chaldrons. The amount of ballast carried by each ship is, not surprisingly, proportionate to the size of the ship, but was in general equivalent to 10 per cent of the ship's coal carrying capacity. The ballast records indicating that the amounts each ship was depositing varied from 10 to 100 tons. The detail in the Accounts does allow us to make an estimate of the amount of the dues charged to ships' masters, and it would appear to have been between 9 and 10 pence for each ton deposited. In an attempt to see how the process of ballast management changed during the eighteenth century, Chamberlains' Accounts for 1702 and 1756 were assessed. The 1702 Accounts are less detailed than the 1756 accounts. The 1702 book lists the amount of ballast carried and the shore on which it was discharged, with the names of the ship and its master and a lump sum to cover the sum of all the dues payable. The 1756 Accounts are much more complex, as on each occasion the master of a ship is recorded as paying a series of separate dues for his ship including ballast dues, duty on coal and a small charge for his ship or boat, which must be a form of harbour dues, separately all on the date shown in the book. On some occasions, however, this entry is followed by a series of other entries paying similar dues for previous visits for earlier dates, which have presumably been previously unpaid. This practice of mixing payments for the date of entry with late payments for earlier visits, together with the inclusion of a very large range of other payments into the town's coffers, ranging from guild payments to rent for land, makes it extremely difficult for the historian to use these documents to estimate the number of ships coming and going over a defined period.

The ballast shores identified in the 1702 and 1756 Chamberlains' Account Books are shown in Table 2.1. The listed sites in many cases represent places that can be recognized today, some others appear on contemporary maps, but there are a few that appear to be named after a person, presumably the person who owned the land or the rights to use it. In most cases, as noted above, the ballast was moved by the women conveyors from the point of landing to a place some distance from the river, as may be seen in the case of the Ewesburn (Ouseburn) ballast hill, which subsequently became the Ballast Hills Burial Ground that lies many metres away from the river. In this context, it is interesting to see ballast recorded as going to the Town Moor, which is a considerable distance from the river.[36] Slightly later than the period covered by this book, a pamphlet published by the Port of Newcastle upon Tyne in 1830, signed by the Town Clerk, lays out the rules to be observed by those involved in the handling of ballast.

---

[36] Perspectives of the Town Moor in relation to the river Tyne may be seen in Figures 2.4 and 2.5.

Table 2.1   Ballast shores listed in Newcastle Chamberlains' Accounts

1702	1756
New Willington	Willington
Jarrow	Jarrow
Ewesburn	Ewesburn
Hebburn	Hebburn
St Anthony's	St Anthony's
New Quay	New Quay
Town	Town
Brandling	Brandling
Haymans	Burdons
Howdon	Dunstan
Walker	Town Moor
Mildam	
Heworth	
Lime Kilns	

The document lays out in some detail the processes required for the deposition of ballast by incoming ships, including the need to obtain a warrant from the ballast office.[37] It is clear that keels are playing a vital role in the movement of ballast, carrying no more than eight chaldrons, but it is particularly interesting to find that there were described specific ballast keels which were permitted to carry up to 10 chaldrons or 30 tons of ballast, and were specially marked to enable them to do so. The process allowed for a strict account of the amount of ballast deposited to be kept and also to control the ballast staith to which it was to be delivered. The key to the process was the ballast warrant, which not only contained the instructions as to where the ballast was to be taken, but was endorsed with the amount of ballast that was landed, presumably as a basis for the consequent ballast charges. It is probable that these processes had evolved over a period of years and were very similar to the processes used during the eighteenth century. It was the deposition of this ballast along the banks of the river that served not only to modify the navigability of the river, but also to influence the development of the riverside communities that are the subject of the following chapters.

---

[37] Port of Newcastle upon Tyne, *Rules and Regulations to be Observed by the Water Bailiff's Boatmen, by the Messengers Employed on Board Ballast Keels, by the Master of Ships and by Ballast Keelmen and Others Employed in the Delivery of Ballast in the River Tyne* (Newcastle upon Tyne: Printed by J. Clarke, 1830), Newcastle University Libraries, Special Collections, Friends 57.

Chapter 3
The Water Trades Community of Tyneside

Having established the economic and geographical environment in which Newcastle and the communities along the lower reaches of the river were developing during the seventeenth and eighteenth centuries, we can now move on to examine the population and community structure of the region. Newcastle upon Tyne, like London and many provincial towns in England during the period, underwent a period of prolonged and progressive expansion (Table 3.1). London was the most dramatic example of a growing city in England, the bulk of its expansion coming from migration from surrounding counties, but unlike many other provincial towns and cities, London had a higher incidence of migrants from further afield who, in general, were better qualified. Many authors have emphasized the magnitude of the migration of young adults into larger towns, particularly London and the port towns where such migration was predominantly female; in some towns between 60 and 80 per cent of the population were migrants.[1] Newcastle was one of many significant Western European port towns in the early modern period that served as a focus for the development of working and trading communities dependent on the inward and outward flow of commodities to other countries and ports throughout Europe and the rest of the known world. Richard Lawton and Robert Lee explored many of the social and demographic aspects of port towns and cities across Western Europe, none of which were the capitals of their respective countries, a role which in itself would inevitably have had a substantial influence on growth and development. In many of these European port cities, the typical features of rapid economic growth were associated with inward migration and an increasing population. Similar changes occurred in port towns in England,

---

[1] J. Ellis, *The Georgian Town 1680–1840* (New York: Palgrave, 2001), p. 28; D. Souden, 'Migrants and the Population Structure of Later Seventeenth-Century Provincial Cities and Market Towns', in *The Transformation of English Provincial Towns 1600–1800*, ed. P. Clark (London: Hutchinson & Co., 1984), p. 133; P. Corfield, 'A Provincial Capital in the Late Seventeenth Century: the Case of Norwich', in *Crisis and Order in English Towns 1500–1700*, ed. P. Clark and P. Slack (London: Routledge, 1972), p. 233; E.J. Buckatzsch, 'Places of Origin of a Group of Immigrants into Sheffield 1624–1799', *Economic History Review*, 2nd ser., 2 (1950), p. 292.

Table 3.1   Population of Newcastle between 1560 and 1831

Year	Newcastle Population
1560	10,000[a]
1600	10,000[b]
1665	10,800[c]
1670	12,000[d]
1700	16,000[e]
1736	20,000[f]
1750	29,000[g]
1801	28,294[h]
1831	53,613[i]

Sources: (a) S. Middlebrook, *Newcastle upon Tyne*, 63. (b) E.A. Wrigley, 'Urban Growth and Agricultural Change', pp. 686–7. (c) R. Welford, 'Newcastle Householders in 1665', p. 49; J. Langton, 'Residential Patterns in Pre-Industrial Cities', 1; T. Arkell, 'Multiplying factors for estimating Population totals from the Hearth Tax', p. 51. (d and e) E.A. Wrigley, 'Urban Growth and Agricultural Change', pp. 686–7. (f). S. Middlebrook, *Newcastle upon Tyne*, p. 116, quoting H. Bourne, *History of Newcastle*. (g) E.A. Wrigley, 'Urban Growth and Agricultural Change', pp. 686–7. (h) S. Middlebrook, *Newcastle upon Tyne*, p. 150, providing separate figures for Newcastle, Gateshead and Sunderland from the 1801 National Census; E.A. Wrigley, 'Urban Growth and Agricultural Change', pp. 686–7, gives a much higher figure of 42,000 which also includes Gateshead, also derived from the 1801 National Census. (i) S. Middlebrook, *Newcastle upon Tyne*, p. 175, derived from the 1831 census.

Scotland and Ireland such as Hull, Bristol, Liverpool, Glasgow and Cork,[2] and many of these characteristics, related to rapid population growth, can be found in Newcastle and the communities along the river Tyne during the seventeenth and eighteenth centuries.[3] Although water trades communities were distributed

---

[2] R. Davis, *The Trade and Shipping of Hull 1500–1700* (Veverley: East Yorkshire Local History Society, 1964); D. Hussey, *Coastal and River Trade in Pre Industrial England: Bristol and its Region 1680–1730* (Exeter: Exeter University Press, 2000); M. Stammers, 'Ships and Port Management at Liverpool Before the Opening of the First Dock in 1715', *Transactions of the Historical Society of Lancashire and Cheshire*, 156 (2007), pp. 27–50; A. Gibb, 'Industrialisation and Demographic Change: A Case Study of Glasgow, 1801–1914', in *Population and Society in Western European Port Cities, c. 1650–1939*, ed. R. Lawton and R. Lee (Liverpool: Liverpool University Press, 2002), pp. 37–73; R. Lawton, 'The Components of Demographic Change in a Rapidly Growing Port- City: The Case of Liverpool in the Nineteenth Century', in *ibid.*, pp. 91–123; J. O'Brien, 'Population Society and Politics in Cork from the Late-Eighteenth Century to 1900', in *ibid.*, pp. 326–46.

[3] R. Lee and R. Lawton, 'Port Development and the Demographic Dynamics of European Urbanisation', in *Population and Society in Western European Port Cities,*

along both banks of the lower Tyne, during this period the largest concentration was based at the east end of Newcastle 'keyside' in Sandgate; the area was notable for the squalor and poverty graphically described by Defoe in 1726.[4] A variety of secondary sources of information about the water trades communities along the Tyne tend to give equally variable and conflicting information about the size and development of the sector and the extent to which inward migration from Scotland and surrounding counties of Northern England contributed to its growing population.

Evidence about the size of the population of Newcastle upon Tyne in the seventeenth century comes from studies of Hearth Tax returns. Welford estimated from the returns for 1665 that in the 24 Wards of the town there were 2510 households, of which 1472 were liable to pay the Hearth Tax and 1038 were not. On the assumption that each household contained an average of five persons, he estimated the Town's population at around 12,250; however, Arkell, in an analysis of the multiplication factors used to estimate population totals from Hearth Tax returns for all areas outside London, recommended a multiplication factor of 4.3, which gives a lower total than Welford's estimate – closer to 10,800.[5] Langton, in a further analysis of Welford's Hearth tax data, related them to information contained in the Newcastle upon Tyne Register of Freemen. He was able to identify the relative wealth of each of the different occupations, as manifested by the average number of hearths in their houses; he also located where in the town the different trades lived, and highlighted the concentration of richer merchant venturers in the areas nearer to the Castle,

---

c. 1650–1939, ed. R. Lawton and R. Lee (Liverpool: Liverpool University Press, 2002), pp. 1–36; D. Levine and K. Wrightson, *The Making of an Industrial Society: Whickham 1560–1765* (Oxford: Clarendon Press, 1991), pp. 221, 230; J. Langton, 'Residential Patterns in Pre-Industrial Cities: Some Case Studies from Seventeenth- Century Britain', *Transactions of the Institute of British Geographers* 65 (1975) p. 1.

4   D. Defoe, *A Tour Thro' the Whole Island of Great Britain*, Vol. 2 (London: 1726; reprint London: Frank Cass & Co., 1927, 1968), p. 659.

5   R. Welford, 'Newcastle Householders in 1665; Assessment of Hearth or Chimney Tax', *Archaeologia Aeliana*, 3rd ser., 7 (1911), p. 49; J. Langton, 'Residential Patterns in Pre-Industrial Cities', 1; T. Arkell, 'Multiplying factors for estimating Population totals from the Hearth Tax', *Local Population Studies*, 28 (1982), pp. 51–7. Arkell provided a detailed critical analysis of the different methods for calculating household size from Hearth Tax returns, paying particular attentions to the work of Peter Laslett who provided a range of multiplication factors for different household circumstances, the most frequently quoted figure being 4.75, in P. Laslett, 'Mean Household Size in England since the sixteenth century', in *Household and Family in Past Time*, ed. P. Laslett and R. Wall (Cambridge: Cambridge University Press, 1972), pp. 125–58.

Guildhall and Quayside.[6] Another study relevant to the population of Newcastle comes from Levine and Wrightson in their study of early modern Whickham, a coal mining community less than 10 miles from Newcastle.[7] They showed that the community underwent a fourfold increase in the number of households between 1563 and 1666. Associated with this change, was only an initial doubling of the rate of marriages and baptisms up to the first decade of the seventeenth century, following which the rates stabilized, notwithstanding the continuing increase in the size of the population. From 1610 there was a rise in the gender ratio at burial from 100 up to 142[8] by 1639; the ratio fell back to 100 in the 1640s, then rose again to 149. These figures were very suggestive of a male dominated population with a very high mortality rate. The authors suggest that these changes are reminiscent of an industrial population rather than a rural community, and they indicate that such population changes could only be maintained by a significant rate of inward migration. To examine migration further, they used the incidence of new surnames appearing in the parish registers, following a method devised by Lasker and Roberts, who used changes in surnames in Whickham parish records to calculate a 'coefficient of relationship by isogony', as a measure of change in population composition and an indicator of the impact of migration upon the community. Lasker and Roberts reported that between 1603 and 1628 58.5per cent of all surnames were new to the parish, with the process continuing up to 1654.[9] This rapid influx of manpower by immigration was a reflection of the intensive exploitation of coal reserves with the opening of new coal mines around Whickham during this period.[10] There are references to migrants from Scotland working in the Newcastle and Tyneside area, but other than a number of Scottish

---

6   J. Langton, 'Residential Patterns in Pre-Industrial Cities: Some Case Studies from Seventeenth- Century Britain', in *The Tudor and Stuart Town, 1530–1688: A Reader in English Urban History*, ed. J. Barry (London: Longman, 1990), pp. 166–205.

7   Levine and Wrightson, *The Making of an Industrial Society*, p. 172; K. Wrightson and D. Levine, 'Death in Whickham' in *Famine, Disease and the Social Order in Early Modern Society*, ed. J. Walter and R. Schofield (Cambridge: Cambridge University Press, 1989), pp. 129– 65 .

8   Gender ratio of 142 implies 142 male burials for every 100 female burials

9   G.W. Lasker and D.F. Roberts, 'Secular Trends in Relationship as Estimated by Surnames: a Study of a Tyneside Parish', *Annals of Human Biology*, 9 (1982), pp. 299–307. It is interesting to note in their conclusions that their results indicate that the main increase in population size occurred at a time when there was no decrease in relationship as shown by change in surnames. This, indicates that either the attribution of population expansion to migration is erroneous, or the migration occurred from nearby populations, which often had with surnames similar to those in Whickham.

10   Levine and Wrightson, *The Making of an Industrial Society*, 178–80; Wrightson and Levine, 'Death in Whickham', pp. 130–38.

surnames appearing in the registers there were few specific references to Scottish migration into Whickham.[11]

Michael Barke undertook an analysis of the changing population of Newcastle in his study of the pre-civil registration population of Newcastle between 1700 and 1840.[12] He used parish registers from Newcastle's four main parishes: All Saints, St Nicholas, St John's and St Andrew's. Barke indicated that a major problem in using such data was that most of these parishes extended beyond the walls of the town, and calculations based on their registers thus would include more people than resided within the city walls. It is unclear in many historical estimates of the population of Newcastle whether the areas within the parish boundaries or the town walls have been used to estimate the size of the population . Barke was able to demonstrate that between 1770 and 1801 there would have been a net reduction in the population of Newcastle, had it not been for inward migration leading to a significant net increase. The source of this new labour force, in both Whickham and Newcastle as a whole, is less clear. It is likely that the intensification of industrial activity associated with coal mining was reflected in a proportionate increase in the activity and demand for labour in trades associated with the export of coal, including the keelmen and watermen working on the Tyne. Migration of labour to the areas of developing industry around the River Tyne appears to be different from migration in other parts of England, where the vast majority of immigrants into major towns and cities travelled less than 50 miles. Around Tyneside there is reported to have been a significant migration of labour from the Borders and Scotland into a variety of industries that would have involved journeys well in excess of 100 miles. Houston argues that seasonal migration from the highlands to the lowland cities in the summer was a feature of Scottish life; this could have involved travel over very long distances and difficult terrain. It is possible that the readiness of the Scots to travel long distances for work in Scotland was reflected across the Border by a readiness to travel similar distances for work in the Tyne valley – starting to some, degree following the Union of Crowns in 1603, but probably growing significantly after the Union of 1707.[13]

---

[11] Levine and Wrightson, *The Making of an Industrial Society*, p. 186. Levine and Wrightson refer to a shortage of labour in the adjacent parish of Winlaton where 'for lack of workmen, women were employed and there was talk of sending to Scotland for men'.

[12] M. Barke, 'The Pre-civil Registration Population of Newcastle upon Tyne', *Northumbria University, Division of Geography and Environmental Management, Occasional Papers*, 37 (2000).

[13] R.A. Houston, *The Population History of Britain and Ireland 1500–1750* (Basingstoke: Macmillan, 1992), p. 58.

The size of the population of water tradesmen in Newcastle and along the River Tyne was the subject of various estimates in eighteenth- and nineteenth-century literature, however many of these estimates appear to be based on anecdotal reports rather than any form of census or head count. Welford provides one of the earliest quotations, which he says was undated, but which he lists as originating from 1637:

> There is in Newcastle upon Tyne, of keelmen, watermen and other labourers, above eighteen hundred able men, the most of them being Scottish men and Borderers that came out of Tynedale and Riddesdale. By reason of the stop of trade occasioned (by) cross winds this year, they have wanted employment, and are thereby in great necessity, having most of them great charge of wives and children. And unless they have employment, they must be relieved by the charity of others, ... the inhabitants of the town, many of whom are so poor that they are scarcely able to maintain themselves, or else we doubt that, in regard of their necessity and rude condition, they will be in danger to assemble themselves and make an uproar in the town.[14]

In a review of the labour conditions in the coal industry Hughes referred to the seasonal nature of both coal mining and the transport of coal to the ships by the keels. He indicated that it was not just the inclement winter weather that prevented ships from sailing, but the additional effect of cold weather on the coal itself, which led to ice breaking up the larger pieces of coal into small pieces that were more difficult to sell. In addition, the roads and wagon-ways became more difficult to maintain during the wet winter months, making the transport of coal to the riverside staiths more difficult.[15] Moller observed that it was a custom to land keels in the winter for an annual overhaul in readiness for the re-opening of the season in May. This was a process designed to prolong the life of the keels, which could be as long as 50 or 60 years in the mid seventeenth century.[16] The use of keels by the authorities in the Town for clearing the river of wrecks is recorded in the Orders and Minutes of the Hostmen for 19 September 1655:

---

[14] R. Welford, *History of Newcastle and Gateshead*, 5 vols (London: Walter Scott, 1885), p. 348.

[15] E. Hughes, *North Country Life in the Eighteenth Century: the North East, 1700–1750*, (London: Oxford University Press, 1952), p. 251.

[16] A.W.R. Moller, 'The History of British Coal Mining, 1500–1750', PhD diss., Oxford University, 1933, p. 552; F.W. Dendy, *Extracts from the Records of the Company of Hostmen of Newcastle Upon Tyne, Surtees Society*, 105 (Durham, Published for the Society, 1901), p. 108.

Ordered that everie Brother and Sister of this Companie who from and after The Makinge of this present Order shall have any of their Keeles pressed or taken for the weighinge of wracks as aforesaid, shall in recompence for everie keele Three shillings and foure pence cleere for everie Tide for and duringe so longe time such keele shall be used and imployed as aforesaid.[17]

It would appear the use of keels in this manner would include the use of the crews, without whom the work would not be possible, and it is clear from other entries that the compensation was partly in response to a degree of damage that the keels sustained in this work. The work was referred to by Hughes, who noted that, in view of the hardship to the water related tradesmen caused by a seasonal layoff, 'it was stated in 1723 that Newcastle had employed keelmen during the slack winter months in taking sand and removing wrecks from the river with a view to improving navigation, but that in recent years this had been discontinued'.[18] In his extracts from the Orders and Minutes of the Company of Hostmen, under a date of July 1707, Dendy includes a reference to an 'Instrument drawn up by William Storey, Scriviner, on the Order of Several of the Skippers and Keelmen of this Town'. He then presents a transcript of this document entitled *The case of the poor Skippers and Keelmen of Newcastle*, which he indicates came from 'Mr Welford's collection of local documents'. The first paragraph states: 'that the said poor Skippers and Keelmen, being in number about 1,600 men besides women and children, for many years past have suffered great misery and distress, and were exceedingly burthensome on the parishes where they lived'.[19] A subsequent document from the Welford collection, under the same date, *A farther case relating to the poor Keelmen of Newcastle*, related to a petition from the keelmen about the mismanagement of the keelmen's charity. This document states that, 'it is well known the whole number of Keelmen is within 1600, near one thousand whereof have put their hands to this petition, 400 are them are yet in Scotland whither they go always in the winter to their families'.[20] In 1770 the keelmen petitioned the House of Commons for a bill to extend an existing Society of Keelmen. Among the evidence presented was a statement by their Agent, Thomas Harvey that 'great numbers of the Keelmen employed at Newcastle are natives of Scotland from the mode of binding and

---

[17] Dendy, *Company of Hostmen*, p. 107.
[18] Hughes, *North Country Life*, p. 251.
[19] Dendy, *Company of Hostmen*, p. 172; *The Case of the poor Skippers and Keelmen of Newcastle Truly Stated* (London, ?1712), Eighteenth Century Collections Online.
[20] Dendy, *Company of Hostmen*, 176; *A Farther Case relating to the poor Keel-men of Newcastle*, (London, ?1712), Eighteenth Century Collections Online.

hiring and service, are not ... allowed to gain settlement in the Parish of All Saints where most of them reside'.[21] A further witness, who had worked five years as a keelmen, testified that,

> 1200 keelmen were residing in All Saints parish, half of whom, if not more were Scotsmen, and also that he had never known sick or infirm Scotsmen to be relieved as parishioners, even though they had been employed a great number of years as Keelmen.[22]

In contrast, a further witness put the number of keelmen in All Saints parish as 800–900.[23] A number of lists of keelmen were published as parts of legal proceedings during the strikes that took place throughout the eighteenth century.[24] It is probable that these do not represent a complete list of all the keelmen, but only those who were perceived to be guilty of a breach of their conditions of work. These lists could not be construed, therefore, as a realistic basis for the estimation of population size, and it is clear that most of these estimates of the population of keelmen and other water trades are anecdotal and conflicting, with little objective evidence to support them. The accounts that describe the keelmen as being particularly poor should perhaps be regarded with some caution, as Baillie indicated that they were particularly well fed 'they live almost entirely upon flesh-meat and flour, of the best kinds'.[25] And Charleton describes keelmen's houses as 'models of comfort', with 'well filled larders', and apparently well furnished.[26] It is likely, however, that, as in any working population, there was a wide spectrum of relative wealth and wellbeing across the whole community of keelmen.

The terms and conditions of work for the keelmen on the Tyne were based on an annual bond with their employer, the hostman. A surviving original bond in the Bell Collection, dating from 28 December 1787, provides details of the

---

[21] J.M. Fewster, 'The Keelmen of Tyneside in the Eighteenth Century, Part I', *Durham University Journal*, 50 (1957), p. 28 and *The Keelmen of Tyneside: Labour Organisation and Conflict in the North-East Coal Industry, 1600–1830* (Woodbridge: Boydell and Brewer, 2011), pp. 117–24.
[22] Fewster, 'The Keelmen of Tyneside, pp. 28–9.
[23] Fewster, 'The Keelmen of Tyneside', p. 29.
[24] Fewster, 'The Keelmen of Tyneside', p. 24.
[25] J. Baillie, *An Impartial History of the Town and County of Newcastle upon Tyne and Its Vicinity* (Newcastle upon Tyne: Vint and Anderson, 1801), p. 142.
[26] R.J. Charleton, *Newcastle Town*, 4th ed. (London: Walter Scott, 1885, rep., 1978), p. 353.

keelmen employed by a single hostman, Anthony Hood.[27] This handwritten document (Figure 3.1 below) outlines the terms and conditions of work, and is signed and sealed by 68 people. Nineteen people are named separately in the document 'to be and go (as) skippers on nineteen severall keels, coal boats or lighters severally belonging, or to be employed by the said Anthony Hood for the term of one year to be reckoned from this date'. The remainder are named as being employed as 'bound men or shovelmen' for the same period. The document goes on to state that Hood,

> has given them the said skippers, and to each and every one of them the like sum of twenty shillings apiece for the binding of them and their said men to the said service, and has lent unto the said skippers and each and every one of them the like sum of twenty shillings. If therefore the said skippers ... do and shall on or before the eleventh day of June next ensuing will truly pay or cause to be paid to the said Anthony Hood ... the sum of twenty shillings so lent.

The document continues by specifying the details of their work: loading and transporting coal from the staiths to the colliers, including the maximum of eight chaldrons of coal to be loaded into each keel.

This example of the keelmen's bond is particularly interesting from a number of different perspectives. The nature of the document is likely to have remained largely the same for many years. Another surviving bond, which originates from the nineteenth century, relates to a hostman Nathaniel Clayton and is dated 2 February 1820. The terms and conditions in this later bond are almost identical to those in the 1787 bond, apart from the fact that the original signatures of the bonded men are not included in the preserved copy. The 1787 bond, shown in Figure 3.1, is notable in that it clearly categorizes the skippers separately from the other 'bound men or shovelmen', implying a distinctly different status. The payment of 20 shilling bonding money is supplemented by an additional loan of 20 shillings; the fact that the payment is made during the winter implies that it is a supplement to assist the keelmen to survive the winter period, when trade was quieter, with the expectation of repayment when trade improved in the summer. Throughout the bond, the boats the keelmen were to work in were referred to as 'keels, coal boats or lighters' implying that there may either have been a variety of different boats used to carry coal in addition to keels, or that there were a variety

---

[27] J. Bell, *Collections Relative to the River Tyne its Trade and the Conservancy*, Vol. 1, 1603–1800, The Bell Collection, Newcastle City Libraries, NCL/LS, L942.8, T987B, f. 211.

Figure 3.1 The bond used by hostman Anthony Hood to bind his keelmen. By permission Newcastle City Libraries

of descriptions of such boats in common usage. The use of the terminology that the boats were 'severally belonging or to be employed by' the hostmen suggests that a hostman did not necessarily own all of the keels that he used, but hired or borrowed any additional ones that he required for the volume of his business. It is notable that the bond describes 19 keels with 19 skippers and 49 bound men as crew, which is insufficient to provide crews of four in all of the keels, indicating that the keel crew numbers employed by Anthony Hood varied between two and three men in addition to each skipper.

The closest we get to a realistic estimate of the size of the general population of the riverside parishes comes from Welford, in his paper on Hearth Tax returns. He includes the returns for the Sandgate Ward in 1665, where there are 644 households listed, of which only 134 were liable to pay the tax and 510 were not, giving, at an average of five persons per household, an estimate of a Sandgate population of 3220.[28] This could be an overestimate, as more recent evidence about multiplication factors for Hearth Tax data suggests household size was closer to 4.3 persons giving a population estimate for Sandgate of 2770.[29] Unfortunately these estimates of population size are not as satisfactory as might have been hoped, displaying varying population sizes, complicated by a degree of uncertainty about the particular part of the population the individual authors might have been describing. There is a clear need to establish more precisely the population that is being examined, and to use more consistent and reliable measures of population size and changes over time of the water trades. A number of other primary sources provide valuable insight into the evolution of the water trades along the Tyne in the seventeenth and eighteenth centuries, including the Parish Registers for all of the parishes surrounding the lower River Tyne. These records are of variable quality and completeness. There is also a significant body of original documentary material in local archives, which refers directly to the changing circumstances of trade on the Tyne and into Newcastle, and which clarifies many of the pressures that influenced the developing population of water tradesmen and their families during this period of significant change.

The principal economic driver of the burgeoning population growth of Newcastle and the other communities along the lower River Tyne was coal. One of the earliest quantitative references to the coal trade on the River Tyne was in 1367, when the Pipe Rolls, 40th of Edward III, refer to 676 chaldrons of coals purchased from Winlaton for Windsor Castle; 33 keels and one boat were used, with 20 Chaldrons to each keel and 16 to the boat. At this time the Newcastle

---

[28] Welford, 'Newcastle Householders in 1665', p. 49.
[29] Arkell, 'Multiplying factors for estimating population totals', p. 51.

Chaldron weighed about 20 hundredweight (cwt), the keels were manned by keelers, paid 6d each, the hire of each keel was 12d, and there were 5 men to a keel and 4 to the boat.[30] By 1566 the keels on the River Tyne were built and owned by the same Newcastle merchants who became the colliery owners. At first, during the sixteenth century, they dealt with the skippers of the keels who undertook the 'fittage' (negotiating the sale and transport of the coal between the coal owners and the masters of the colliers), giving the skippers some savings and social standing in the Town, but subsequently this role was taken over by agents or hostmen. Close examination of the documents indicate that, although the hostmen managed the process and had access to enough keels for their purposes, there is little objective evidence as to whether they also owned the keels.[31]

The measurement of coal depended on the use of the Newcastle Chaldron, but the precise amount of coal this represented varied, progressively increasing with time. In 1421 it weighed as little as 18 hundredweight (cwt), it had increased to 30 cwt by 1566, and to 52.5 cwt by the beginning of the seventeenth century, where it stabilized.[32] The amount of coal carried by a keel had been standardized, because the crown raised taxes from the coal exported from the Tyne. As a result, the keels that carried the coal from the coal staiths to the colliers were marked so that they carried a standard weight of 8 Chaldrons, which amounted to just over 21 tons per keel; indeed, the term 'keel' was sometimes used as a quantitative term for this measure of coal. This allows a comparison of data from differing sources about the export of coal from the Tyne in terms of tonnage, and also enables computation of the potential number of keel trips required and the manpower, based on a crew of a skipper and two (or three) crew members. In 1602 the Hostmen's records show that during that year there were 29 hostmen divided into four groups, or 'quarters', who moved 190,680 tons of coal in 85 keels.[33] This represents at 21 tons (8 Newcastle Chaldrons) per keel load, 9080 keel loads, which is equivalent to 107 trips in each of 85 keels during that year. At a minimum of 3 crew in each keel, this implies a pool of at least

---

[30] T.J. Taylor, 'Archaeology of the Coal Trade', *Proceedings of the Archaeological Institute of Newcastle upon Tyne* (1852), 159; J. Guthrie, *The River Tyne, its History and Resources* (Newcastle upon Tyne: Andrew Reid, 1880), 18; Charleton, *Newcastle Town*, p. 324.

[31] J.U. Nef, *The Rise of the British Coal Industry*, 2 vols (London: George Routledge & Sons, 1932), Vol. 1, p. 440.

[32] Nef, *The Rise of the British Coal Industry*, Vol. 2, Appendix C, p. 368. The interpretation of published data is confused by the fact that the Newcastle Chaldron was almost twice the weight of the London Chaldron, by a ratio of 217:136; see J. Hatcher, *The History of the British Coal Industry*, Vol. 1, *Before 1700: Towards the Age of Coal* (Oxford: Clarendon Press, 1993), pp. 483–500.

[33] Charleton, *Newcastle Town*, p. 325; Dendy, *Company of Hostmen*, p. 44.

255 skippers and keelmen in 1602. In 1604–05 the hostmen's records outline serious problems being encountered in the coal trade. It would appear that a significant number of 'unauthorized persons' were conspiring with the keepers of the keels, and without the knowledge of the owners of the keels, to load and sell coal to the ships in the Tyne secretly, and without a record being kept, and by implication without taxes being levied. The response of the 28 hostmen and those merchants listed was to appoint eight 'factors and book-keepers in general' to deal with the selling of coal to the ships on behalf of the hostmen. One of these men possibly appears in the list of those admitted as members of the Hostmen's Company.[34] The hostmen then allocated 95 of the keels owned between them, and distributed them among the bookkeepers/factors, with instructions that the sales of coal should be distributed evenly amongst the keel owners. The hostmen appointed six of their number to act as 'surveyors' to supervise the work of the bookkeepers, hiring and firing them as necessary depending on their performance. In addition, the surveyors would visit every one of the coalworks involved in the scheme to monitor progress every 7–14 days. This account indicates a more complex hierarchy, with the hostmen being the coal owners and surveyors, and the bookkeepers/factors being employees from a very early stage.[35]

The estimates of the coal exports from the River Tyne between 1606 and 1700, which have been analysed critically and published by John Hatcher, show annual coal exports increasing from 300,232 tons in 1606 to 518,483 tons by 1700, with a proportionate increase in the number of keels and keelmen.[36] From 1700 to 1790 the coal exports increased further, to 1,150,350 tons.[37] The computation of the number of keels required to move this coal, based on the data from 1602 suggests that the average number of trips made each year by a Tyne keel, on the basis that a keel held 21 tons (8 Newcastle Chaldrons), was 107. In addition, the keel was crewed by a skipper and either two or three crewmen.[38] This appeared to continue until 1634, when a statement is made in the Hostmen's records that it was 'wasting keel time to take coal to Shields, and that ships would have to come up the river to a place above

---

[34] Dendy, *Company of Hostmen*, pp. 265–84.
[35] Dendy, *Company of Hostmen*, pp. 51–5.
[36] Hatcher, *The History of the British Coal Industry*, p. 497.
[37] Dendy, *Company of Hostmen*, p. 260.
[38] P.D. Wright, 'Water Trades on the Lower River Tyne in the Seventeenth and Eighteenth Centuries', PhD diss., Newcastle University, 2011', pp. 59–63. Evidence for the number of keelmen in a keel varies between three and four, in a variety of sources implying that it was not a fixed number and probably varied.

Bill Point to load at least half their coal'.[39] Previously, ships had been able to load coal above Ouseburn; however, shortly after this period, the increasing size of the ships and their cargoes meant that they all needed loading at or around Shields. This meant that twice the number of keels were required, due to increased damage and loss of keels as a result of the greater distances covered over a longer time, and the increased risk of damage and loss of life from the high seas and weather encountered towards the mouth of the river. This resulted in an increase in the rates of keel rent and a doubling of keel numbers, which must have resulted in a reduction of the average number of trips made by a single keel to around 55 in a year.[40] The detailed list that exists, of the amounts of coal shipped coastwise from 1606 to 1710 and both coastwise and overseas from 1723 to 1786, allows us to estimate the changing number of keels and keelmen at intervals between 1606 and 1786, and to compare these with estimates that appear in the secondary literature (Table 3.2). There is the opportunity to compare the figures for coal shipments from Newcastle, included in Dendy's Hostmen's records, with Willan's figures based on Newcastle Port Books,[41] as well as with those shown by Nef and Hatcher,[42] who used a combination of figures from Dendy, the port books and a number of other sources. It is interesting to note that the figures for 1683 are identical in these sources, at 210,972 Newcastle Chaldrons or 553,751 tons. Both sets of figures from Dendy and Willan are stated to be coastwise figures only. A similar comparison, of 1731, shows that the figure provided by Dendy, of 311,278 Chaldrons (824,886 tons), is for both coastwise and overseas, whereas Willan's figures for coastwise shipments alone are 280,353 Chaldrons (735,926 tons), 10 per cent less than Dendy's estimates of the total shipments. This is probably a reasonable estimate of the proportions of coastal to overseas shipments for the same year,[43] and suggests overseas shipments of 30,925 (81,178 tons). Nef has attempted to correct the overall figures by obtaining data from the relevant port books to calculate the overseas shipments and consequently the total shipments for the year.

Further comparisons with estimates of keel numbers in the Hostmen's records with those made by other authors can be found. Bourne wrote in 1736

---

[39] Dendy, *Company of Hostmen*, p. 74.
[40] Dendy, *Company of Hostmen*, p. 107.
[41] T.S. Willan, *The English Coasting Trade, 1600–1750* (Manchester: Manchester University Press, 1938), p. 210, TNA, Exch.K.R. Port Books 200/15.
[42] Nef, 'The Rise of the British Coal Industry', Vol. 2, Appendix D, p. 388; Hatcher, *The History of the British Coal Industry*, p. 497.
[43] Willan, *The English Coasting Trade*, p. 211, TNA, Exch.K.R. Port Books 236/7.

Table 3.2 Estimated populations of Newcastle keels and keelmen from coal exports

Year	Newcastle[a]	Coal Exports (Tons)	Keels	Keelmen[b]	Keels (Literature)	Keelmen (Literature)
1560	10,000					
1602		190,680	85	255–340		
1610		300,232	132	396–528		
1630		349,935	156	468–624		
1665	10,800	484,447	419	1,257–1,676		
1670	12,000					
1671		439,563	381	1,143–1,524		
1700	16,000	518,483	449	1,347–1,796		
1704		525,489	455	1,365–1,820	400	1,500[c]
1707		558,095	483	1,449–1,932		1,600[d]
1709					338[e]	
1710		445,239	385	1,156–1,540		1,600[f]
1736	20,000	787,966	682	2,046–2,728	688	2,064–2,752[g]
1750	29,000	752,727	652	1,956–2,608		
1760		748,667	648	1,944–2,592		
1790		1,150,350	996	2,998–3,984		
1801	28,924					

Sources: (a) Newcastle population as shown, with sources, in Table 3.1. Keel numbers are calculated from coal export figures in Table 1.2, assuming a keel held 8 chaldrons or 21 tons of coal, and undertook an average of 107 trips per keel per year up to 1634, and an average of 55 trips each year thereafter. The figures closer to 1800 are probably an overestimate, because other methods of loading coal into ships were beginning to be used after 1770 including coal chutes directly into colliers. (b) Figures throughout this table assume a keel crew ranging between 3 and 4. (c) Charleton, *Newcastle Town*, p. 325. (d) Dendy, *Company of Hostmen*, p. 176; *A Farther case of the poor keelmen*. (e) M.W. Flinn, *The History of the British Coal Industry*, p. 168; Heslop MS article NEI Misc Bell and Coatsworth Papers, 60/ZA/3a. (f) Fewster, 'The Keelmen of Tyneside', p. 28. (g) Bourne, *The History of Newcastle upon Tyne*, p. 159. This provides an estimate of keel numbers, after which the numbers of keelmen have been given as a range depending on 3 or 4 keelmen.

that there were 400 keels and 1500 keelmen in 1704,[44] and Charleton quotes identical numbers, which, although unreferenced, are likely to have been quoting Bourne,[45] whereas our estimate from the coal exports in the Hostmen's records

---

[44] H. Bourne, *The History of Newcastle Upon Tyne* (Newcastle upon Tyne: John White,1736), p. 161.

[45] Charleton, *Newcastle Town*, p. 325.

indicates 455 and 1365 respectively. Flinn reported that between 1709 and 1719 there were said to be 400 keels, but more precise accounts indicate 338.[46] Although the data was deficient in the Hostmen's records for 1709, the figures for 1710 were 385 and 1156 respectively. In addition, Bourne wrote that in 1736 'Coal was shipped at 300,000 chaldrons a year, also vast exports of grindstones, salt, lead and salmon'.[47] This equates to 795,000 tons of coal, 688 keels and 2064 keelmen. The equivalent Hostmen's record for that year indicates 297,346 chaldrons or 787,966 tons of coal, from which a very similar estimate of 682 keels and 2047 keelmen is obtained. All of these comparative figures tend to suggest a high degree of consistency in the estimates of keel and keelman numbers, which give some confidence in their validity. It is notable, however, that the close similarity between the estimates of keel numbers and the number of keelmen and those in the literature depend on the keels being crewed by only three men. This is somewhat at variance with the evidence, both in the literature and in contemporary art, for crews of four manning each keel. In view of this, Table 3.2 shows a range of values for the numbers of keelmen. The issue of keelmen numbers is further complicated by the reports indicating that the keel crew often included a boy; it is uncertain whether this boy was a member of the family of the skipper or keelman.[48] The keelmen were never able to form themselves into an incorporated company, and thus they were unable to take formal apprentices; nevertheless, it is possible to speculate that, in light of the powers of parish overseers and justices to 'bind out' poor children into apprenticeships, poor children were indeed deployed to work on the keels in an informal apprenticeship.[49]

Contemporary evidence for the number of bound men comes in a further document in the Bell Collection: this is a notice dated 'Newcastle, April 28th 1750', printed at the time of a keelmen's strike (Figure 3.2). The notice reads:

---

[46] M.W. Flinn, *The History of the British Coal Industry*, Vol. 2, *1700–1830: The Industrial Revolution* (Oxford: Oxford University Press, 1984), p. 168.

[47] H. Bourne, *The History of Newcastle upon Tyne* (Newcastle upon Tyne: John White, 1736; rep, Newcastle upon Tyne: Frank Graham, 1980), p. 159.

[48] J. Brand, *The History and Antiquities of the Town of Newcastle Upon Tyne*, 2 vols (London, 1789), pp. 261–2. Brand notes that the labourers working the keels were also known as keel-bullies, and he quotes Stukeley as saying that there were three keelmen and a skipper to a crew; but he also quotes Pennant as saying that the crew consisted of a skipper, one man and a boy. He also notes that the wives and daughters of the keelmen were used to sweep the keels and to keep the sweepings for their pains. The women were known as keel-deeters. At the time 'to deet' meant to sweep or keep clean.

[49] Richard Burn, *The Justice of the Peace, and the Parish Officer* (London: Printed by W. Strahan and M. Woodfall for T. Cadell, 1772), Vol. 1, pp. 54–92.

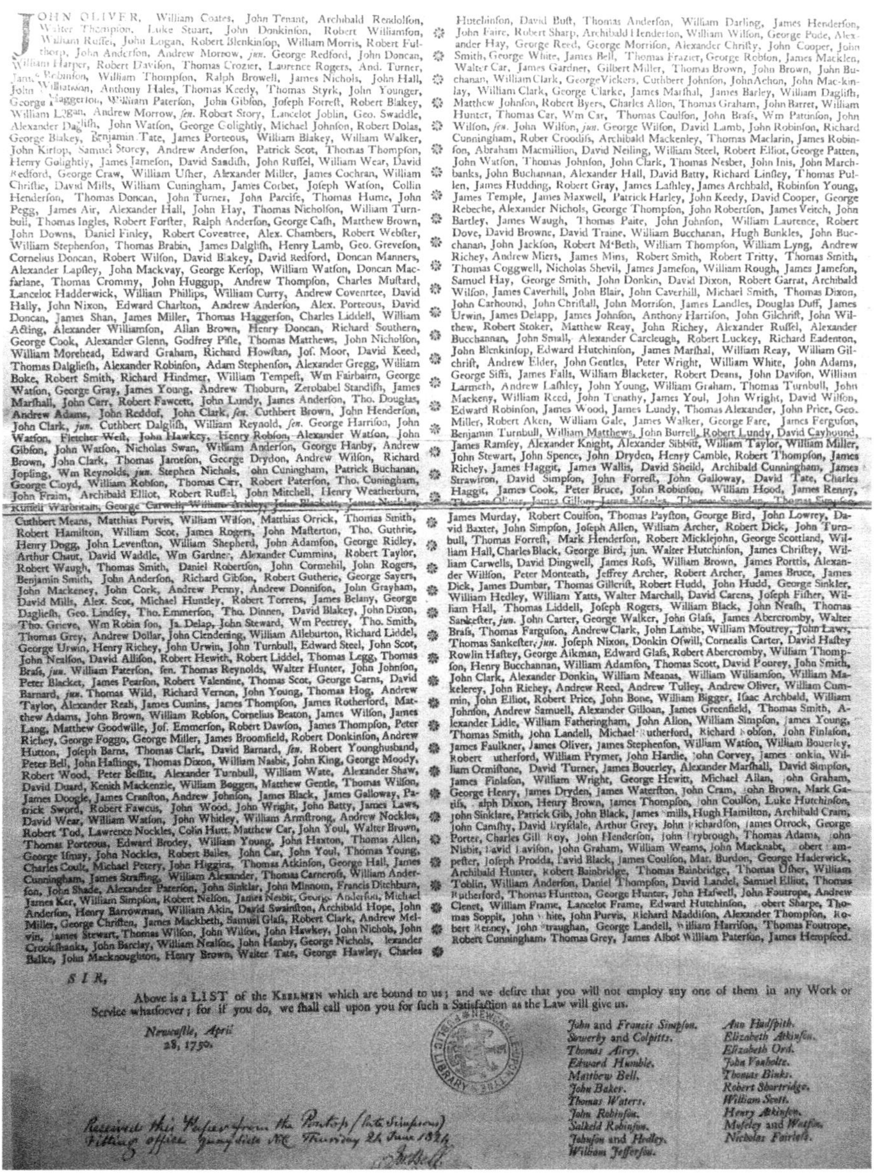

Figure 3.2   Handbill listing keelmen employed by hostmen in 1750. By permission Newcastle City Libraries

'Sir, Above is a list of the keelmen which are bound to us; and we desire that you will not employ any one of them in any work or service whatsoever; for if you do we shall call upon you for such satisfaction as the law will give us'. This notice is preceded by a very long list comprising the names of over 800 keelmen, followed by the names of 25 hostmen. This list of hostmen is interesting in itself, in that it includes the names of three women, and also includes William Jefferson, whose apprentice Ralph Jackson is considered in some detail in Chapter 7. It is notable that the list of keelmen amounted to only just over 800, when the calculated number of keelmen shown in Table 3.2 for 1750 was between 1,900 and 2,600. It might be speculated that the list of hostmen adding their names to the notice represented only a proportion of those hostmen who were active at the time. However, an insight into the number of active hostmen at the time is provided by the Newcastle Chamberlains' Accounts, in which the names of the hostmen were entered each time they cleared a ship loaded with coal through the process of paying the local coal taxes.[50] Figures from the Accounts for 1756 show the names of 22 hostmen entered, most of whom were represented among the signatories of the notice. This implies that the list does indeed represent most of those hostmen who were active at the time. There are a number of possible reasons for this discrepancy. First, lists of keelmen made out during a period of industrial unrest in 1740 not only listed by name the keelmen working for each hostman, but also identified that for some hostmen at least one of the crew was not a bound man but a free man.[51] Second, there is inevitably an element of uncertainty about the exact number of keels, which for 1750 were estimated at around 650, and it is possible that the 800 names were those of bound skippers rather than shovelmen. This is perhaps a more plausible explanation, as 800 keelmen in total would enable the working of only 265 keels, which is far too few to move the coal that we have good evidence was indeed transported.

In 1711, William Cotesworth (1668–1726) and five other coal owners formed what they described as 'The Regulation', which was designed to control and regulate the coal trade and maximize their profits. They re-measured the keels used by the regulation and marked them with a 'scrivening' iron, then sent agents to accompany them down to the ships to make sure the keelmen did not throw the coal overboard and properly loaded it into the ships. They reduced the number of keels, so that for every 100 keels used previously they used only 92. They employed a total of 260 keels for the year, making sure that they were

---

[50] TWAM MD.NC/FN/1/1/108.
[51] Keelmen's Papers, TWAM GU, 394/11.

used fully, delivering approximately 300,300 tons of coal.[52] If these figures are compared with those found in the Hostmen's records for the nearest year 1710 we find that the total export figure for the Tyne was 445,239 tons, indicating that 'The Regulation' only provided 67 per cent of the coal exported that year. Throughout eighteenth century there were continual disputes between the coal owners, the keelmen and the masters of the colliers, and also with the purchasers of the coal, mainly in London. This resulted in the formation of a number of 'combinations' at every level in the trade, with many strikes, and refusals to transport coal.[53] Notwithstanding this turbulence, it is clear from the figures of coal exports in the Hostmen's records that there was a continuing increase in the volume of coal exports throughout the period. Towards the end of the eighteenth century and into the nineteenth, the nature of coal transport changed with the increasing use of railways to move the coal greater distances, and coal spouts at the staiths, particularly those below the Tyne Bridge, enabling the loading of coal directly into the colliers without the use of keels. This resulted in a reduction in the number of keels and a weakening of the previously close association between the amount of river traffic and the amount of coal exported.[54] However, coal was not the only commodity to be exported, there was a significant import and export trade, particularly of foodstuffs and other domestic consumables. Much non-coal import and export activity apparently occurred at the commodious Newcastle quayside. However, the extent to which the shallow and tidal nature of the Tyne meant that some of the general cargo for export had to be carried in small boats to deeper water closer to the mouth of the river, for loading onto ships, remains unclear; and the reverse process would be true for imports. The published data on the amounts of coal exported each year, and the computations on the numbers of keels and keelmen necessary to undertake the work involved, provide a perspective on the potential size of the water- trades community involved in the coal trade. The calculations appear to give very reasonable comparisons with those figures appearing in the literature, particularly during the eighteenth century. However, there are fewer useful estimates in the

---

[52] Hughes, *North Country Life*, pp. 170–72.

[53] Charleton, *Newcastle Town*, p. 325; Nef, *Rise of the British Coal Industry*, Vol. 2, pp. 178–9; S. Middlebrook, *Newcastle upon Tyne: Its Growth and Achievement* (Newcastle upon Tyne: Newcastle Journal, 1950), p. 108; Fewster, 'The Keelmen of Tyneside', p. 28, 'The Last Struggles of the Tyneside Keelmen', *Durham University Journal*, 55 (1963), pp. 5–15; Fewster, *The Keelmen of Tyneside*, pp. 70–86.

[54] Fewster, 'The Keelmen of Tyneside', 1–15; D.J. Rowe, 'The Decline of the Tyneside Keelmen in the Nineteenth Century', *Northern History*, 4 (1969), pp. 111–31.

literature for the seventeenth century; for example, an estimate for 1637 of 1,800 men included other types of labourer. This makes comparisons more difficult; but, overall, relating keel and keelmen numbers to published levels of coal exports appears to give more realistic estimates. However, these estimates take no account of the section of the water-trades community that may have been involved in the non-coal trade – unless those workers involved in the coal trade were also working to support the non-coal trade. This emphasizes the need for a closer examination of the water-trades community as a whole.

Chapter 4
All Saints:
The Growth of a Riverside Parish

Given that there are reasonably reliable estimates of the number of keels and keelmen operating on the Tyne during the seventeenth and eighteenth centuries, those living and working in the water trades at a more local level can be examined more closely. During this period, the largest concentration of the water trades community was based at the east end of Newcastle 'keyside', in Sandgate, which lay within the Parish of All Saints. Many contemporary records survive for all of the Anglican parishes in Newcastle and along the lower River Tyne, however the four parishes in Newcastle, those of St Nicholas, St John, St Andrew and All Saints, have particularly full and complete surviving parish registers, including details of occupation in burial, baptism and marriage registers dating back to 1557 (Figure 4.1).

From these records it is clear that the vast majority of those who had occupations in the water trades lived in the parish of All Saints, with few if any living in the other three parishes, and this provides the opportunity for a case study of the evolution of this part of the working population along the river. Any study using Anglican parish registers as a tool for studying the population dynamics of a parish or a particular group within a parish requires an understanding of the limitations of these records. The All Saints parish registers are appropriate for analysis, in that they are complete and thus satisfactory. In addition, the minimum register size is substantially greater than 100. Extra-parochial registration does not appear to be a problem, but under-registration is a significant issue, particularly with diminishing burials in the last 50 years up to 1800, associated with the increasing numbers of dissenters using non-conformist chapels and the use of the unconsecrated Ballast Hills burial ground.[1]

The three types of registers, burial, baptism and marriage, each have their own problems. Stuart Basten examined the impact of religious dissent upon the

---

[1] M. Drake, *Population Studies from Parish Registers* (Oxford: Open University Press, 1982), pp. v–xxxiv; S. Basten, 'Registration Practices in Anglican Parishes and Dissenting Groups in Northern England 1770–1840', PhD diss, Cambridge University, 2008.

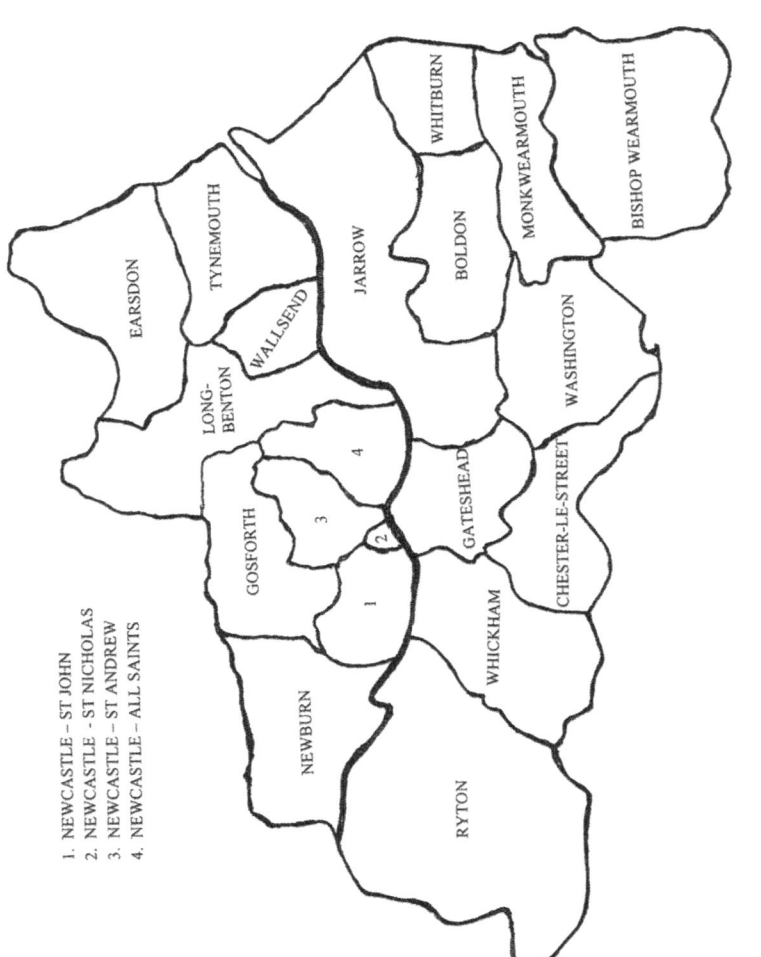

Figure 4.1   Anglican parishes around the lower River Tyne, 1600–1800

registration practices in Anglican parishes in the North of England, including those in Newcastle, and highlighted the magnitude of the problems arising from the high levels of under-registration, particularly in burial registers. This makes it almost impossible to make reliable estimates of population size, particularly from burial records, without a very significant use of a variety of adjustment factors, some of which may be of more value than others.[2] Baptism records under-represent the real number of births during the seventeenth and eighteenth centuries, largely because of the relatively high peri-natal mortality rates, which resulted in many babies who died in the first weeks of life not being registered at all. These elements of under-registration were addressed by Wrigley and Schofield, who introduced a number of correction factors in an attempt to rectify this problem.[3] However, in his review of vital registration in Newcastle, Barke points out that even after Wrigley's adjustments the estimates seem abnormally low, possibly due to groups in the poorer urban areas who probably escaped any form of registration.[4] Wrigley, in his analysis of English county populations in the eighteenth century after the introduction of Hardwicke's Marriage Act in 1753, points out that the registration of marriages in Anglican parishes became virtually complete, making it a more useful parameter for estimation of population dynamics.[5] Notwithstanding the undoubted elements of under-registration that occurred in Newcastle, making accurate calculations of total population size potentially unreliable, Wrigley indicates that, even if it is not possible to derive accurate estimates of population size, estimates of the proportions in which different occupations are distributed in a community may well be significant.[6] In view of these considerations, it is legitimate in this context to regard those registrations that did occur in All Saints as representative of a minimum population size, and as such are worthy of consideration. In addition, the *proportions* of those described as working in the water trades are probably valid for the parish population as a whole. It is reasonable to expect that the descriptions of the various occupations that appear in parish registers are those that were supplied by the families of those members of the community

[2] Basten, 'Registration Practices in Anglican Parishes'.

[3] E.A. Wrigley and R.S. Schofield, *The Population History of England 1541–1871, a Reconstruction* (London: Edward Arnold, 1981).

[4] M. Barke, 'The Pre-Civil Registration Population of Newcastle Upon Tyne', pp. 7–11.

[5] E.A. Wrigley, 'English county populations in the later eighteenth century', *Economic History Review*, 60:1 (2007), 35–69; E.A. Wrigley, 'Rickman revisited: the population growth rates of English counties in the early modern period', *Economic History Review*, 2nd ser. 62 (2009), pp. 711–35.

[6] Wrigley, 'English county populations', pp. 38–9.

whose life events were being recorded. Alternatively, they were the descriptions supplied by the parish clerk, which one would expect to be very similar to the names by which the occupations were known in the community at the time.

Notwithstanding the historical accounts that have suggested that there was a higher incidence religious dissent among the keelmen, particularly because many of them may have originated from non-conformist Scotland, the occupations listed in the All Saints registers reveal a large number of water-trades people in the parish. There was a change in the descriptions of these water-trades occupations over 200 years (Table 4.1).[7] Parish burial registers for the 50 years from 1600 to 1650 show that the water tradesmen were most commonly described as keelmen, who we must assume were those labourers who worked in the keels on the River Tyne. After the peak between 1600 and 1650 there is a rapid decline in the use of the term 'keelman', with a corresponding rise in the use of the term 'waterman'. In view of these striking changes, we must assume that there was a change in the terms used to describe the keelmen, using this more generic title of waterman. Whether this term was used to describe a larger community of water tradesmen, of which the keelmen were only a part, remains uncertain. Similarly the records indicate that the term 'skipper' was commonly used, almost certainly to describe the skipper of a keel, a term that persists in lists of keelmen prepared by hostmen in 1740,[8] even though the term had ceased to be used in the lists of occupations in the parish registers by the beginning of the eighteenth century. From 1700, the term waterman was used to describe around 90 per cent of the water tradesmen, with only two mentions of keelmen in the entire eighteenth century. The term 'wherryman' is present throughout the period studied, representing around 10 per cent of the water trades population by 1750. These were watermen who worked on the wherrys, which were different from the coal carrying keels, being, at this time, quite possibly smaller and simpler passenger-carrying craft. In the presence of a body of literature apparently describing the origins, work and the lifestyle of the keelmen, it is a little surprising that the parish records of All Saints, where a large proportion of the keelmen lived, use the term with decreasing frequency over the seventeenth century, and scarcely at all during the eighteenth century. It is unlikely that this choice of nomenclature was the result of a whim of a particular parish clerk, as this process continues over 200 years, and covers the tenure of a number of different clerks. In addition, the records of burials in these parish registers show that throughout the period

---

[7] P.D. Wright, 'Water Trades on the Lower River Tyne in the Seventeenth and Eighteenth Centuries', PhD diss., Newcastle University, 2011', pp. 46–89.

[8] Keelmen's papers TWAM, GU 394/11.

Table 4.1   Water tradesmens' occupations from parish burial register

Years	Boatmen	Skippers	Keelmen	Watermen	Wherrymen	Total
1600–1649	14	44	315	15	33	421
1650–1699	8	109	24	360	12	513
1700–1749	0	0	0	720	80	800
1750–1800	0	0	2	246	27	275

studied there are many clusters of three watermen or keelmen buried within a day or two, which is very noticeable in the context of relatively few burials each month. There is a high probability that this represents burials of crews of keels or equivalent, probably resulting from accidents at work. These groupings of possible work related deaths occur throughout the year, implying that keels crewed by at least three men were working both in the summer and winter.[9]

Accurate measurement of the size of a population in the seventeenth and eighteenth centuries is difficult and requires reference to contemporary documents, which cover a substantial proportion of the whole population – most likely legal documents of some kind. In most parts of England, such a document would be either a parish register or a mandatory tax return such as the Hearth Tax. The use of parish burial registers as a tool for estimating changes in the size of an urban population is fraught with difficulty, particularly in the presence of variable factors such as under-registration associated with poverty and religious dissent. However, notwithstanding these problems, in the absence of more satisfactory sources they have been used with a number of correction factors to estimate changes in population.[10] As Vanessa Harding has noted, John Graunt and Sir William Petty used parish burial records as a basis upon which to estimate population size in London.[11] The records from the burial registers in the parish of All Saints are remarkably complete, and according to calculations based on the methods used by Graunt and Petty, the population size of All Saints parish rose from 8,785 in the decade 1621–30 to an apparent peak in population, near the end of the seventeenth century, of around 10,000. An apparent decline in

---

[9] Wright, 'Water Trades on the Lower River Tyne' pp. 46–89.
[10] Wrigley and Schofield, *The Population History of England*.
[11] V. Harding, *The Dead and the Living in Paris and London, 1500–1670* (Cambridge: Cambridge University Press, 2002), pp. 16–17; J. Graunt, *Natural and Political Observations on the Bills of Mortality*, 3rd ed. (London, 1665), p. 141; W. Petty, 'Another Essay in Political Arithmetick Concerning the Growth of the City of London', in C.H. Hull, *The Economic Writings of Sir William Petty* (Cambridge: Cambridge University Press, 1899) p. 459.

population towards 6,000, during the eighteenth century, is most likely to be spurious, and related to the decline in registrations in Anglican parish registers. This decline was almost certainly due to the rise in non-conformism and burial in un-consecrated burial grounds, which became more prominent in the latter half of the century. The Reverend Emerson, Vicar of All Saints, was so concerned about under-registration in his parish that he employed a woman to count the burials in Ballast Hills burial ground for one year in 1800. She found 612 unregistered burials, of which she claimed 466 originated in All Saints; this emphasizes the magnitude of the problems associated with the use of Anglican parish burial registration in studies of population size.[12] Details in the Ballast Hills burial registers,[13] however, indicate that, overall, around 50 per cent of the burials there were of people living outside All Saints parish, making a calculation of population size from burial registers even more unreliable. Indeed Emerson's observer, having counted 466 additional burials of All Saints parishioners in Ballast Hills, made the annual total of burials in the parish 637, which would have given a parish population of over 19,000 in the year 1800. This was clearly a gross overestimate, as the population of the whole of Newcastle in the 1801 census was shown to be 28,294. When compared with the population estimates for the whole town of Newcastle shown in Chapter 3, these figures for All Saints parish appear higher than we would expect, particularly during the seventeenth century, as they would represent almost three quarters of the town's population. It is likely that this is partly due to a large section of the parish being outside the town boundaries, but it may also represent the presence of a large proportion of the town's trade and business activity taking place within the parish boundaries. Many secondary sources reflect the seasonal nature of the coal trade and suggest that many of the keelmen returned to families in the Borders or Scotland for the winter. If this were indeed the case, one might expect a relative absence of water tradesmen in winter to be reflected in the monthly burial rates. There was no clear seasonal pattern of burials in the decadal monthly patterns of burial of water tradesmen in All Saints during the seventeenth century, with the number of burials of water tradesmen during the winter usually very similar in number to those in the summer. However, during the eighteenth century a clearer seasonality emerges, with a significant increase in deaths over the winter and early spring. Although this increase would be an expected seasonal increase in death rate, the fact that there were still water tradesmen remaining in the

---

[12] Commentary by the Rev. Emerson, All Saints Parish Registers, Newcastle City Libraries Local History Section, (NCL/LS) L929.3/N536, Vol. 11.
[13] TWAM Ballast Hills Cemetery Burial Records, 1792–1853 CE. BA (MF).

parish that died, does not seem to support the view that significant numbers of watermen left All Saints in the winter.[14]

Like the burial registers, marriage registers in the parish are almost complete throughout the seventeenth and eighteenth centuries, with the exception of the period around 1650. For most of the period they also contain details of the husband's occupation, however when the structure of the record changes, after the introduction of the Hardwicke Act of 1754, occupational details are no longer included. Table 4.2 shows the details of the total number of marriages registered, together with the numbers in the water trades, at 25-year intervals during the seventeenth century, and 10 year intervals during the eighteenth century, up to the end of the old system in 1753. In the light of the observations in the literature about the effect of under-registration caused particularly by religious dissenters on the completeness of the marriage registers before 1754, it is notable that the numbers of marriages registered in All Saints before 1754 were no lower than those registered afterwards. This calls into question the validity either of the claim that under-registration of marriages was occurring before the implementation of Hardwicke's Act, or of the claim that the Act had eliminated under-registration. The estimates of the population of All Saints can be compared with those of Newcastle at the same time; for example, in 1750, when Newcastle's population was 29,000, the estimated population of All Saints was 16,414, or 57 per cent of the population of the city. Again, this percentage must be an overestimate, as a significant part of All Saints parish lay outside the Newcastle town walls. All of the figures for the parish population seem to be relatively high, and this may be due to the fact that the marriage rate in this urban parish may have been very much higher than any of those described in Wrigley's paper on county populations.[15] Comparison between the estimates of All Saints parish population and, where possible, the relevant water trades populations, can also be seen in Table 4.2. The estimates using marriage registers are much higher than those using burial registers; and although an element of this difference may be due, once again, to the choice of marriage rate used for the calculations, the majority of the difference is likely due to the better quality of the marriage registers as a source of data for population studies.[16]

An important issue in the historical accounts of the water-trades community in Newcastle has been the impact of immigration, particularly from Scotland,

---

[14] Wright, 'Water Trades on the Lower River Tyne', pp. 46–89.
[15] Wrigley, 'English County Populations', 44; It is notable that M. Barke (in 'Pre-Civil Registration') described a marriage rate for Newcastle in the late eighteenth century as 8.297, which is lower than the rate used in Table 4.2.
[16] Wright, 'Water Trades on the lower River Tyne' pp. 46–89.

Table 4.2   Marriages from All Saints parish registers, 1600–1800*

Year	Marriages	Water Trades	Est. Population	Est. Water Trades
1601	51	12 (24%)	5,937	1,397
1625	77		8,964	
1650	41		4,773	
1675	95	31 (33%)	11,059	3,650
1700	74		8,615	
1710	76	26 (34%)	8,847	3,027
1720	83	30 (36%)	9,662	3,492
1730	119	35 (29%)	13,853	4,075
1740	127	58 (46%)	14,785	6,752
1750	141	57 (40%)	16,414	6,636
1753	121	41 (34%)	14,086	4,773
Hardwicke's Act				
1755	104		12,107	
1760	102		11,874	
1765	133		15,483	
1770	106		12,340	
1775	111		12,922	
1780	121		14,086	
1785	125		14,551	
1790	115		13,388	
1795	124		14,435	
1800	146		16,997	

Source: All Saints Parish Marriage Registers, NCL/LS, L929.3/N536

* These figures from the All Saints parish marriage registers are divided into those before and those after the introduction of Hardwicke's Act in 1754. Not all of the years had details of occupation, those that did have the figures under 'water trades' to include keelmen, watermen, skippers and wherrymen. After E.A. Wrigley, 'English county populations', 40–50, the marriage register data was used to calculate serial populations of All Saints and the number of those in Water Trades families. Wrigley's estimates of the marriage rate per 1000 people for Northumberland was a very low 6.84, as it represented a more rural population than that of All Saints, with its industrial community, which was likely to have a rate closer to that of Lancashire's 9.9. As a compromise, the figure for England as a whole of 8.59 has been used for calculation of the All Saints population sizes.

which was often stated to have made a substantial contribution to the numbers of keelmen. The All Saints parish records give an impression of the dynamics of the water-trades population, and particularly the true contribution of inward migration to the community. The use of baptism and burial data from parish records has been proposed by Kitch and Corfield as a method of estimating the level of migration into a parish; they suggested that a parish with a large migrant population might be expected to show a large excess of burials over baptisms. The corresponding figures for All Saints indicate that, throughout the period studied, there appeared to be a substantial excess of baptisms over burials, which, on its own might indicate that there was not a significant inward migration into the All Saints parish as a whole.[17] However, these figures for both baptisms and burials must be viewed with extreme caution, as they are likely to be a substantial underestimate due to the high levels of under-registration, which has been shown to prevail in all Newcastle parishes. From these figures it would appear that the effect of significant under-registration of burials, due to increasing levels of non-conformist dissenters, was already at work by the beginning of the seventeenth century, and it is most probable that the apparent excess of baptisms over burials represents no more that the fact that the levels of under-registration of burials was even greater than that of baptisms, making the data of little value for estimating population dynamics of any kind. However, marriage registers, which appear to be of more value for estimates of population size,[18] indicate that there was a progressive increase in the population of All Saints from 5,937 in 1601 to a maximum of around 16,997 in 1800, with the water tradesmen's proportion rising from 24 per cent of the parish population in 1601 to 46 per cent in 1740. It would be expected that in a growing urban community with a thriving trade there would be significant population growth from inward migration, in addition to an element of endogenous growth, which is difficult to quantify in the absence of good population data.

An alternative way of estimating the degree of migration was used by Levine and Wrightson, who used the ratio of male to female burials as an indicator of migration in nearby Whickham. Applying this technique to All Saints, all years except 1750 show male burials to be in great excess of female, which, as the authors note, might be indicative of a male dominated society with an excess of males in the population. In addition, there would have been an inevitable rise in male mortality rate, consistent with the inherent risks existing in the industrial community that we know existed in All Saints at the time, and within which Levine and Wrightson suggest the working population could only be maintained

---

[17] M.J. Kitch, 'Capital and Kingdom: Migration to Later Stuart London', *London 1500–1700: the Making of the Metropolis*, ed. A.L. Beier and R. Finlay (London: Longman, 1986), p. 224. P. Corfield, 'A Provincial Capital in the Late Seventeenth Century: the Case of Norwich', in *Crisis and Order in English Towns*, ed. P. Clark and P. Slack (London: Routledge, 1972), p. 233.

[18] E.A. Wrigley, 'English County Populations'.

by significant migration.[19] Although such conclusions might be justified when looking at the population of the parish as a whole, they would not be satisfactory when applying the male to female burial ratios in the context of occupation. The quality of parish burial register data in All Saints would make any occupation-related conclusion difficult, as uncertainty about whether female burials would necessarily be associated with occupations such as the water trades would affect the conclusions. The same authors used a further marker of migration into a community, using the work by Lasker and Roberts referred to earlier, and their 'coefficient of relationship by isogonomy'. Studying Whickham they suggested that the appearance of a surname that had not previously existed in a community was highly suggestive of the arrival of a new individual or family, and they used this supposition to estimate the impact of immigration upon the community. They estimated that between 1608 and 1623 58.5 per cent of the names in the parish of Whickham were new, implying that this increase was due to migration.[20]

Applying the same concept to All Saints, the percentage of new surnames in the parish over the 50 year interval from 1600 to 1650 was 76.5 per cent, falling to 58–60.5 per cent for the remaining intervals up to 1800. Notably, apart from 1600, the percentage of new surnames is very similar to that found in Whickham. Although there appear to be a significant number of new surnames amongst the water trades in All Saints, this apparent migration does not appear to be any greater than that which might be expected in any other rapidly developing industrial community, such as Whickham, at that time. In addition, unlike Whickham, there is considerable written evidence to suggest an influx of labour from Scotland into the water trades of All Saints. However, there does not appear to be an undue predominance of new Scottish names among the population. Like Whickham, the period of maximum growth in the population between, 1646 and 1750, was not accompanied by an equivalent increase in the number of new surnames, indicating that either the increase in the water trades population was not entirely due to migration, or that, like Whickham, any migration was from places relatively close by with a similar pattern of surnames.[21]

In her study of social relations in Newcastle upon Tyne in the seventeenth and eighteenth centuries, Joyce Ellis described evidence, from a census of keelmen taken in 1740, of a degree of migration of water tradesmen. At this time, there had been serious hunger riots, in which the keelmen had taken a leading part.

---

[19] D. Levine and K. Wrightson, *The Making of an Industrial Society: Whickham 1560–1765* (Oxford: Clarendon Press, 1991), p. 179.

[20] Levine and Wrightson, *The Making of an Industrial Society*, p. 180.

[21] G.W. Lasker and D.F. Roberts, 'Secular Trends in Relationship as Estimated by Surnames: a Study of a Tyneside Parish', *Annals of Human Biology*, 9 (1982), pp. 299–307.

The magistrates wrote to the hostmen on 16 July 1740 asking them for 'as soon as maybe, an exact list of all skippers (and bound men) ... with an Account of the time they have respectively been in Town, and the place respectively they came from and were born or settled in'.[22] The original letter and the returns from the hostmen are preserved in the Tyne and Wear Archives.[23] These returns show that they employed a total of 428 keelmen, which is clearly not the whole of the community of keelmen when compared with the estimated of keelmen numbers shown in Chapter 3, but does appear to provide a representative sample. They show a number of revealing features: First, the hostmen appear to include a woman, which corroborates the observations made earlier that among 25 hostmen signing a letter three were women. The involvement of women as active hostmen has not been widely reported in the literature.[24] Second, the keelmen are almost universally recorded in groups of three or four with a 'skipper' and two or three bound men, often with a line between each group, probably indicating that each group was the crew of a single keel. A relatively small proportion of these list four men, often with a note that one has recently left, corresponding with accounts in the literature of the size of a keel crew being three or four men. Third, the place of birth of most of the keelmen was noted and indeed, of the 150 whose origin was stated, 46 per cent originated outside the Newcastle area.[25] Most of these originated in Scotland or the Borders, but some came from other places, such as Cumberland and the town of Wakefield. Similarly, of those keelmen who had moved to Newcastle from elsewhere and whose duration of stay was noted, 81 per cent had been there for more than 10 years.[26] Of those keelmen originating from and still living in the Newcastle area, a considerable number originated from Tyneside parishes outside Sandgate, and some still lived in places such as Gateshead and North Shields. Fourth, the information requested by the magistrates about recent absences of keelmen showed that 61

---

[22] J. Ellis, 'A Dynamic Society: Social Relations in Newcastle-Upon-Tyne 1660–1760', in *The Transformation of English Provincial Towns 1600–1800*, ed. P. Clark (London: Hutchinson & Co., 1984), p. 209.

[23] Keelmen's Papers, TWAM, GU 394/11.

[24] Jane Watson appears in the 1740 list of hostmen, filing a return on the details of her keelmen for the Mayor. There are a number of males named Watson entered in the lists of members of the Company of Hostmen, and it is quite possible that she could be the widow continuing her late husband's business.

[25] This is 46 per cent of those keelmen employed by the nine hostmen who reported place of birth or settlement.

[26] From the seven hostmen who gave the necessary information, 81 per cent of the keelmen born outside the Newcastle area had been in the City for more than 10 years, with most having been there for considerably longer.

recently had left their employer. Some of the hostmen gave details of where they had gone, and it would seem that most of them had gone to work on another keel for a different hostman, but a significant number had joined the marines, or otherwise gone to sea as pressed men.

It would appear that once migrants came to Newcastle they tended to stay for long periods, suggesting a natural process of migration rather than a transient population of seasonal workers. From the information available, it is clear that All Saints was a growing community, with the water trades increasing in proportion to the rest of the population up to the mid eighteenth century. Contributing to this growth was an element of immigration from those areas immediately surrounding the parish, as well as some from a greater distance. The fact that a significant proportion of those listed appeared to originate from Scotland or the Borders probably reflected trends that were also taking place in a range of other local heavy industries such as coal mining. These changes were similar in magnitude to those in most major developing industrial centres in England at that time. In addition, as Barke has shown, the balance of deaths and births in Newcastle would have resulted in a fall in the population of over 1,500 between 1770 and 1801 if it were not for over 8,000 migrants. The result was a net increase in population, during that period, of just under 6,500. This was followed by a net fall in population between 1801 and 1810 when outward migration increased during a period of near famine.[27] The predominance of males in the population of All Saints is unusual for a growing community in the early modern period, and, as has been noted by Levine and Wrightson, is more consistent with a developing industrial community.[28]

A further indicator of the impact of immigration into the community of All Saints comes from the settlement records. The settlement laws in the seventeenth and eighteenth centuries were complex and open to interpretation, not just by the courts, but also by the parish authorities, which could choose the extent to which they enforced them. Norma Landau has pointed out that parishes in the South of England could be demonstrated to be using the settlement laws as an instrument to manage immigration, which extended far beyond controlling the problem of the poor becoming a burden on the parish. The laws were often

---

[27] M. Barke, 'The People of Newcastle: A Demographic History', in *Newcastle upon Tyne, A Modern History,* ed. R. Colls and B. Lancaster (Chichester: Phillimore, 2001), p. 137; S. Middlebrook, *Newcastle Upon Tyne: Its Growth and Achievement* (Newcastle upon Tyne: Newcastle Journal, 1950), p. 164. Failure of the cereal crops in 1800 led to serious food shortages, with corn riots in Sunderland, and soup kitchens and relief funds opened for the poor.

[28] Levine and Wrightson, *The Making of an Industrial Society*, p. 179.

applied to relatively wealthy members of the community who could be subjected to a settlement examination and required to be in possession of a settlement certificate from their parish of origin, guaranteeing to take responsibility if they later became a burden on the parish. Some workers or apprentices who had worked for an employer for over one year could gain rights of settlement in a parish, provided their employer also had settlement in the parish.[29] As noted by Dendy and Fewster, because of the nature of their bonded contract of work with its attendant holidays, the keelmen were regarded as being employed for less than a year; it is said that because of this, they were not entitled to settlement in the parish. Consequently, when the keelmen or their families became poor or elderly they were not entitled to settlement and would have been returned to their parish of origin.[30] However, this only applied to those who originated in parishes in England, as Scotland and Ireland had no settlement laws and paupers could not be returned to Scottish or Irish parishes.[31] It might be expected that such a trend would be shown in the parish settlement records or the pauper records. Sadly, the only settlement records that have survived for All Saints are those from 1771 to 1800.[32] These records include the names of all those who were either returned to All Saints from other parishes for poor relief, or sent away from All Saints to other parishes. Out of over 600 entries in the records, 67 per cent were records of people being sent away from the parish to their original homes, making All Saints a net exporter of the poor. The vast majority of these people originated from other parishes in the immediate Newcastle and Tyneside area, with a smaller number coming from the wider Northumberland and Durham counties. Only 11 of those removed were sent to destinations

---

[29] N. Landau, 'The Regulation of Immigration, Economic Structures and Definitions of the Poor in Eighteenth Century England', *The Historical Journal*, 33 (1990), pp. 541–72, and 'Who was Subjected to the Laws of Settlement? Procedure under the Settlement Laws in Eighteenth Century England', *Agricultural History Review*, 43 (1995), pp. 139–59; K.D.M. Snell, 'Pauper Settlement and the Right to Poor Relief in England and Wales', *Continuity and Change*, 6 (1991), pp. 375–415.

[30] F.W. Dendy, *Extracts from the Records of the Company of Hostmen of Newcastle Upon Tyne*, Surtees Society, 105 (Durham, Published for the Society, 1901), pp. 205–6; J.M. Fewster, 'The Keelmen of Tyneside in the Eighteenth Century, Part 1', *Durham University Journal*, 50 (1957)', p. 28n and *The Keelmen of Tyneside: Labour Organisation and Conflict in the North-East Coal Industry, 1600–1830* (Woodbridge: Boydell and Brewer, 2011), pp. 20–49; K. Wrightson, *Earthly Necessities: Economic Lives in Early Modern Britain* (New Haven and London: Yale University Press, 2000), pp. 215–21.

[31] R. Burn, *The Justice of the Peace, and Parish Officer*, 4 vols (London: Printed by W. Strachan and M. Woodfall for T. Cadell, 1772), Vol. 3, pp. 290–92.

[32] All Saints Parish Settlement Records, TWAM, MF 356.

further away, and none of these had any previous occupation listed in the records, so it is impossible to say whether any of them had worked in the water trades.

In the light of the predominance of the water trades in All Saints it is likely that a number of those removed from the parish had worked in the water trades. The records demonstrate that there was significant immigration from areas other than Scotland into All Saints; indeed, the fact that the vast majority of those being returned came from relatively local parishes tends to support the observation that the profile of new names appearing in the parish register was consistent with more local origins. The frequent references in the hostmen's records to the problems of supporting the care of the poor in Sandgate, culminating in the establishment of the keelmen's charities and the building of the Keelmen's Hospital, may well have been a reflection of the inability to return poor immigrants originating from Scotland.[33] A further source, which might have given some idea of the make-up of those who were requiring poor relief in the parish, were the parish overseers accounts in the pauper records.[34] Although many of these still survive for All Saints, they contain only the names, dates and sums paid out, with no note of their occupations or parish of origin, meaning that they are of little value for clarifying the nature of the inward immigration into All Saints. In addition to the crude numbers of baptisms, marriages and deaths, the parish registers contain more personal details, including family names; this makes it possible to identify the family names that appear most frequently, possibly enabling the recognition of family 'dynasties' in certain trades. All Saints parish registers certainly allow identification of the larger family groups and the duration of their prominence in the community. Analysis of the names of over 750 water tradesmen and their families, identified from a sample of parish registers from All Saints between 1600 and 1800, yields a number of groupings; but the largest family surname group, the Wilsons, totalled only 16 over a period of 200 years. It is possible that some of these groupings were a result of co-incidence rather than a single family, and there were clearly no obvious very large family groups or 'dynasties' among the water trades community. Notwithstanding the overall deterioration in the quality of parish registration towards the end of the eighteenth century, there was an improvement in the quality of information regarding details of age and occupation, as well as place of birth. From this information, we can get an impression of the age and occupational structure of the population in All Saints parish between 1750 and 1800. It was not until 1778 that sufficient ages were

---

[33] Dendy, *Company of Hostmen*, pp. 205–6.
[34] All Saints parish Overseers Accounts, TWAM, MF 349.

included in the burial registers to make the data suitable for analysis; however, using the register from that date until 1800 we can get a very limited view of the spectrum of the age distribution at burial of the male working population in All Saints, and this shows a normal distribution pattern. Although the numbers are very small, we find that there are only five burials of watermen registered in this period, which is too small a number to analyse, other than to observe that their distribution fitted the trends shown by the male working population as a whole.

Analysis of the occupational profiles of this small sample of the male population of All Saints parish, based on burial register details from 1750 to 1800, shows a diverse working community, with around 35 different occupations in a population of around 14,800. The range of occupations changes over the period, with the water tradesmen still featuring very high in the lists up to 1800, although it is possible to speculate that the size of certain occupations were more likely to be underestimated because of their association with religious dissent. Sadly, the small numbers available make it difficult to draw firm conclusions from parish registers about how the full occupational profile of the Newcastle parishes developed towards the end of the eighteenth century and into the nineteenth. However, the Cambridge Population Studies Group have examined the occupational structure of many of the Tyneside parishes using baptism registers from between 1813 and 1820. They show clearly the redistribution of occupations along the river with the preponderance of keelmen and watermen in All Saints being replaced by ships' masters and mariners, with the river water tradesmen reappearing, distributed throughout the other riverside parishes.[35] Few other sources of occupational information are available. The censuses of 1801, 1811 and 1821 did not collect occupational details, and it was not until the 1831 census that a limited number of occupational details were collected; but unfortunately, in the summaries that are available there are no records of the water-trades occupations. The 1841 census gives a much more complete occupational profile of all of the riverside parishes including All Saints, and it includes many of the occupations associated with the water trades. However, by this stage in the nineteenth century many social and industrial changes had taken place, which influenced the patterns of occupation and employment.

Although only one of the riverside parishes, All Saints, has been examined in detail, it contained such a concentration of the water-trades community that its population and their dynamics provide a very strong indication of how the

---

[35] Leigh Shaw-Taylor, personal communication, 6 January 2009. The author is indebted to Dr Shaw-Taylor for so freely sharing his occupational population data for this period.

water-trades community associated with the lower River Tyne was developing as a whole during the seventeenth and eighteenth centuries. It is clear that a significant number of the water tradesmen will have been resident in some of the other parishes along the river, however there is no evidence to suggest that the members of the community who lived in parishes other than All Saints displayed characteristics that were different from those resident in that parish. The analysis of this parish population show that it was consistent with an industrial community that was growing in a manner very similar to those that were occurring in many other provincial and port towns at the time, with both growth, and the proportion of migrants to the rest of the population being almost identical to that described elsewhere. The often-repeated suggestion that the population of water tradesmen was largely of Scottish origin does appear to be at least partially true; though less than half the census of keelmen claimed origin from outside Newcastle, most, but not all, of those who did were from Scotland. That there should be a significant proportion of Scots is not surprising, considering its relative proximity to the Tyne; but of those who came, most seem to have taken up long-term residence in Newcastle. In addition, because of the nature of the settlement laws and the absence of equivalent legislation in Scotland, there was no evidence of destitute Scotsmen being returned to Scotland when they fell upon hard times. Scottish labourers were certainly recruited into the coal industry surrounding the Tyne; Levine and Wrightson describe shortages of labour in the coal mines around Whickham, which had resulted in the employment of women in the mines and the need to recruit additional labour from Scotland.[36] The relatively high proportion of Scotsmen among the immigrants did give rise to some concern about their loyalties during the Jacobite uprisings, however keelmen were prominent among the volunteers to defend Newcastle against any rebels in 1715, and were noted for their 'conspicuous loyalty'.[37]

A major problem, in comparing the changing size of the populations of Newcastle, All Saints parish and the water-trades communities, with the estimates of the local population in the literature, has been that some of the latter estimates vary considerably. However, although based on a number of assumptions, the figures for keelmen numbers, using the recorded levels of coal exports as described in Chapter 3, produced estimates of the size of the water-trades population which were not too dissimilar from those appearing in the literature. In addition, particularly for the beginning of the eighteenth

---

[36] Levine and Wrightson, *The Making of an Industrial Society*, pp. 185–6.
[37] Fewster, *The Keelmen of Tyneside*, p. 71.

century, the figures compared well with those obtained from the All Saints parish registers; the fact that the estimates obtained from the coal trade were always lower than those from the parish registers may possibly be indicative of the number of water tradesmen who worked in water trades other than the keels and the coal trade. A changing pattern of the different occupations in the riverside communities was shown in the last 50 years of the eighteenth century, when the parish registers indicate a wider range of tradesmen working in the community. However, throughout this period of accelerating change in the industrial community along the river Tyne, the water tradesmen remained a significant part of the working people of the parish.

Chapter 5
Who Were the Owners? Networks of Working Boat and Ship Ownership

A significant feature of urban and industrial communities in the seventeenth and eighteenth centuries was the importance of interrelated social and business networks, which had become essential to the functioning of the business life of the community, and particularly amongst those of the 'middling sort'.[1] One's position within these networks, particularly those involving the coal industry along the River Tyne, was very much a consequence of the power exercised by virtue of ownership, either of the coal itself or the mode of transport or both. The power exercised by those who controlled the modes of transport of coal is not easy to identify, partly because evidence of ownership of ships was not always well documented. Although registration of seagoing shipping did not become necessary until towards the end of the eighteenth century, notes of the ownership of a seagoing vessel and the name of its master were often included in some of the Customs House Shipping Records. However, this was inconsistent, and thus insufficient to provide an overall picture of the patterns of ship ownership during the years before registration. Records were not necessary for river craft,[2] and the ownership of river craft, such as keels, thus has no readily available documentation at all. There are a number of anecdotal accounts of keel ownership, but none supported by objective evidence. Nef observed that the Tyne keels: 'were built and owned by the same Newcastle merchants who became the colliery owners. At first during the sixteenth century they dealt with the skippers who undertook the "fittage" giving them some savings and social standing in the Town,'[3] subsequently this role was taken over by agents or hostmen. In contrast, after the implementation of the Navigation Act of 1786, all vessels greater than 15 tons

---

[1] S. D'Cruze, 'The Middling Sort in Eighteenth Century Colchester: Independence, Social Relations and the Community Broker', in *The Middling Sort of People*, ed. J. Barry and C. Brooks (London: Palgrave, 1994), pp. 181–96.

[2] M. Stammers, *Sailing Barges of the British Isles* (Stroud: The History Press, 2008), p. 34.

[3] J.U. Nef, *The Rise of the British Coal Industry*, 2 vols (London: George Routledge & Sons, 1932), Vol. 1, p. 440.

had to be registered at one of the designated ports of registry. This was usually a port from which the ship normally traded, or where her owners lived, and Newcastle upon Tyne became such a port. This Act was intended to distinguish British shipping, entitled to the privileges of the navigation laws, from American shipping, in the aftermath of the American War of Independence. Registration gave a more precise estimate of the maritime strength of the country, and helped to minimise abuses of the tonnage dues and smuggling. The registration details of a ship after the introduction of the Act included full details of the dimensions and rig of the ship, together with details of the names, addresses and occupations of the owners and a record of their respective share of ownership in sixty-fourths.[4] However, once again, small, working river craft were not included, and hence their ownership continued to go unrecorded.

One of the few primary sources of evidence about the ownership of property and personal effects in the seventeenth and eighteenth centuries are wills and probate inventories. Probate inventories were lists of moveable items and property that had belonged to a person who had died; the size of the estate needed to require an inventory varied between different ecclesiastical court jurisdictions across the country. These inventories were usually prepared by friends or relatives of the deceased, and were required to be exhibited at the time of probate. They were made throughout the sixteenth and seventeenth centuries, but only a few survive after the mid eighteenth century.[5] Notwithstanding the limitations of probate inventories as a source, both in terms of their availability and scope, they can provide a valuable source of information about the ownership of both ships and working riverboats.[6] Before the Court of Probate Act of 1857, the proving of wills and granting of administrations lay with the ecclesiastical courts, the process of deciding in which court a will would be proved was complex and depended on the size of the deceased's estate and its distribution. Where an estate was spread over a number of archdeaconry court districts, the will would be proved in the next higher court, which was usually the diocesan court. In circumstances where

---

[4] S.P. Ville, 'Shipping in the Port of Newcastle 1780–1800', *Journal of Transport History*, 9 (1988), pp. 60–61; S.P. Ville, 'Patterns of shipping investment in the Port of Newcastle upon Tyne, 1750–1850', *Northern History*, 25 (1989), pp. 205–21; S.P. Ville, *English Shipowning During the Industrial Revolution: Michael Henley and Son, London Shipowners 1770–1830*, (Manchester: Manchester University Press, 1987), pp. 2–15.

[5] T. Arkell, 'The Probate Process', *When Death Do Us Part*, ed. T. Arkell, N. Evans and N. Goose (Oxford: Leopard's Head Press, 2000), pp. 3–13; J. Cox and N. Cox, 'Probate 1500–1800: a System in Transition', in When Death Do Us Part, pp. 14–37; L. Weatherill, *Consumer Behaviour and Material Culture in Britain, 1660–1760*, 2nd edition (London and New York: Routledge, 1996), p. 2.

[6] T. Arkell, 'Interpreting Probate Inventories', *When Death Do Us Part*, pp. 72–102.

the estate was distributed over more than one diocese, the will came under the aegis of one of the provincial courts, either the Prerogative Court of York (PCY) or the Prerogative Court of Canterbury (PCC). In addition, whenever an estate included property in London, or the death occurred abroad, the will was proved in the PCC, wherever in England the deceased resided.[7] There are very few relevant surviving inventories in the records of either the Canterbury or York Prerogative Courts;[8] however, there remain a significant number of surviving probate inventories in the Durham diocesan probate registry for the parishes surrounding the lower River Tyne between 1600 and 1750. Fortunately, a large percentage of these inventories have details of parish of origin and occupation, enabling an examination of the extent to which the ownership of boats or ships was recorded, and how they were distributed through the local community (Figure 4.1; Table 5.1). A small number of wills mention the existence of boats or ships, but the details are usually too vague and imprecise, when compared with the detail included in the inventories. An understanding of the patterns of ownership of boats and ships enables a clearer view of the structure of the business networks that enabled the coal and other trades to function, and, in addition, many inventories give a valuation of both the boats and ships, enabling an insight into the relative wealth of individuals who owned these different craft. Among 2,095 surviving probate inventories originating from the parishes surrounding the lower River Tyne from the Durham probate registry, 796 show evidence of boat or ship ownership.[9] Among these inventories, 864 ships and boats are identifiable, with details of their skippers or masters. These demonstrate not only the very wide range of working boats present on the river, but also the range of valuations, which varied according to age and condition. The inventories show the range of occupations of the owners of these boats and ships, and illustrate the wide spectrum of people who had a major share in the ownership of working riverboats, and by implication were major players in the trading networks. In addition, the inventories illustrated how cargo ships were owned in fractions, from a whole ship to division into sixty-fourths; the majority

---

[7] Arkell, 'The Probate Process', pp. 3–7; Weatherill, *Consumer Behaviour and Material Culture*, p. 2; M. Overton, J. Whittle, D. Dean and A. Hann, *Production and Consumption in English Households, 1600–1750* (London: Routledge, 2004), pp. 13–32.

[8] The National Archives, in Kew, has records of wills and inventories in the Canterbury registry. Out of 37,308 records, only 12 are related to Tyneside. None of these related to people or material relevant to the study. The Borthwick Institute in York holds records from the York Prerogative Court. Only 67 wills originated from Newcastle and the other Tyneside parishes, of which 25 were identifiable as relating to hostmen or merchants; none of these included an inventory or reference to boats and ships.

[9] Wright, 'Water Trades on the Lower River Tyne', pp. 90–131.

Table 5.1 Distribution of probate inventories showing boat or ship ownership among parishes surrounding the lower River Tyne

Parish	Inventories	Per cent of Total
Blaydon	2	0.25
Gateshead	64	8.0
Hebburn	4	0.5
Howdon	1	0.125
Heworth	1	0.125
Jarrow	8	1.0
Newburn	5	0.6
Newcastle	582	73.1
North Shields	31	3.9
Ryton	25	3.1
South Shields	47	5.9
Tynemouth	9	1.1
Wallsend	4	0.5
Whickham	13	1.6
Total	796	

of ship shares being in eighths, sixteenths and thirty-seconds. This ability to invest in a defined fraction of the ownership of a merchant ship made it much easier for an interest in ship ownership to be spread amongst a wider spectrum of the population, many of whom may have had only a modest amount of money to invest. This almost certainly led to the potential for a wider ownership of shares in cargo ships among trades not normally associated with maritime trade, implying that there was an opportunity for the development of an investment market in ships and sea trades,[10] with many tradesmen and women taking advantage of this growing investment opportunity.

The numbers of working boats on the lower River Tyne listed in the probate inventories during the seventeenth and eighteenth centuries are shown, by decade, in Figure 5.1. The number of records decline rapidly after 1720, as few inventories remain in the Durham registry after this date. The inventories show a substantial excess of boats over owners, as many individuals owned more than

---

[10] R. Grassby, *The Business Community of Seventeenth-Century England* (Cambridge: Cambridge University Press, 1995), pp. 16–17, 82–98.

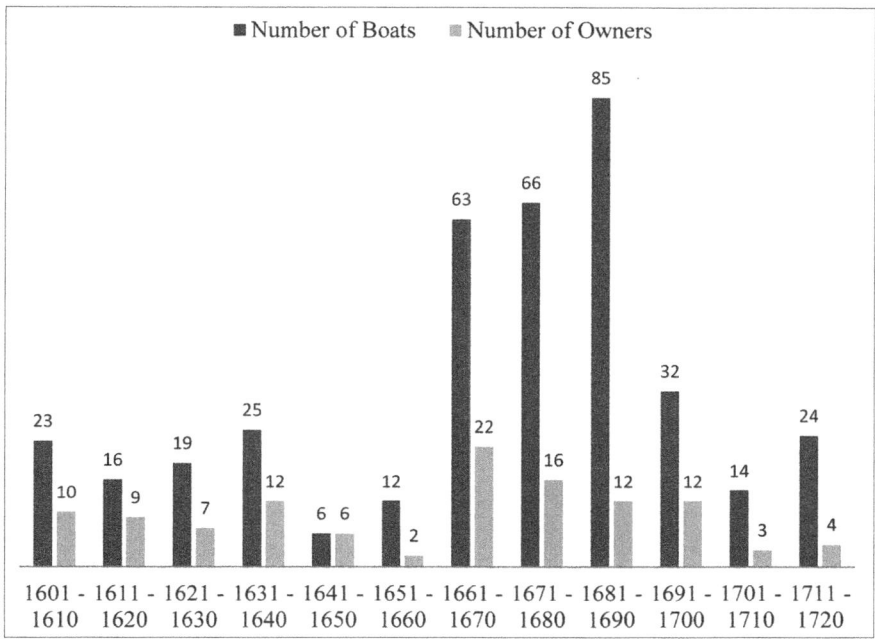

Figure 5.1   Boat ownership on the River Tyne by decade

one boat. The distribution of boats and owners peak between 1660 and 1690 partly due to an increase in both the number of surviving inventories and the number of boats owned by an individual owner. Even allowing for the fact that these figures represent only those inventories that have survived, this sample clearly illustrates a trend toward ownership being concentrated in fewer hands, as the number of boats increased in response to increasing trade. The wide variety of riverboats described and valued in the inventories totalled 396; the types and their respective numbers are illustrated in Figure 5.2. It is clear that the commonest type of boat was the keel, making rather less than half of the total. The remainder were composed of a wide variety of boats of varying sizes and functions, including small numbers of fishing boats and a ferry; the types of working boat described changed with the passage of time. It is notable that keels continued to be the predominant type of boat listed throughout, however 'chalder boats' appeared in the first half of the seventeenth century and 'coal boats' were a feature of the second half, almost equalling keels by the last decade. Wherrys, however, appeared in small numbers throughout the whole period.

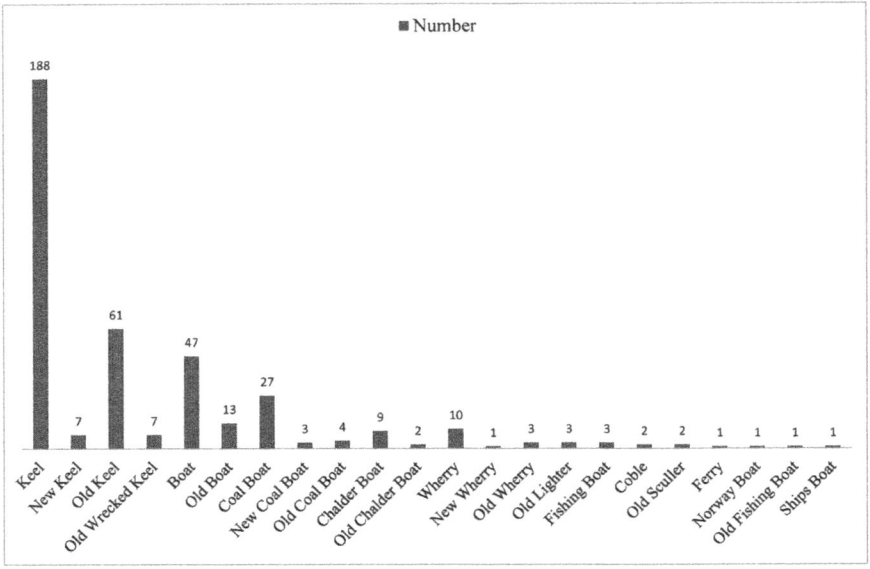

Figure 5.2   Types of working boat on the River Tyne, 1600–1750

Keels remained consistent in size and construction for many centuries.[11] As taxes were raised on the basis of a keel load of coal weighing 8 chaldrons or 21 tons, they were measured on a regular basis by being loaded with a known weight of lead and then marked with a nail on the water line, to ensure the accuracy of their load capacity. A note in the Company of Hostmen's records from 1713 reports that a John Clutterbuck, the Officer for the Admeasuring of Keels, had a certain quantity of lead delivered to him, but was causing much anger by charging more to measure the keels than the cost of the lead.[12]

Sadly, no examples of a keel have survived. Viall provided the most comprehensive description of a keel, in 1942, when he published a line drawing of a keel based on models currently held in the Discovery Museum in Newcastle upon Tyne.[13] The exact dates of the models are unknown, but are believed to

---

[11]   R.J. Charleton, *Newcastle Town*, 4th ed. (London: Walter Scott, 1885, rep., 1978), p. 254; S. Middlebrook, *Newcastle Upon Tyne: Its Growth and Achievement* (Newcastle upon Tyne: Newcastle Journal, 1950), p. 42; Nef, *Rise of the British Coal Industry*, Vol. 1, pp. 387–8; Hatcher, *The History of the British Coal Industry*, Vol. 1, *Before 1700: Towards the Age of Coal* (Oxford: Clarendon Press, 1993), p. 467.

[12]   Dendy, *Company of Hostmen*, p. 181.

[13]   H.R. Viall, 'Tyne Keels', *Mariner's Mirror*, 28 (1942), 160–62; Tyne Wear Archives and Museums (TWAM).

originate from the early or mid nineteenth century. Having done much local research, including an extensive search for archaeological evidence of remains of keels, Viall combined evidence from a number of indirect sources to prepare the drawing of a keel and gave what appears to be a reasonably accurate idea of its construction. The characteristic feature of keels was that they were of smooth sided, or carvel, construction with the planks being fixed to frames edge to edge. They were about 42 feet in length, 19 feet wide and 6 feet deep; they were steered by a large oar called a swape, and either were propelled by a large oar or pole, or carried a square sail.[14] Viall wrote:

> The earliest type (of keel) was double ended and rudderless, being steered by an oar held by one man, the skipper, and propelled by a very large oar or 'swape' managed by three men. ... At some later stage a rudder was introduced. ... The floor of a keel was about 2 feet from the deck line, and the coals were piled up on this and kept in place by deals stacked on end, this was done to ease the labour of unloading the cargo. ... The early keels carried only square sails; later on a staysail was introduced and in their latter days we find a large spritsail and staysail to be the common practice ... In construction the keels were extraordinarily strong. In the best, i.e. the highest priced examples. The timbers of grown oak were so close that only the width of a man's fist would go between them. This space was a matter of price; the wider the space the cheaper the keel. Planking was mainly of English oak, but elm was used in many cases below the water line.[15]

A number of illustrations in art works from the eighteenth and nineteenth centuries showing keels at work on the river illustrate both the means of propulsion of the keels and the nature of the crew and pattern of loading. A detail from the engraving by Samuel and Nathaniel Buck, from 1745,[16] clearly shows the keels with a crew of three keelmen and a skipper steering. In one case the keel is propelled by three men using a large single oar, and is steered by the skipper using a single oar – the swape, over the stern (Figure 5.3). Another boat is propelled by a square sail, which could be lowered with its mast to pass

---

[14] J. Brand, *The History and Antiquities of the Town of Newcastle Upon Tyne*, 2 vols (London, 1789), Vol. 2, pp. 261–2; Charleton, *Newcastle Town*, pp. 324–8; T.S. Ashton and J. Sykes, *The Coal Industry in the Eighteenth Century* (Manchester: Manchester University Press, 1929), p. 196; W.S. Mitcalf, 'The History of the Keelmen and Their Strike in 1822', *Archaeologia Aeliana*, 4th ser., 14 (1937), p. 3; Nef, *Rise of the British Coal Industry*, Vol. 1, pp. 387–8.

[15] Viall, 'Tyne Keels'.

[16] National Maritime Museum, Images ref. B2547. See also Figure 2.4.

Figure 5.3   Keels off Newcastle Quay. Detail from Buck Brothers' engraving of Newcastle upon Tyne, 1745. © National Maritime Museum, Greenwich, London

under the bridge, once again steered by a skipper using a single steering oar. The keels in the Buck engraving can both be seen to be loaded with coal, in a hold in the centre of each boat and piled up high above the deck making it easier for the keelmen to shovel the coal up into the seagoing colliers, as described in the literature.[17]

A number of other boats apparently involved in the coal-carrying trade were described in the inventories as 'coal boats'.[18] There are no boats of this description, either in the historical texts relating to Newcastle during this period or in maritime historical texts. From the valuations of the coal boats that appear in the probate inventories, they appear of similar value to keels. This is consistent with the change in nomenclature in other documents, such as parish registers, used to describe those working in the water trades, such that between 1650 and

---

[17]   Brand, *History and Antiquities*, Vol. 2, pp. 261–2; Charleton, *Newcastle Town*, pp. 324–8; Ashton and Sykes, *The Coal Industry*, p. 196; Mitcalf, 'History of the Keelmen', p. 3; Nef, *Rise of the British Coal Industry*, Vol. 1, pp. 387–8.

[18]   The description occurs in a number of Durham Probate Inventories, including those of two Yeomen/Watermen, Matthew Grant (DPRI/1/Inv 1690) and John Whitehead (DPRI/1/ Inv 1696).

1750 the term 'keelman' progressively disappeared to be replaced by the term waterman. It is possible that a similar change occurred in the terminology used to describe the boats, with the term 'keel' partially being replaced by the term 'coal boat'. Amongst the lists of other boats appearing in the probate inventories was a group of boats called chalder boats; these may well have been used in the coal trade, but they were clearly of a smaller carrying capacity than the keels. Their capacity was described using the number of chalders they could carry – a one-chalder boat or three-chalder boat, for example. The chalder, or chaldron, was a measure used almost exclusively in the coal trade. The smaller size of these boats may be inferred not just from the smaller number of chaldrons carried, but the lower valuations they were given in the inventories.[19] Once again, there is no account of such boats appearing in the historical literature relating to Newcastle or in the maritime historical literature.[20] Coal was used in significant quantities by many of the early industries along the Tyne, such as lead and iron smelting and glass making, and it is probable that such smaller coal-carrying craft were used to ferry coal to such industrial complexes, or to consumers based along higher tributaries of the Tyne that were too shallow to take a keel.

Wherrys were probably smaller than keels, at this time, and, in contrast to keels, they were constructed using an overlapping plank, or clinker construction. This was a simple and economical boat-building technique, which had been used in Northumbria and elsewhere since the time of the Anglo-Saxon and Viking settlers, and was probably derived from boats used as small passenger ferries. References are made to the hire of a wherry for 9s 6d in the records of the Masters and Mariners Society, also known as Trinity House, on 14 September 1635, for work on the ground where the Low Light now stands at North Shields.[21] In the seventeenth and eighteenth centuries wherrys were probably rather small and lowly craft, as their value shown in probate inventories was always quite small

---

[19] An example of the variations in size and value of chalder boats may be found in the Inventory of George Waugh (DPRI/1/Inv. 1668), which described a 7-chalder boat valued at £30, quite close in capacity and value to that of a keel; another, at 6 chalders, was valued at £28, and on at 5 chalders was valued at £10. In contrast, an inventory of Richard Carr (DPRI/1 Inv. 1609) describes a 3-chalder boat valued at £3.

[20] Brand, *History and Antiquities*, Vol. 2, pp. 261–2; Charleton, *Newcastle Town*, pp. 324–8; Ashton and Sykes, *The Coal Industry*, p. 196; Mitcalf, 'History of the Keelmen', p. 3; Nef, *Rise of the British Coal Industry*, Vol. 1, pp. 387–8; Viall, 'Tyne Keels', pp. 160–2; Stammers, *Sailing Barges*, pp. 29–36.

[21] E. Mackenzie, *Descriptive and Historical Account of the Town and County of Newcastle upon Tyne* (Newcastle upon Tyne: Mackenzie and Dent, 1827), p. 681.

when compared with those of keels.[22] Although smaller during the seventeenth and eighteenth centuries, boats described as wherrys in the nineteenth century became progressively larger. Surviving illustrations of wherrys suggest that, in contrast to most keels, they used a fore and aft sailing rig with a mast and two sails.[23] There are references in the records of the Company of Hostmen of wherrys being used, probably illicitly, to carry coal.[24] During the nineteenth century wherrys eventually took over from keels as a form of lighter, often towed by steam-powered tugs. The later examples, in the twentieth century, reached about 55 feet long and were powered by a diesel engine; an example of this still exists in preserved form, and five examples also survive as remnants of wrecks along the banks of the upper reaches of the navigable Tyne near Newburn. These wrecks of five remaining wherries have recently been subjected to an archaeological study providing an analysis of the methods of construction of wherries in the later nineteenth and early twentieth centuries.[25] Uncertainty exists about the construction of the other boats described in the inventories, however it is likely that many of them were of clinker overlapping planked construction, similar to many small boats that are seen on rivers and lakes today.

The basis upon which probate valuations of working boats on the River Tyne were made is uncertain. In his detailed analysis of the pitfalls of estimating prices from probate inventory valuations, Overton noted that appraisers of an inventory were bound in law to use the price that an item would fetch at auction. In all probability, the valuations were based on a perceived market value or potential auction price. The mechanisms by which the market price of a boat such as a keel was derived are not clear. It is likely that it was a combination of the costs of the materials used in construction, plus an element related to the time and skill

---

[22] Probate Valuations of Tyne Wherries: Synceler (DPRI/1/Inv. 1613), £6; Langstaffe (DPRI/1/Inv. 1633), £4; Young (DPRI/1/Inv. 1679), £2; Gatenby (DPRI/1/Inv. 1706), £2; Taylor (DPRI/1/Inv. 1707), £11.

[23] Charleton, *Newcastle Town*, p. 328; Stammers, *Sailing Barges*, pp. 37–8. A fore and aft rig constitutes a mast with a foresail or jib in front of the mast and a mainsail behind the mast, in contrast to a square sail usually used by a keel which is a transversely mounted sail on a yard (or beam of wood) fixed to the front of the mast.

[24] Dendy, *Company of Hostmen*, p. 198. There is a record of several wherrys being used by a ship's master Mr Hart to carry coal from a Mr Sivertops, a matter which was to be investigated by the Company. There is s subsequent reference some days later (203) of Mr Silvertops 'exercising the trade of a hostman, not being a free Burgess or free of the fraternity', and the Company making efforts to restrain him from doing so.

[25] P. Taylor and A. Williams, 'The Newburn Wherries: Remnants of the River Tyne's Industrial Past', *Archaeologia Aeliana* 5th ser., 39 (2010), pp. 401–25.

of the shipwrights and boat builders, allowing them to make a decent profit.[26] There is little evidence to say whether there was an element of either scarcity or excess that would have tended to increase or decrease the prices of working boats in a competitive market. From the probate valuations given in the inventories the keels were listed at a number of different values, and were sometimes described as new keels valued at around 40 pounds, keels valued at about 20 pounds and old keels valued at about 10 pounds, and even wrecked keels were listed in some inventories, at an even lower value. It is perhaps surprising that the values of all types of keel varied very little throughout the period, showing a modest increase in the middle of the seventeenth century and decreasing towards the eighteenth century. When comparing the values of keels of all types with the valuations of the other types of boat, we find that the values of coal boats in the second half of the seventeenth century were very similar to those of keels, tending to confirm that the term was used to describe a boat very similar to a keel. It is probable that the relative values of the different types of boats as described in the inventories might also be a reflection of the relative size and complexity of the boats. It is interesting to note that *The London Tradesman* in 1747 suggests that a Thames Waterman, on completion of his apprenticeship, could purchase a boat for between £12 and £17, which is much lower that the valuations of Tyne keels in the inventories. Whether this difference is due to differences in size or complexity remains unclear.[27] It is possible that such differences between the values of the Thames and the Tyne river craft were a reflection of a greater need for smaller simpler boats to provide passenger transport on the London Thames. The ownership of working boats on the river was spread widely across members of 23 different occupations, many of whom owned one or two boats of varying type. It is not surprising that the hostmen owned a large proportion of the keels, given that their occupation included managing the movement of coal in keels from the staiths to the ships at the mouth of the river. However, it is surprising to discover that the largest single group of working boat owners were the shipwrights, who owned substantially more than any other occupational

---

[26] M. Overton, 'Prices from Probate Inventories', in *When Death Do Us Part*, pp. 121–41; L. Weatherill, *Consumer Behaviour and Material Culture*; Newcastle Courant, 237 (January 2 1725), p. 11. Although advertisements for the sale of keels and lighters appear in the local newspaper, there is no evidence of an asking price, which appears to be the subject of negotiation with the advertiser, in this case: 'Four Keels or Lighters, in good repair and condition, now in the work of Mr John Robinson jun., Fitter are to be sold. Enquire of Mr Thomas Burdus, Notary Public who will treat with any persons about the sale thereof'.

[27] R. Campbell, *The London Tradesman*, Vol. 1 (London: T. Gardener, 1747, Reprint, Newton Abbot: David and Charles, 1969), Appendix Section 26, Watermen, p. 327.

group. A group of merchants, knights and gentlemen were together a significant though much smaller group of owners of keels and other working boats.[28]

Ownership of cargo ships is frequently described in some detail in probate inventories. It was common to include the name of the master, and the fraction owned, usually up to sixty-fourths, with a valuation of the fraction owned, enabling an estimate of the value of the entire ship to be made. Later in the eighteenth century, when registration of cargo ships became a requirement, this information would have been included in the Register of Shipping.[29] The pattern of ship ownership between 1600 and 1720, suggests an increase in ship ownership being reported in the latter half of the seventeenth century (Figure 5.4). The extent to which this is a real increase or a reflection of the larger number of inventories remains uncertain. Unfortunately, the tonnage of a ship was rarely included, making it very difficult to estimate the size of a ship other than by assuming that value increased with size, making the assumption that the most valuable ships were the largest. The values of the ships are displayed by decades in Table 5.2. The range of ships described is very wide with the lowest value ships probably being no larger than a keel,[30] whereas the highest value, and by implication the largest vessels were likely to have been long-distance heavy cargo ships. Although the median value of the ships varied little throughout, there was a steady increase in the value and therefore the size of the large ships, smaller ones probably being small coasting vessels. Alternative perspectives on the valuations of shipping in the seventeenth and eighteenth centuries are difficult to obtain. Robin Pearson examined insurance valuations in the eighteenth century and noted that the Sun Fire Office had an agent in Newcastle from 1720 to 1793. As the insurers usually made the owner carry 25 per cent of the risk himself, the value in the policy registers was always unlikely to represent the full market value or replacement value of a ship.[31]

Names of ships that are shown in probate inventories, from Newcastle and parishes along the Tyne, have a tendency to recur over a period of some years in inventories of a number of different individuals. Ships are of necessity robust and would, if not subject to the risks of shipwreck and warfare, normally have a working life of up to 50 years, making it possible to track their ownership

---

[28] Wright, 'Water Trades on the Lower River Tyne', pp. 90–131.
[29] Stammers, *Sailing Barges*, p. 34; Ville, 'Shipping in the port of Newcastle', pp. 60–61.
[30] Stammers, *Sailing Barges*, p. 34.
[31] Professor Robin Pearson, Personal Communication, 06 January 2009; M. Freeman, R. Pearson and J. Taylor, 'Technological Change and the Governance of Joint-Stock Enterprise in the Early Nineteenth Century: The case of Coastal Shipping', *Business History*, 49 (2007), pp. 573–94.

Table 5.2   Estimated ship valuations from probate inventories, by decade

Years	Number of Ships	Minimum	Median	Maximum
1601–1610	12	£13	£240	£800
1611–1620	7	£40	£100	£216
1621–1630	30	£9	£254	£1,280
1631–1640	48	£12	£430	£1,472
1641–1650	27	£240	£720	£1,600
1651–1660	32	£160	£568	£1,600
1661–1670	97	£56	£400	£2,400
1671–1680	75	£60	£384	£2,488
1681–1690	25	£48	£176	£960
1691–1700	15	£50	£640	£2,912
1701–1710	2	£24		£288

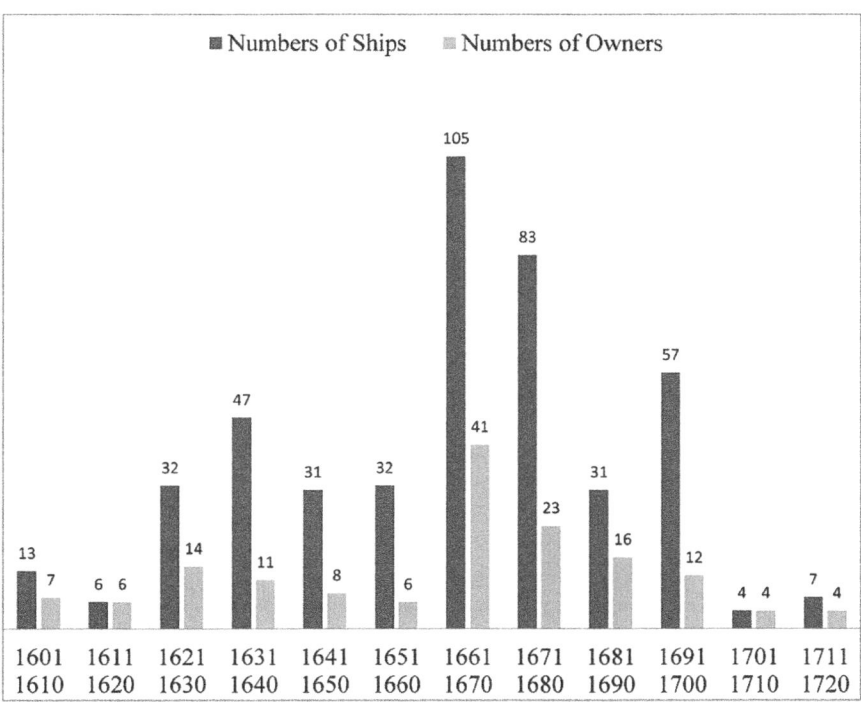

Figure 5.4   Ship ownership on the River Tyne by decade

through probate records. In addition, most of the inventories state the name of the ship's master. For example, probate inventories are preserved from five separate owners of fractions of the 'John of Newcastle', with estimates of the total value of the ship, which would exclude cargo. There was an increase in value of the ship from £360 in 1636 to £576 in 1645, which would seem appropriate for inflation at that time. However, it is notable that by 1660 the value had fallen to £160, less than 30 per cent of its former value; this may indicate that with the passage of time it had become more decrepit and getting towards the end of its useful life, or alternatively that the original ship had been lost and replaced with a smaller, lower-value ship of the same name.[32] The patterns of ownership of another ship, the 'Tryall of Newcastle' are a little more consistent: over a period of 30 years five owners can be identified, four of whom have what appear to be meaningful valuations starting with £375 in 1643 and ending with £320 in 1673, all of which are within the ranges expected for the period. This appears to confirm an apparent useful life expectancy of a ship to be at least 30 years. In addition the name of the master would frequently appear mong the owners of shares, and was likely to remain the same for a significant period.

There is an even wider spectrum of occupations owning ships than occurred with working boats, with 25 separate occupations being identified. Once more, the main occupations were hostmen, shipwrights, merchants, masters and mariners. As we have seen, it was the custom for most masters of ships to own a share of the ship they commanded, and consequently a share in the profits. There was a small though significant group of those working at a more menial level in the water trades who also showed evidence of boat or ship ownership. The wide range of people within occupations other than those related to the sea and the water trades who had a modest investment in shipping would tend to confirm that their ownership was a speculative investment with a view to sharing in the profits.[33] There was a smaller group who showed evidence of both ship

---

[32] W.J. Hausemann, 'Size and Profitability of English Colliers in the Eighteenth Century', *Business History Review*, 51 (1977), pp. 460–73; S.P. Ville, 'Size and Profitability of English Colliers in the Eighteenth Century, A Reappraisal', *Business History Review* 58 (1984), pp. 103–20. In his re-appraisal Ville describes the recently discovered records of the Henley Family, following their fleet of ships over some years and emphasising the increased profitability that came from a high degree of vertical integration; see also W.J. Hausemann, 'Profitability of English Colliers in the Eighteenth Century, Reply to a Reappraisal', *Business History Review*, 58 (1984) pp. 121–5; S.P. Ville, 'Patterns of Shipping Investment in the Port of Newcastle upon Tyne, 1750–1850', *Northern History*, 25 (1989), pp. 203–21; Ville, 'Shipping in Newcastle 1780–1800', pp. 60–77.

[33] Wright, 'Water Trades on the Lower River Tyne' pp. 110–16. It is notable that there were a significant number of widows amongst those who owned shares in ships, and it is

and boat ownership in their inventories, with a predominance of hostmen and shipwrights among this group of owners. Notwithstanding the large numbers of ships and boats owned by some of these groups, when looked at in the context of each occupational group as a whole, the combination of boat and ship ownership occurred in only a minority of all groups.

Exploring the patterns of ship or boat ownership among those occupations most closely associated with the water trades, it became apparent that it was extremely uncommon for an individual water tradesman to have sufficient wealth to require the preparation of a probate inventory at the time of death. Out of the many thousands of watermen and keelmen who must have lived between 1600 and 1720 there were only 42 surviving inventories, and only 14 of those showed evidence of boat ownership. The mean inventory value was substantially higher in the boat-owning water tradesmen, at £26, than in those who did not own boats, who were valued at £9. In the sixteenth century ownership of property, including boats by keelmen, was more common, as can be seen from the will and inventory of John Robinson, a Keelman of All Hallows parish, dated 11 May 1592:[34]

> To Mr Raphe Jennisone the half of my carvel lighter, whereof James Bell hath the other half, in consideration, that he shall pay for my mortuarie, and stand a good friend and maister unto my wife. To Katherine my wife, all my houses, that I have in Sandgate, during all the term of years that I have in my two leases yet to come. If it shall please God to call my wife to His mercy, before the end of my two leases, then I do give unto my maister, Raphe Jennisone, my four slait houses, wherein I now dwell; and my other two thatched houses to James Bell after my wife her decease. To my wife my clinker lighter, with all her gear. The rest of my goods to my foresaid wife. Inventory: 'One clinker lighter, with her furniture, that is 1 anker and a cable, and a mast, and a sail, and a line, and 5 shovels, 2 hookes, 2 oars, a swape, and 5 plankes, and 2 half planks, before the dower, 24l. half a carvel lighter, with her furniture, that is, 1 oar and a swape. And an old line, with the planks in the waist.

likely that many of these had inherited from a deceased husband whose occupation may have been related to trade and the sea. It is also possible that a number of owners of shares in ships whose occupations are not normally associated with ship ownership, gained their shares as a result of marriage to a ship-owning widow. The role of women in business in the seventeenth and eighteenth centuries is well described in P. Earle, *The Making of the English Middle Class: Business, Society and Family Life in London, 1670–1730* (London: Methuen, 1989), pp. 158–66.

[34] W. Greenwell, 'Durham Wills and Inventories, Part II'. *Surtees Society*, 38 (1860), p. 414: 'Henrie Robinsone, May 11th 1592. of Newcastle upon Tyne, Keillman of the Parish of All Hallows'.

There appears to have been a very small group of those immediately involved in the water trades during the seventeenth and eighteenth centuries, the skippers and watermen, who also owned both boats and ships. The ownership of boats was mainly confined to those described as skippers and watermen, although there were a few fishermen and a ferryman who also owned their own boat. The occupational groups are slightly confused by some watermen also being described as yeomen. There are two particularly well-preserved probate inventories from boat owning water tradesmen. The first is the inventory of Matthew Grant, which is dated 7 November 1690. Grant is described in the inventory as a yeoman, but he can be found in the All Saints parish burial register described as a waterman. The inventory describes his very modest possessions. At the end of the list of his domestic property comes what is described as:

> One Coalboat or Lightner whereof Rich: Bowey is Skipper
> Together with all her furniture.   £21–0–0d

In addition at the end of the inventory there is an item:

> One moiety of a Coalboat   £02–10–0d

This description of a boat as a coal boat almost certainly represents a keel by another name, particularly because the valuation at £21 is almost identical to the values placed on keels in other inventories of a similar date. The change in nomenclature is of interest in view of the apparent disappearance of the term 'keelman' to be replaced by 'waterman' in parish registers at the same time. The ownership of this coal boat by Matthew Grant represents over 75 per cent of his entire estate which was valued at £29–01–02d; the value of his residual domestic goods was £5–11–2d, which was barely enough for his family to need to prepare an inventory. An indicator of the cohesiveness of the different occupations in his community is demonstrated by the inclusion of Roger Durham, a shipwright, as one of the group who prepared his inventory. As there was no list of outstanding debts attached to the inventory it is more likely that this was a duty undertaken by a friend or professional acquaintance rather than a creditor looking for recompense.

The second probate inventory is that of John Whitehead, which was prepared on 4 March 1696. This is an even more modest inventory than that of Matthew Grant; once again, the deceased is described as a Yeoman and appears in the All Saints parish burial register described as a waterman.[35] The majority of the items

---

[35] Newcastle All Saints Burial Register, NCL/LS. L929. 3/N536.

in the inventory are small, very simple domestic items, however towards the end is listed his boat:

'One Old Coalboat with the Appurtenances £13–14–0d'

The total value of the estate is £15–01–08d, the old boat representing over 90 per cent of his whole estate, with the remainder of his property being valued at only £1–7-8d. Once again, we find that the valuation of his old coal boat matches almost exactly that of equivalent old keels, tending to confirm the association between keels and coal boats. It is interesting to note that like the inventory of Matthew Grant, a shipwright also prepared John Whitehead's inventory. Once again, this may have been a reflection of friendships between trades, but may also imply an interest by the shipwright in the estate, notwithstanding the absence of any explicit debts owed to him in the inventory.

One of the largest groups of owners of both working boats and ships were the shipwrights. Although the ownership levels were very high compared with other trades and professions, it was clear that not all shipwrights owned boats or ships, indeed out of 97 inventories from shipwrights between 1600 and 1720, only 38 (39%) owned boats or ships, with 27 (28%) owning 119 working boats and 10 (10%) owning shares in 58 ships. One of the reasons for this could be that not all of those who described themselves as shipwrights were of the same status. Skilled workers who worked in a shipyard owned by another shipwright may still have described themselves as a shipwright, but clearly would have owned neither the stock nor the boats, whereas the owner of the yard, stock and vessels who also described himself as a shipwright was clearly of different status and relative wealth. A case worthy of study is that of Thomas Campion, a shipwright of some substance, whose inventory was dated 1720. In addition to his household and personal property, he owned 13 keels valued at £39 each, totalling £507, with a total estate of £1,934; his inventory included a large amount of boat-building supplies:

Unfinished Keel on stocks and other timber belonging to Thomas Campion:
Timber great and small £70–0-0; Planks £41–0-0; Stabbs £2–4-6;
Keel gunwale £5–2-8; New bottom for Keel £2–0-0;
Keel on stocks part built £20–0-0; Spars for Keel oars and mast £9–12–0;
Deals £3–12-0; Other bits £1–15–0, £2–10–0, £2–11–0;
Stocks for Keel £0–15–0.[36]

---

[36] Durham University Library, DPRI/1/Inv. 1720.

It is understandable that a shipwright might keep a share in the ships that he built as an investment, with a view to sharing in the profits of its trade. However, the ownership of large numbers of river craft such as keels is a little more difficult to understand, unless there was a trade in hiring keels to end users such as hostmen. Though little evidence of such a trade appears in existing literature, it seems implausible that shipwrights would be building such a large number of keels speculatively and carrying such a large capital risk without the prospect of either an early sale or the ability to generate and income from a boat hiring trade.

Evidence does exist, however, of shipwrights making a business out of hiring keels to other traders in the records of the Company of Shipwrights. In the Minutes and Order Book of the Company there is an Order dated 24 June 1731 that clearly states the rules and fees to be charged by shipwrights for the let or hire of keels:

> It is further ordered by the Consent and upon the Consideration aforsd. that no Brother of the sd. Society Free or to be Free of the sd. Society or Widow or Widdows as aforsd. shall at any time or times hereafter Directly or indirectly lett out to ffarm any New Keel or keels fitted with furniture by the year greater or lesser term for less than fourteen Pounds a Year or proportionable in relation to time after the same Rent upon pain & penalty of Six shillings and eight pence a week to be forfeited for every week such Keel or Keels is or are left to Farm Contrary to the true Meaning of these presents by every Brother Widdow or Widdows So letting to Farm and the said penalty to be paid upon demand to the Steward for the time being of the Society to the use of the sd. Society.[37]

The level of annual rent suggested by this order of £14 per year gives an idea of the potential profit from renting a keel. If the value of a new keel was £40, as indicated by the probate inventories, it is likely that this represented the cost to the shipwright of building the keel; at the end of three years, then, the shipwright would have more than recouped the costs of building and be starting to make a profit. In reality the real cost to the shipwright of building a keel would have been less than £40, as the new price would have inevitably included his profit margin, meaning that the profit to a shipwright who was also a hirer of keels would appear even earlier in the first three year period. If these figures are applied to Thomas Campion, whose inventory was discussed above, with his

---

[37] *Minutes and Orders of the Company of Shipwrights*, TWAM GU/SH/4/1; Wright, 'Water Trades on the Lower River Tyne, 121–123. D.J. Rowe, "The Records of the Company of Shipwrights of Newcastle upon Tyne, 1622–1967"', *Surtees Society,* 181 (1966), p. 29.

13 keels valued at £39 each, at a rent of £14 each year, each keel would be fully paid for and generating a profit after 2.8 years, giving an annual income of £182 from his 13 keels. This level of income, when added to his income from any other ship and boatbuilding activities he might have had, goes some way towards accounting for the size of his estate – just under £2,000 – and would have underpinned the underlying financial security of his business.[38] This recognition that a significant part of the trade of a shipwright had been expanded to include the hire of the products of his labours to other end users has not been described before in the literature, and it further emphasizes their place as key players in the business networks that underpinned the coal trade and shipping in general. An example of the tensions that existed between the different trades working along the river were the frequent disputes between the shipwrights, the hostmen and other boat and ship owners about the charges made by the shipwrights for their work. There are a number of references in the hostmen's records in 1719 to shipwrights being paid extravagant wages 'exceeding those of any other part of the country'. In addition, they insisted on using their own supplies of timber for their work, for which they charged far more than it would have cost the boat owner to obtain the timber himself.[39] As shown in the cases of Ralph Gardener and Thomas Cliffe, the shipwrights were assiduous in protecting and enhancing their own interests.[40]

It would be expected that merchants might have a significant role in the ownership of those ships that traded into Newcastle and the Tyne, or the river craft that facilitated the trade. Although a number of inventories of merchants do show evidence of boat and ship ownership, the proportion is relatively small when compared with shipwrights. There survive 208 inventories of merchants who were not also hostmen from the years between 1600 and 1740, and of those 43 (20%) show evidence of boat or ship ownership, leaving 165 who did not own boats or ships. It is possible that this is partly because a significant number of the merchants who did not own boats themselves took advantage of their ability to rent them from the shipwrights. It is also important to recognize that the generic term merchant covers a wide range of people who, although

---

[38] P. Earle, *The Making of the English Middle Clas*, pp. 112–23. Earle emphasises the importance of maintaining adequate cash flow in ensuring the survival of a business, characteristics that are exemplified by Thomas Campion as he maximises every possible source of income from his shipbuilding skills.

[39] Dendy, *Company of Hostmen*, pp. 184–5.

[40] R. Howell, ed., *Monopoly on the Tyne, 1650–58: Papers Relating to Ralph Gardner* (Newcastle upon Tyne: The Society of Antiquaries of Newcastle upon Tyne, 1978); Original papers in TWAM.

all merchants, varied substantially in the size and nature of their business. For example, many of those merchants may have traded locally and had only a small export or import business, with no incentive to invest resources in ship or boat ownership. Alternatively, a number of very substantial merchants had trading links extending throughout Britain and abroad, and for them investment in shipping was a natural complement to the rest of their business.

Being a hostman and a member of the Hostman's Company was a very prestigious position and was actively sought after by many of the merchants in the city of Newcastle. Many of those who had inventories in which the occupation was described as a merchant were also listed as hostmen in the lists of admissions as members of the Hostman's Company,[41] and were in reality a distinct group within the community of merchants as a whole. In view of their links with both river and seaborne trade, it might be expected that many of them might own shares in ships and boats. From the years between 1600 and 1740, 93 inventories of hostmen survive, and of these 32 (34%) showed evidence of boat or ship ownership. Eighteen of these 93 hostmen (19%) owned 99 working boats between them, 14 (15%) owned shares in 94 ships, and 10 (11%) owned 144 ships and working boats together. This level and breadth of ownership is not surprising given the extent to which participation in the river trades was integral to the work of a hostman. However, almost two thirds of the hostmen did not own ships or working boats such as keels. It seems clear that because the hostmen employed the skippers and keelmen who worked the keels and managed their work, it has been wrongly assumed that they must also have owned the keels. This was not always the case; a significant number of hostmen must have been renting their keels from other owners such as shipwrights or other boat owners, possibly merchants and coal owners. In addition to working boats, a number of hostmen also owned ships, however the proportion owning both ships and boats was quite large. The significant level of ship ownership by some hostmen does suggest that they had a very strong grip on many aspects of the coal trade, being able to influence the trade from the coal staiths to its arrival at London or other destinations. When viewed in the context of the very wide range of estate size, this spectrum of ship and boat ownership suggests that some hostmen were much more successful than others. While some were very wealthy and successful, others were clearly of lesser means, either as a result of a relative lack

---

[41] Dendy, *Company of Hostmen*, pp. 265–84; Charleton, *Newcastle Town*, p. 256; Middlebrook, *Newcastle upon Tyne*, p. 67; Hatcher, *The History of the British Coal Industry*, p. 474.

of success in business or of retirement, and this may reflect the complexities and risks involved in the coal trade at this time.[42]

One of the most prominent merchants and hostmen in Newcastle, Henry Maddison, illustrates the significance of the wealthy trading dynasties in the town during the seventeenth century. The Maddison family was typical of those members of the small inner governing ring of hostmen and merchants described by Howell.[43] Henry Maddison was born in 1574 in Newcastle upon Tyne to a prominent merchant Lionel Maddison, who was one of the group who shared the Grand Lease, becoming mayor of Newcastle in 1605 and 1617.[44] Henry flourished, after joining the 'family business'. He was admitted to the Company of Hostmen on 22 March 1600, and joined his father Lionel as sheriff during the latter's term as mayor in 1605, becoming mayor himself in 1623. His son, also called Lionel, became sheriff in 1624 and subsequently, as Sir Lionel Maddison, became mayor in 1632, two years before the death of Henry in 1634. After Henry's death an imposing family memorial was built, which can still be seen, in the south transept of St Nicholas Cathedral in Newcastle.[45] On the death of Henry Maddison his probate inventory displayed the full scope of his wealth, which included coal reserves, land and shipping valued in total at £3,768–9-2d. In addition to his shipping the estate included:

> Three Waggon Horses £3; Six wagons with all furniture belonging them £12; Two riding horses £10; Five hundred tons of coal at pit and staiths, and a lease of a colliery at Fidgerfield having part of it £100; A part of a lease of a colliery at Lingefield £100; A part of a lease of a colliery at Rydingfield £66–3-4d; A part of a lease of a colliery at Faddonsfield £30; In stock with Thomas Cleborne £300; In corn that was sown at Marshallands £14.[46]

---

[42] Earle, *The Making of the English Middle Class*, pp. 143–57; Grassby, *The Business community of Seventeenth Century England*, pp. 242–7.

[43] R. Howell, 'Newcastle and the Nation: The Seventeenth-Century Experience', in *The Tudor and Stuart Town, 1530–1688: A Reader in English Urban History*, ed. J. Barry (London: Longman, 1990), pp. 275–96.

[44] D. Levine and K. Wrightson, *The Making of an Industrial Society: Whickham 1560–1765* (Oxford: Clarendon Press, 1991), p. 35.

[45] The memorial includes a list of Henry's 16 children from his wife, Elizabeth, who died in 1753. The list includes 10 sons: Sir Lionel, Raphe, Robert, William, Henry, Peter, George, Timothy and Thomas who were all still alive at the time of her death and John, who died on an expedition to Cadiz. Henry and Elizabeth had six daughters: Jane, Susan, Elizabeth, Barbara, Eleanor and Jane, whose survivals at the time of her death were not stated on the memorial.

[46] Durham Probate Inventories, Durham University Library, Henry Maddison, DPRI/1/Inv 1636.

All of his shipping interests were listed separately, and these are shown in Table 5.3. Maddison had one of the largest portfolios of shipping and keels in the seventeenth and eighteenth centuries. Ships and boats represented over 30 per cent of his fortune, epitomizing the concentration of both commercial and local political power in the hands of the group of oligarchs that ran Newcastle upon Tyne during this period; indeed, Grassby used Maddison as an example of a successful merchant in a provincial city.[47] One of the most striking features of Maddison's ownership of ships was the wide spread of East-coast ports at which they were based, implying a wide range of business interests

Table 5.3   Henry Maddison's probate inventory, ships and boats 1634

Ship	Share	Value	Total Value
9 Keels	each	£22	£198
Henry and John of Colchester	5/16	£52	£166
Blessing of Ipswich	3/8	£200	£650
Prymrose of Newcastle	1/4	£25	£100
Isabell of York	1/4	£20	£80
Content of Colchester	1/8	£80	£640
Marigold of York	1/4	£90	£360
Neptune of Newcastle	1/4	£30	£120
Blessing of Rochester	3/16	£120	£640
John of London	1/16	£40	£640
Elizabeth of Malding	1/16	£40	£640
Mary of Malding	1/16	£40	£640
Mary Bonaventure of Hull	1/16	£20	£320
True Love of Albrough	1/16	£40	£640
Dove of Ipswich	1/32	£30	£960
Elizabeth of Selby	1/8	£50	£400
Gift of Ipswich	1/8	£50	£400
Indevour of London	1/4	£30	£120
Denis of Lynn	1/16	£25	£400
Protection of Ipswich	1/16	£25	£400
Total Values		£1,316	£8,870

[47] R. Grassby, 'English Merchant Capitalism in the late Seventeenth Century: The Composition of Business Fortunes', *Past & Present*, 46 (1970), pp. 87–107; Grassby, *The Business Community*, pp. 139–70; Earle, *The Making of the English Middle Class*, p. 143.

and a degree of integration of the ownership of the coastal merchant fleet. The fates of the remainder of the large Maddison family are relatively unknown. Sir Lionel Maddison played a central role in the Puritan movement, being a member of the key Puritan group in the town and related by marriage to a number of the leading Puritans in the area.[48] There is a reference in the Common Council minutes to a Thomas Maddison 'who has fallen on difficult times' being appointed a Ballast Assessor by the town council in 1660. The Maddison tomb in Newcastle Cathedral lists a Thomas Maddison among the younger sons of Henry Maddison. If this was the same person, it may well be a sign that in 1660 the family retained some residual influence. However, apart from another Henry Maddison becoming mayor in 1665, there were no further records of the Maddison family in local government in Newcastle up to 1800.[49]

Although there are limitations in the value of probate inventories as a source, the information they contain is likely to be reliable, particularly as it is very likely that if an item such as a boat or ship is listed as belonging to a certain individual on a particular date, in a document witnessed by three or four individuals, then this item did indeed exist and its ownership was as stated. The valuations of the boats and ships are probably accurate for the time, with any variations reflecting differences in the age and quality of the individual boat or ship. A more cynical view might suggest that the valuation may be influenced by a desire to either increase or decrease the recorded value of the estate, for whatever reason. This might explain why there was quite a wide range of valuations for seemingly very similar boats at similar dates.[50] The numbers of keels or hostmen identified are a reflection of the evidence available from the surviving probate inventories, and should not necessarily be taken as representing the absolute number that existed. Although a large number of keels were identified, the probate inventories they came from were widely distributed across many years, making any estimate of the proportion they represented of total keel numbers unreliable. Notwithstanding these limitations, there is evidence from sufficient inventories to draw some very clear qualitative conclusions, and provide a basis for a number of legitimate,

---

[48] Howell, *Newcastle upon Tyne and the Puritan Revolution* (Oxford: Oxford University Press, 1967), p. 127; Levine and Wrightson, *The Making of an Industrial Society*, p. 35.

[49] It is possible that the Henry Maddison who was mayor in 1665 was one of Henry's sons or even a grandson. One of the reasons the Maddison family played a less prominent role on public life after the middle of the seventeenth century may have been the relative dilution of Henry Maddison's fortune when it was spread across a family of 16 children, leaving each one with relatively less wealth to underpin a career in business and public life.

[50] Arkell, 'Interpreting Probate Inventories', pp. 72–102; Overton, 'Prices from Probate Inventories', pp. 120–41.

but cautious quantitative conclusions. Although the extent to which probate inventories have survived from year to year varies, the large number that have been identified and studied has enabled a realistic analysis of the patterns of ship and boat ownership between 1600 and 1750. Many of the owners of small numbers of working boats were of quite modest means, with the value of their boat contributing the vast majority of their wealth. An example is those working in the water trades, the watermen and skippers, a number of whom owned boats, the value of which constituted more than 80 per cent of their entire estate, in contrast with owners of larger numbers of vessels, or more valuable boats or ships where the contribution of this part of their estate to their overall wealth was much less. The owners of shares in ships often had a portfolio of shares in quite a large number of ships, each of quite modest individual value, but in total amounting to quite a large sum, this sum being often much less than half of the total estate. This does tend to confirm that investment in shipping was a considered strategy, with risk being reduced by developing a portfolio consisting of a larger number of separate small investments.

It was not a surprise to find that merchants and hostmen featured prominently in the list of those who owned both working boats and ships, particularly because much has been made in the secondary literature of the role of the merchants and hostmen in the ownership of the working boats, notably the keels which were integral to the coal trade. Whereas there can be little doubt that the hostmen acted as agents, facilitating the coal trade and hiring and managing the skippers and keelmen who carried the coal to the ships, the evidence suggests that not all of them owned the keels themselves. It is clear that some of the wealthier merchants, who also owned or leased the coal mines, owned many keels and supplied them to the hostmen. It is notable that among the most significant owners of keels were the shipwrights who built them. The large numbers that many owned were significantly more than would be anticipated if their only role was to make keels, when it might be expected that they might have one or two in stock pending sale. It has become clear that ownership at this level was an intentional strategy designed to balance the large amount of capital tied up in the keels, by generating a significant income derived from hiring the keels to hostmen, who would find skippers and crews with a view to using them to ferry coal to the ships. Many of the shipwrights additionally had significant ownership of shares in ships, apparently maintaining a financial interest in the ownership and performance of the ships they had built. The major contribution of shipwrights to these trading networks, which has not been described before, demonstrates their participation in the wider business and trading networks that existed on the River Tyne. The nature of the keel rental trade is less clear.

Whereas it is possible that the hostmen rented them and then employed skippers and keelmen to work them, there is some anecdotal evidence that those hostmen who owned keels charged a rental fee to the keelmen who used them. If this was indeed the case, it is equally possible that the skippers hired the keels directly from the shipwrights, and then made themselves and their crewed keel available to an employing hostman. Evidence for this comes from letters and diaries of the time, which often talked in terms of a keel being 'Mr Robinson's keel', where Mr Robinson was the skipper of the keel, implying a degree of responsibility if not ownership.[51] The wide discrepancies between the estate sizes of those who owned boats or ships and those who did not, in all of the occupational groups studied, may be indicative of an economic, and by implication social, hierarchy within each of the different occupational groups. This heterogeneity in the patterns of ownership of working river craft along the lower River Tyne contrasts with the conventions found on other working rivers, such as the Severn, where most of the working craft were fully owned by the ships' masters, who as individuals were more significant members of their local business communities than the skippers and keelmen of Tyneside.[52]

This exploration of the pattern of ship and boat ownership shown in probate inventories originating from Newcastle and its surrounding communities has allowed a glimpse into the wider aspects of life amongst the 'middling sort' in this industrial riverside community. It is clear that those involved in the coal and water trades participated in business networks that were essential to the success of Newcastle at this time; however, they were deeply embedded in the population and constituted only part of the wider business and trading community of the town. Like merchants and tradesmen in other non-water-related trades there was a spectrum of success and relative wealth within each of the water trades that was manifest by the contents of probate inventories. Many of the more successful merchants and hostmen had inventories that showed evidence of extensive holdings of land property and often livestock, whereas there were others who died in relative poverty, notwithstanding their apparent status implied by their occupation. Similar patterns were found in the inventories of those of similar status who had no involvement in the water trades. The inventories from those who were of the 'middling sort' from all of the main trades and occupations in Newcastle and the surrounding communities displayed evidence of a wide range of property ownership and the acquisition of significant amounts of soft

---

[51] See Chapter 7, an analysis of the diaries of Ralph Jackson, an apprentice hostman.
[52] B. Trinder, *Barges and Bargemen: A Social History of the Upper Severn Navigation 1660–1900* (Chichester: Phillimore, 2005), 65–6.

furnishings, books and domestic equipment, indicating active participation in the general culture of consumption that appeared to be flourishing in the community at that time.

Chapter 6
The Shipping Trade on the River Tyne

Having become a flourishing port stimulated by the dynamic coal trade, during the seventeenth and eighteenth centuries, Newcastle had developed a thriving community of merchants and tradesmen. As the community grew, with the development of an urban middle class, relative wealth and spending power, manifested in an increasing demand for consumables, also grew. This 'consuming culture' was a major feature of the seventeenth and eighteenth centuries, and it has been the subject of extensive analysis relating the increased demand associated with consumption to the development of markets and increasing sociability within the community.[1] The impact of these changes upon consumption and regional identity, particularly in the North East of England, has been lucidly presented in a series of essays edited by Helen Berry and Jeremy Gregory, in which a number of distinct features characteristic of the local industrial and trading community dominated by coal are highlighted.[2] The effect of this increasing consumption of a wider range of food and luxury products was to fuel both an increase in the production of consumables locally and an increase in the import of goods that were not locally produced into the Tyne. These imports came not just from London and other ports in England but also from abroad, including timber and cloth from Northern Europe and wines from Southern Europe and the Mediterranean. Many of these commodities came into Newcastle as part of return cargoes in ships that were coming back to the Tyne to pick up further outward cargoes of coal and other local products such as glass, lead and grindstones, particularly as part of the flourishing Baltic trade that was so important to many Newcastle merchants.[3]

---

[1] N. McKendrick, J. Brewer and J.H. Plumb, *The Birth of the Consumer Society: The Commercialisation of Eighteenth-Century England* (London: Europa, 1982); J. Brewer and R. Porter, eds, *Consumption and the World of Goods* (London: Routledge, 1993); J. Brewer and A. Bermingham, *The Consumption of Culture, 1660–1800: Image, Object, Text* (London: Routledge 1995).

[2] H. Berry and J. Gregory, 'Introduction', in *Creating and Consuming Culture in North-East England, 1660–1830*, ed. H. Berry and J. Gregory (Aldershot: Ashgate, 2004), pp. 1–11.

[3] P. Salmon and T. Barrow, eds, *Britain and the Baltic* (Sunderland: Sunderland University Press, 2003).

These changes became manifest in the type and quantity of property owned by householders, and are displayed in surviving probate inventories, which provide an insight into the range of domestic household goods available in the seventeenth and early eighteenth centuries in the North East. In her studies of the ownership of property, Lorna Scammell compared the ownership of consumer durables described in probate inventories in the North East of England with those in other parts of the country. She was able to identify differences between areas with a rural as opposed to an urban economy and suggested that the features of the North East were more akin to those of an area with a mixed economy, and also that the population were clearly benefitting from an improving quality of life. A large proportion of the wide range of domestic goods she found were not made locally but traded from London, almost certainly by sea in ships that were intending to return to their home port with a cargo of coal.[4] The ability to sustain such a reliable and consistent import of goods of all types into Newcastle and its surrounding region influenced the development of trade and industries in the region in both positive and negative ways. Whereas many industries benefited from the ready availability of coal as an energy source and developed locally, some of the smaller industries, which provided what might be considered as luxury goods, did not develop and relied on imports from elsewhere. An example of this effect was the relative absence of a significant distilling industry in the North East. With the increasing taste for gin and other spirits in the seventeenth and eighteenth centuries there was an increasing demand, particularly from those in the flourishing middle classes.[5] This was largely supplied by imports from the significant number of large-scale distillers based in and around London. Chartres, in his analysis of the consumption of gin and other spirits in the North East of England in the seventeenth and eighteenth centuries, highlights the extent of spirit consumption in the region and the extent to which the demand was adequately supplied by manufacturers in London through their agents in London, regionally and locally. Imports also came from the Scottish distilleries and from abroad, not to mention a contribution made by smuggling.[6]

---

[4] L. Scammell, 'Was the North East Different from Other Areas? The Property of Everyday Consumption in the Late Seventeenth and Early Eighteenth Centuries', in *Creating and Consuming Culture*, ed. H. Berry and J. Gregory (Aldershot: Ashgate, 2004), pp. 12–23; L. Weatherill, *Consumer Behaviour and Material Culture in Britain, 1660–1760*, 2nd edition (London and New York: Routledge, 1996).

[5] P. Clark, 'The "Mother Gin" controversy in the Early Eighteenth Century', *Transactions of the Royal Historical Society*, 5th ser., 38 (1988), pp. 63–84.

[6] J.A. Chartres, 'Spirits in the North East? Gin and Other Vices in the Long Eighteenth Century', in *Creating and Consuming Culture*, pp. 37–56; Clark, 'The "Mother Gin" controversy', pp. 63–84.

One of the most important contributors to the overseas trade from Newcastle and the Tyne during the seventeenth and eighteenth centuries was the Baltic trade. Throughout this period, there was a regular traffic of ships from the Tyne to Norway and through The Sound of Denmark into the Baltic, usually carrying cargoes of coal, salt and glass to the Baltic ports. The iron trade from Sweden to England became particularly strong as the trade between Sweden and Holland diminished, with Newcastle and other East Coast ships loading iron in large quantities in both Gothenburg and Stockholm.[7] The trade between Newcastle and Narva (a coastal port in what is currently in Estonia, close to the Russian border) was of particular significance in the latter half of the seventeenth century, as the town was used as an access point into the Russian trade. A number of English merchants became resident in the town to benefit from the flourishing tobacco import trade that developed.[8] In addition to iron from Stockholm, the returning cargoes included large amounts of timber, particularly from Norway, and flax, pitch, tar and hemp from the other Baltic ports.[9] One of the best examples of a successful eighteenth-century Newcastle merchant was Ralph Carr (1711–1806).[10] Carr followed his father into the business of a merchant trader in Newcastle, and began his career, while still an apprentice, with a long tour of the continental trading centres in Northern Europe, including northern France, Amsterdam, the Low Countries and the Baltic, eventually spending some time in St Petersburg. The Baltic was to remain one of his main business interests for the rest of his life. On his return to Newcastle he began trading on his own account, even though he had not yet completed his apprenticeship. The contacts he had made on his trip, particularly those in Amsterdam and elsewhere in Holland and the Baltic were essential to the future development of his Baltic trading network. Carr developed a series of interrelated business interests, including becoming a proprietor of the British Linen Company, founded in 1746, which corresponded nicely with his imports of flax from the Baltic and Hamburg. A further interest was in

---

[7] L. Muller, 'Britain and Sweden: The Changing Pattern of Commodity Exchange 1650–1680', in *Britain and the Baltic*, ed. P. Salmon and T. Barrow (Sunderland: Sunderland University Press, 2003), pp. 61–76; D. Aldridge, 'English East Coast Trade with the Baltic in the Closing Years of the Great Northern War 1714–1721', in *Britain and the Baltic*, pp. 119–30.

[8] E. Kung, 'English Commercial Activity in Narva During the Second Half of the Seventeenth Century', in *Britain and the Baltic*, pp. 77–108.

[9] R. Davis, *The Rise of the English Shipping Industry in the Seventeenth and Eighteenth Centuries* (London: Macmillan, 1962), p. 213.

[10] B. Purdue, 'Ralph Carr: A Newcastle Merchant and the Baltic Trade in the Mid Eighteenth Century', in *Britain and the Baltic*, pp. 157–68.

buying and selling corn, importing it from Scotland and the Baltic and, using close links with London dealers, re-exporting it to the most profitable centre. The financial mechanisms of the Baltic trade were complex, and depended on bills of exchange often drawn upon at Amsterdam or Rotterdam, the entire trade being a tri-partite arrangement financed largely by Dutch money, which was then repaid by English merchants. Ralph Carr became deeply involved in international bill-broking, both for himself and for other merchants with less capital and experience; this was later to lead him, with others, to found Newcastle's first Bank, the 'Old Bank'.[11]

Ralph Carr's connection with Amsterdam merchants was to lead him to become associated with the American trade through Newcastle. Amsterdam had developed a flourishing trade with ports on the eastern seaboard of America, particularly New York and Boston;[12] however, before American independence ships heading from Europe to America were required to clear customs in England, and Carr provided a service for Dutch merchants to clear their ships in Newcastle before going to America, for which he charged commission. The funds raised by these commission charges generated funds to pay bills in Amsterdam for trade undertaken in the Baltic. Although he had not solicited the American trade, Carr used it in an attempt to develop his network further. As well as clearing the Dutch ships through customs, Carr provided them with some ballast cargo for their transatlantic trips, which consisted of relatively cheap bulky goods easily obtainable in the Newcastle area such as coal, anchors and grindstones. In addition, he corresponded with a number of American merchants in an attempt to develop the American trade, trying to persuade them to accept a larger range of products, such as woollen goods, pottery and glassware, in addition to the ballast cargoes, maintaining that he could obtain them at cheaper prices than could be found at other English ports. In spite of his best efforts Carr failed to interest his correspondents and develop an American trade, partly because the products he could offer were not of the quality required, but more importantly because

---

[11] Purdue, 'Ralph Carr', p. 165. Carr's experience in the Corn market led to an association with the Coutts brothers John and James in Edinburgh and London, with whom he made large profits shipping grain during periods of shortage, particularly in 1741, to the most profitable markets. This experience in the Baltic and corn trades gave him the financial experience and capital to facilitate his entry into banking in Newcastle.

[12] Purdue, 'Ralph Carr', p. 166; J. Ellis, 'The "Black Indies": The Economic Development of Newcastle, c1700–1840', in *Newcastle Upon Tyne: a Modern History*, ed. R. Lancaster and B. Colls (Chichester: Phillimore, 2001), 5; W.I. Roberts, 'A Newcastle Merchant and the American Colonial Trade', *Business History Review*, 42 (1968), pp. 271–87.

he was not prepared to offer them the credit facilities they were demanding. The impact of this flourishing and varied import and export trade along the River Tyne would necessarily have been felt by the wider community at all levels. It is striking how the relative efficiency of the internal local transport system on the river would have affected the efficiency of the import and export trades and vice versa. The increased activity by merchants would have been reflected not just by their increasing need for finance and cash flow, as exemplified by the developments in the career of Ralph Carr, but also by increased demands placed on shipping into and out of the river and all of those involved in supporting this increased traffic. The effect of the development of such a varied non-coal import and export trade on those working in the river-related trades would have been substantial, with the increased amount of shipping and the variety of imported goods that were to be unloaded, marketed and distributed to the various end users, stimulating and diversifying the local economy.

The extent to which commodities and other materials associated with the relative boom in consumption in the North East arrived in the region by sea may be seen in the contents of the cargoes listed in the various surviving sources. One of the few sources available for such a study are the Exchequer Port Books. These volumes provide contemporaneous lists of the ships involved in both coastal and overseas trade departing from and arriving at a port. The port books were compiled at 122 maritime centres around the coast of England and Wales between 1565 and 1799. The purpose of the books was to enable the Customs authorities to enforce the collection of customs duties. The major ports, such as Newcastle, were designated Head Ports, and were responsible for a number of lesser ports; Newcastle, for example, had a number of 'member' ports under its aegis, such as Stockton, Whitby and Sunderland, some of which would have their own port books. Usually the larger ports included in their books lesser 'creeks', which in the case of the Newcastle books included Cullercoats, Seaton Sluice and Blyth Nook.[13] There were three officials responsible for collecting the overseas duties, the 'customer', the 'controller' and the 'surveyor' (or searcher),

---

[13] E.E. Hoon, *The Organization of the English Customs System* (Newton Abbot: David & Charles, 1968 [orig. pubd. 1938]), pp. 5–25, 36–8; R.C. Jarvis, 'The Appointment of Ports', *Economic History Review*, 2nd ser., 11 (1958), p. 463; R.C. Jarvis, 'Critical Historical Introduction', in E.E. Hoon, *The Organization of the English Customs System* (Newton Abbot: David & Charles, 1968 [orig. pubd. 1938]), pp. xii–xvii; Davis, *The Rise of the English Shipping Industry*, pp. 396–7; D. Woodward, 'Sources for Maritime History (III): The Port Books of England and Wales', *Maritime History*, 3 (1973), pp. 147–65; D. Hussey, *Coastal and River Trade in Pre-Industrial England: Bristol and Its Region 1680–1730* (Exeter: Exeter University Press, 2000), pp. 7–17.

the customer and controller being responsible for the coastal duties. Each of these officials kept their own duplicate copy of the records. The books recorded all goods coming in and going out of a port, the object being to prevent goods coming or going from abroad being passed off as goods going to or from local coastal ports, thus avoiding customs duties. In addition, there were a number of commodities, including coal, for which internal duties needed to be paid. Even internal coastal shipping was liable to customs fraud and smuggling, and to prevent this there was a substantial bond, payable at the port of departure, which was returned to the bondsman on successful completion of cross checks at the end of a domestic voyage. Notwithstanding these precautions, there was still a significant amount of fraud, often involving corrupt customs officers, particularly in the smaller ports.[14]

There are a number of problems associated with using port books as a historical source, the most important of which is the relatively restricted number of books that have survived the passage of time and remain legible. Even in those that have survived, Woodward emphasized that 'they do not provide trade statistics, but only a record of a part of the trade passing through particular ports'. There were several reasons for this: in addition to the possibility of there being corrupt customs officers, clerical errors and the evasion of duty by merchants all contributed to the problems.[15] In his detailed study of Bristol port books, Hussey noted that, in the late seventeenth century, around 500 coastal voyages cleared that port each year; each record contained details of the ship, destination ports, masters, merchants and cargoes, all amounting to around 30,000 discrete items of data each year. A further 900 voyages were similarly recorded entering Bristol each year. In the light of the vast amount of information contained in each port book, it is not surprising that even the most comprehensive of works are based on a relatively superficial analysis.[16] A number of studies include reference to the contents of the Newcastle Port Books during the seventeenth and eighteenth centuries. One of the earliest was by Willan, in his classic studies *The English Coasting Trade 1600–1750,* and *Studies in Elizabethan Foreign Trade*.[17] Willan

---

[14] Hoon, *English Customs System*, pp. 19, 195, 203; Woodward, 'The Port Books of England and Wales', pp. 147–65; P.A.M. D'Sena, 'Perquistes and Pilfering in the London Docks 1700–1795' (M.Phil Thesis, Open University, 1986).

[15] Hoon, *English Customs System*, p. 203; Woodward, 'The Port Books of England and Wales', pp. 157–8.

[16] Hussey, *Coastal and River Trade*, p. 17.

[17] T.S. Willan, *The English Coasting Trade, 1600–1750* (Manchester: Manchester University Press, 1938), pp. 115–18; Willan, *Studies in Elizabethan Foreign Trade* (Manchester: Manchester University Press, 1959), pp. 67–9; see also Davis, *The Rise of the English Shipping Industry*, p. 213.

noted that in 1547 Newcastle had an active export trade of coal, grindstones, salt, wool and skins to ports in France, such as Rouen, the Low Countries, Danzig, Emden and Hamburg, together with an import trade of timber pitch, tar, flax and hemp from Norway and the Baltic. This was supplemented by a wide range of more exotic goods such as ginger, prunes, aniseed and figs from France and the Low Countries. Willan noted that 'the town was so industrialized and so dependent on food from a distance that it appears almost an anachronism in the northern parts of Elizabethan England'. He also observed that, in 1634, when Newcastle was already a major centre of coal mining, glass-making and salt-making, together with the production of grindstones, that there were coastal exports of around 400,000 tons of coal and around 6,022 wheys of salt. There was no glass exported that year, but, by 1640 1,200 cases of window glass were exported to London.[18] Throughout the remainder of the seventeenth century, the main destinations for coastal exports from the Tyne were London and a range of eastern coastal ports such as Hull, Lynn and Yarmouth. Most of the imports were of grain and other cereals from these east coast ports and a variety of household goods, haberdashery and wines from London. This trade continued during the eighteenth century, with the addition of butter as a major export particularly to London.[19]

The sea trade from Newcastle was relatively unusual when compared with other ports in England, in that its most prominent coastal and overseas exports were relatively high-volume low-value cargoes, as opposed to exports from other ports such as Bristol or London, where the cargoes tended to be of lower volume and higher value. The consequence of this was that proportionally more vessels' movements were required to move cargo of a given value from Newcastle than other ports, partially explaining the very high volumes of sea traffic in and out of the Tyne, with up to 50 arrivals and departures each day.[20] The effect of this was that a very large proportion of the ships arrived carrying ballast alone or another cargo in addition. As shown in Chapter 2, this in itself became a cause of conflict within the town because the volume of ballast discharged was such as to cause obstruction to the river and a hindrance to navigation, but was also a source of income, as the Burgesses of Newcastle charged a fee to deposit ballast on shores within its jurisdiction. The ballast did have some benefits to the town, however, as the sand became an essential component in the flourishing glass manufacturing industry that lined the banks of the river, which had been one of the earliest sites

---

[18] Willan, *The English Coasting Trade*, p. 116; U. Ridley, 'The History of Glass Making on the Tyne and Wear', *Archaeologia Aeliana*, 40 (1962), pp. 145–62.
[19] Willan, *The English Coasting Trade*, p. 116.
[20] Ellis, 'The "Black Indies"', p. 2.

where plate glass was made. During the seventeenth and eighteenth centuries the region was a major manufacturer and exporter of window glass and glass bottles, in addition to particularly fine drinking glasses.[21] In her examination of trade in Newcastle, and particularly the salt trade between 1660 and 1790, Joyce Ellis examined the port books between those years, producing a detailed analysis of the annual salt exports, both coastal to other ports in England, particularly Hull, Lynn and London, and abroad, mainly to Scandinavia and the Baltic. This trade continued until the 1730s, when the Cheshire salt mines began to produce better quality salt at lower prices, reducing the English trade in sea salt. The North-East trade was further undermined by the discovery of salt reserves in Denmark, near Christianshaven. Imports into the Baltic from Iberia also lowered the demand for English sea salt from the Baltic countries. These changes resulted in a progressive decline of the sea-salt trade on the Tyne, as these other sources of better quality salt became readily available.[22]

In a re-evaluation of the Newcastle port books, I chose to study books from years for which other authors had examined port books for comparable provincial ports. The work of David Hussey with port books for ports in the Bristol Channel, including Bristol and Gloucester, proved a particularly appropriate comparator, since it concentrated on a provincial port with a similar magnitude of trade but with a mix of imports and exports very different to that of Newcastle. Hussey chose 1699 as a sample year because it lay between the conclusion of the Anglo-French war, in 1697, and the outbreak of the War of the Spanish Succession, in 1702, representing a period of relative stability in overseas trade.[23] The availability of surviving Newcastle port books covering this period is rather limited. Although the National Archives hold a number of Exchequer Port Books from close to this date, unfortunately overseas and coastal port books for the same year no longer survive. There are, however, complete volumes surviving including the Christmas 1688 to Christmas 1689 Overseas Inwards and Outwards books, and the Christmas 1702 to Christmas 1703 Coastal Inwards and Outwards books; each of these books contains huge numbers of entries recording individual shipments. Two further port books were examined: both Coastal and Overseas for January to December 1756.[24] These

---

21   Ridley, 'The History of Glass Making', pp. 145–62.
22   Ellis, 'The "Black Indies"', p. 3; Ellis, 'The Decline and Fall of the Tyneside Salt industry', pp. 45–58; Davis, *The Rise of the English Shipping Industry*, p. 350.
23   Hussey, *Coastal and River Trade*, p. 18.
24   P. Wright, 'Water Trades on the Lower River Tyne in the Seventeenth and Eighteenth Centuries' (PhD diss., Newcastle University, 2011), pp. 132–57; Port of Newcastle, Sunderland and Stockton, Controller Overseas, Christmas 1698–Christmas 1699 (Includes

latter port books illustrating the changes in the patterns of shipping, as recorded in the port books, over the first 50 years of the eighteenth century. In addition to these Newcastle Port Books, an important further series of documents relevant to imports and exports from the Tyne is the Newcastle Chamberlains' Accounts of Receipts and Disbursements, which are complementary to the port books. They record the payment of local city taxes on the export of coal and salt, and fees for deposition of ballast, the payments often being made on the same day as the customs duties recorded in the exchequer port books. These documents record payment of a variety of other local taxes and charges in addition to the payment of fees for depositing ballast and local taxes on the export of coal, including those for the attainment of freedom following an apprenticeship, and numerous payments for the rent of land and property and fines that have been imposed. The details of the shipping taxes tend to corroborate the entries in the port books, containing the names of both the ship and that of its master together with the amount of coal carried and the amount of tax paid. The ballast records show both the amount of ballast deposited and the ballast shores where it was deposited, together with the fees paid. Ships that arrived with incoming cargo, instead of ballast, were also identified if they left with coal or salt, for which local taxes were paid.[25]

The Coastal Outwards port book for 1702–03 is very much larger than the Coastal Inwards book,[26] and is relatively well preserved. It is mostly legible, although there are one or two areas of damage to the pages and text. The book is arranged in two parts, the first part records the coastal outwards shipments, arranged in five columns. These include the name of the Bondsman underwriting the voyage,[27] the date and the name of the ship and its master, together with any

---

Inwards and Outwards shipments), TNA: E/190/207/4; Port of Newcastle, Customer and Controller Coastal, Christmas 1702–Christmas 1703 (Includes Inwards and Outwards shipments), TNA: E/190/209/1; Port of Newcastle with Blyth, Stockton and Sunderland, Customer and Controller Coastal, Jan 1756–Jan 1757 (Outward shipments only), TNA: E/190/256/9; Port of Newcastle with Blyth, Stockton and Sunderland, Searcher Overseas, Jan 1756–Jan 1757 (Inward and Outward shipments) TNA: E/190/257/5. Those for 1756 were selected in the light of information contained in the diaries of Ralph Jackson, apprentice hostman, whose final year of apprenticeship was 1756, and whose diaries are considered in Chapter 7.

[25] Newcastle Chamberlains' Accounts of Receipt and Disbursements, TWAM, MD.NC/FN/1/1; E.M. Halcrow, 'Chamberlain's Accounts, Newcastle upon Tyne', *Journal of the Society of Archivists*, Vol. 1, Issue 10 (1955), pp. 289–91; Ellis, 'The "Black Indies"', p. 17.

[26] TNA E/190/209/1.

[27] Although the Port Books include the name of the bondsman underwriting the voyage, they do not include the amount of the bond that he paid. In addition, the details of the

Table 6.1 Shipments in 1702–03 coastal outwards port book

Month	Shipments	London[a]	Coal + cargo[b]	Coal only[b]	Salt + coal[b]	Salt[b]	Cargo only[b]
January	80	21(26%)	33(41%)	14(17%)	31(39%)	2(2%)	5(6%)
February	37	22(59%)	17(46%)	14(38%)	2(5%)	1(3%)	3(8%)
March	183	120(66%)	33(18%)	125(68%)	9(5%)	9(5%)	7(4%)
April	277	152(55%)	51(18%)	212(77%)	8(3%)	2(0.7%)	4(1%)
May	206	116(56%)	28(14%)	164(80%)	9(4%)	2(1%)	3(1%)
June	185	105(57%)	27(15%)	142(77%)	11(6%)	3(2%)	2(1%)
July	270	163(60%)	47(17%)	194(72%)	21(8%)	3(1%)	5(2%)
August	430	227(53%)	72(17%)	322(75%)	17(4%)	16(4%)	3(0.7%)
September	299	175(59%)	41(14%)	227(76%)	22(7%)	3(1%)	6(2%)
October	232	82(35%)	64(28%)	136(59%)	25(11%)	2(0.8%)	5(2%)
November	56	26(46%)	23(41%)	22(39%)	4(7%)	4(7%)	3(5%)
December	25	3(12%)	18(72%)	1(4%)	3(12%)	3(12%)	0
Totals	2280	1,212(53%)	454(20%)	1,568(69%)	162(7%)	50(2%)	46(2%)

Note: (a) These percentages represent the proportion of the total shipments that went to London; (b) These percentages represent the proportion of total shipments for each commodity or combination of commodities.

additional cargo other than salt or coal, the amount of salt, the amount of coal in chaldrons, the destination port and the date of clearance at the port of arrival (allowing the bondsman to be repaid his bond). The second part, the Coastal Inwards book, is also arranged in columns, including the date of arrival, the name of the ship, its master, the name of the merchant and the nature of the cargo, the port of origin and the date of departure. The format makes it relatively easy to identify the details of the coastal trade from the Tyne over the year. An analysis of the coastal outwards port book by month showed the number of shipments leaving the Tyne, the proportion which were London bound, and the extent to which they were coal alone, other non-coal cargo, salt or a combination of these (Table 6.1). There were 2,280 coastal shipments out of Newcastle in 1702–03. Many of the authors of histories of Newcastle have stated that the coal trade by sea out of Newcastle to London and other ports stopped over the winter, partly because of bad weather and sea conditions and partly because frost damaged the quality of the coal.[28] The port books clearly show that although there was a

---

cargo shipped on any particular voyage include the size of each shipment but unfortunately neither its value nor the full value of the shipment as a whole.

[28] R. Welford, *History of Newcastle and Gateshead*, 5 vols (London: Walter Scott, 1885), Vol. 3, p 348; E. Hughes, *North Country Life in the Eighteenth Century: the North*

great reduction in voyages over the winter months, there were still a significant number of shipments of all cargoes, including coal leaving the Tyne throughout the winter. In addition to coal and salt, there was a significant amount of general cargo shipped out of the Tyne to coastal ports throughout the year: 2,184 of the 2,280 coastal shipments included coal in their cargo (96%), but 20% (454 of 2,184) of the coal shipments were accompanied by general cargo, and 7% (162 of 2,184) were accompanied by salt. If one assumes that the coal cargo, being in bulk, was loaded on board the ships first, then it is likely that the general cargo was loaded last while the ship was anchored at the mouth of the river; the clear implication is that the same mode of transport, probably the keel, was used to move the general cargo from land to the ship. The range of general cargoes carried out of the Tyne was very wide (Table 6.2) and was taken to a very wide range of coastal ports in addition to London (Table 6.3). The port books also show the names of the bondsmen who underwrote each coastal voyage. It is notable that the names recur very regularly, and in many cases they appear to be the same names as those that appear in the lists of members of the Hostman's Company. For example, Robert Wallis's name appears as bondsman for 57 shipments in 1702–03. This name appears as an apprentice hostman in 1698, who was admitted to the company as a member in 1705, suggesting either that he was acting as bondsman while still an apprentice or this was another individual of the same name. Unfortunately the books do not contain details of the size of the bond or the value of the cargo. The wide range of commodities other than coal exported to other English coastal ports is very remarkable, and, whereas the most common exports were those which were produced locally, such as lead, grindstones and glassware, the list includes many items that were not produced in Newcastle or its hinterland. This implies that significant amounts of consumables that had been imported into Newcastle from London or abroad were being re-exported to other coastal towns, and were included in the general cargo that accompanied so many coal and salt shipments.[29]

The coastal inwards port book is very much smaller than the outwards book, confirming the gross excess of outward shipments when compared to those inwards. The number of inward shipments is shown in Table 6.4, and their ports of origin in Table 6.5. The majority of coastal shipments into the Tyne were of foodstuffs, particularly large quantities of grain from the East Anglian ports and a very wide range of domestic consumables from London (Table 6.6). Unfortunately, because

---

East, 1700–1750 (Oxford: Oxford University Press, 1952), p. 251.

[29] Willan, *English Coasting Trade*, pp. 115–16; Ellis, 'The Decline and Fall of the Tyneside Salt Industry', pp. 45–58.

Table 6.2 Number of shipments of commodities other than coal or salt carried coastal outwards, 1702–03

Cinders 108[a]	Linsley Wolseys 5	English Wheat 2	Flannel 1
Lead 115	Juniper Berries 5[b]	Feathers 2	Galletia Wine 1
Glass 71	Woolen Yarn 5	Old Ropes 2	Hollands Damask 1
Skins 58	Tobacco Pipes 4	Pitch 2	Hollands Diper 1
Tallow 45	Clarritt Wine 4	Red & White Port 2	Hollands Linen 1
Grindstones 42	Gloves 4	Sugar 2	Kelseys 1
Butter 36	Brass 3	Alum 1	Kendall Cottons 1
Glass Bottles 36	Deals 3	Apothecary Wares 1	Nails 1
Flagstones 15	Flax 3	Bags of Shot 1	Oats 1
Leather 12	Quills 3	Beans 1	Oyl 1
Beef & Pork 11	Soap 3	Bottled Ale 1	Paper 1
Course Hats 11	Starch 3	Chains 1	Sherry Wine 1
English Spirits 8	Tar 3	Chairs 1	White Callico 1
French Wine 8	Tobacco Stalks 3	Clapboard 1	White Crepe 1
Candles 7	Woolen Stockings 3	Copperas 1[c]	Woollen Cloth 1
Cottons 6	Trim'd & Squared Iron 2	Currants 1	Worsteds 1
Wrought Iron 6	Baskets Violes 2	Cut Tobacco 1	Yellow Canvas 1
English Steel 5	Beeswax 2	English Malt 1	
Linnen 5	English Iron 2	Fish, Cod & Ling	

Note: (a) Cinders: 'A small piece of coal from which the gaseous or volatile constituents have been burnt, but which retains much of the carbon so that it is capable of further combustion without flame' (OED Online). Cinders appeared to be regarded as different from coal, and were used for different purposes, see C.E. Thornton, *Bound for the Tyne: Extracts from the diary of Ralph Jackson, Apprentice Hostman of Newcastle upon Tyne 1749–1756*, 15. Coal was burnt at the pit heads to make cinders in a primitive coking process. There was a ready market for this product at glassworks, in smithies and in maltmaking. (b) Juniper berries used for making gin. (c) Copperas, or green vitriol, is a form of ferrous sulphate.

of serious fading and deterioration in some pages of the port book it is not possible to obtain an accurate quantity of each of the imported goods, as some parts of the cargo lists have become obscured or disappeared completely, making a detailed quantitative analysis similar to the Coastal Inwards book impossible.[30]

---

[30] Willan, *The English Coasting Trade*, p. 116; B. Purdue, 'Ralph Carr', pp. 157–67; T. Barrow, 'Corn, Carriers and Coastal Shipping: The Shipping Trade of Berwick and the Borders 1730–1830', *Journal of Transport History*, 21 (2000), pp. 6–27. The main coastal imports into Newcastle from ports other than London were rye, barley, wheat, peas and beans. The most prominent exception was Hull from which were imported numerous coal

Table 6.3 Newcastle outward coastal destination ports used other than London, 1702–03

Lynn 161	Deal 15	Brighton 4
Yarmouth 107	Blakeney 13	Cowes 4
Sandwich 72	Bridlington 13	Poole 4
Wells[a] 56	Dover 10	Scarborough 4
Portsmouth 54	Grimsby 9	Woodbridge 4
Kingston upon Hull 54	Stockton 9	Weston 4
Southampton 41	Newhaven 7	Arundel 3
Colchester 38	Wisbeach 7	Folkstone 3
Exeter 30	Guernsey 6	Sunderland 3
Rochester 28	Maldon 6	Hartlepool 2
Ipswich 25	Weymouth 6	Plymouth 2
Faversham 21	Harwich 5	Berwick 1
Whitby 18	Southwold 5	Lewes 1
Boston 17	Aldbrough 4	Wainfleet 1

Note: (a) Now known as Wells-next-the-sea in North Norfolk.

Table 6.4 Newcastle inward coastal shipments, 1702–03

January	30
February	13
March	10
April	51
May	14
June	12
July	12
August	15
September	9
October	12
November	12
December	16
Total	206

wagon wheels, English spirits, underfelt, flax, ironmongery and linen, probably sent from the Midlands through the river system to Hull. In addition, there were shipments of tobacco pipe clay from Poole and Southampton, and alum from Stockton.

Table 6.5 Ports of origin of inward coastal shipments to Newcastle, 1702–03

London 58	Blakeney 8	Whitby 3
Wells 45	Lynn 8	Stockton 2
Bridlington 26	Yarmouth 4	Hartlepool 1
Hull 21	Woodbridge 4	Ipswich 1
Colchester 9	Boston 3	Southampton 1
Grimsby 9	Poole 3	

Table 6.6 Imports listed from London into Newcastle, 1702–03*

White Wine	English Spirits	Vinegar	Wooden Hoops
Lime Juice	Oranges	Cheese	Copperas
Wrought Iron	Bay Salt	Saltery Wares	Brown Paper
Hopps	Florence Wine	Saddles	Pipe Staves
Red Lisbon Wine	Woolen Drapery	Cyder	Currants
Spanish Red Wine	Upholstery	Sugar	Raisins
Bone Ashes	Pewter	Verdigrease	Groceries
Cherrys in Spirit	White Lead	Soap	Port Wine
Tobacco Pipe Clay	Canary Wine	Cotton	Whalebone
Sweets	Haberdashery	Chain	Tin Plates
Gingerbread	Pimento	Earthenwares	Aniseeds
Chariot with Furniture	Apparell	Corks	Hankerchiefs
Apothecary Wares	Tobacco	Trees	Seeds
White Lisbon Wine	Mens wares	Flannel	Old Shoes
Whitening	Paper	Hats	Chairs
Lanthorne Lights	Linen Drapery	Spades	Red Lead
Stationery Wares	Dyed linen	Candle Wick	White Port Wine
Confectionary Wares	Ironmongery	Sieves	Frying Pans
Sturgeon	Bellows	Course Hats	Glasses
Crooked Lane Wares	Oylemens Wares	Indigo	Lemons
Dyers Wares	Gardeners Wares	Chocolate	Boxes of Drugs

* Because of the variable legibility of some of the records in the port books, it was difficult to make an accurate quantitative estimate of the number of individual shipments of each commodity; hence, this table is designed to provide a qualitative rather than a quantitative perspective of the inward London trade.

Most of the ships that would subsequently carry cargo outwards came to the Tyne in ballast, and although they are not recorded in the port books, they can be found in the Newcastle Chamberlains' Books of Receipts and Disbursements, where they are entered as having paid their taxes to the city for the deposition of ballast, and also the local city taxes on coal exports. The fact that of the 2,280 coastal shipments that left the Tyne, only 206 (9%) had arrived with coastal inbound cargo suggests that no fewer than 2,074 ships arrived in the Tyne carrying ballast in that year. It is interesting to find that among the very wide range of commodities imported from London, a relatively small proportion were materials intended for local manufacturing industry. In light of the observations made by the various scholars in Helen Berry and Jeremy Gregory's compilation of different perspectives upon the developing consumer culture in the North East of England at the time, it is notable that the vast majority of the imports were foodstuffs or wine and spirits, and a large proportion of the remainder were cloths and fabrics associated with clothing and soft home furnishings.[31]

The Newcastle Overseas Inwards and Outwards Port Book dates from 1698–9; it is rather fragile, and much more difficult to read than the Coastal Port Books because of fading and damage, once again making a detailed quantitative analysis of the contents of individual cargoes impossible. The Outwards Overseas Port Book section is the most legible.[32] Each shipment and its destination is clearly identified, giving a clear picture of the scope of the overseas mercantile connections of Newcastle at the end of the seventeenth century. The number of outwards overseas shipments, when combined with the coastal shipments, give an estimate of the total export trade of the port, which at over 3,000 shipping movements out of the Tyne in a year, implies an average of between nine and ten departures daily (Table 6.7).

A wide range of foreign ports were visited (Table 6.8), but the most common destination was Amsterdam, which was the recipient of almost half of the shipments, with the North Sea coast of Europe and the Baltic being most often frequented as has been reflected in the literature.[33] The commonest export cargo was coal, with a significant amount of salt, and a variety of general goods (Table 6.9). Drammen, near Oslo, was the second most frequently visited port, and is notable because it was a major source of the timber products which were imported into the Tyne, in exchange for which the return voyages from the Tyne carried almost exclusively salt, with a few shipments of glass bottles. In his review

---

[31] Berry and Gregory, *Creating and Consuming Culture*; Ellis, 'The "Black Indies"', pp. 21–6.
[32] TNA E/190/207/4
[33] Salmon and Barrow, *Britain and the Baltic*.

Table 6.7 Shipments in 1702–03 coastal and 1698–99 overseas outward port books

Month	Coastal	Overseas	Total
January	80	40	120
February	34	54	88
March	183	136	319
April	277	105	382
May	206	64	270
June	185	96	281
July	270	99	369
August	430	68	498
September	299	60	359
October	232	22	254
November	56	10	66
December	25	6	31
Total	2,280	760	3,040

of English east coast trade with the Baltic in 1715, Aldridge records a total of 125 voyages to the Baltic from Newcastle and the North East ports, with a lesser number from ports such as Hull Bridlington and Yarmouth.[34] Conversely, in our study of the 1699 Newcastle port book we find no fewer than 274 shipments to Norway and the Baltic ports, the most frequented being Drammen, which receives no mention in Aldridge's study of 1715. Particularly interesting were shipments to the New World, with no fewer than five shipments to Barbados, and also shipments to Boston and Virginia.[35]

The Newcastle Inwards Overseas book is more difficult to assess because, in addition to being very fragile with many areas of illegibility, there is some confusion in the layout, with the occasional shipment being identified by the importing merchant's name without including the name of the importing ship and its master. This makes the number and source of some of the shipments

---

[34] Aldridge, 'English East Coast Trade', p. 123. There are fewer shipments from Newcastle to the Baltic in Aldridge's figures from the 1715 port books, the reasons for this are unclear, but it is possible that the declining salt trade was having an impact on the number of shipments leaving for ports such as Drammen.

[35] The Shipments to Barbados, Boston and Virginia were notable for being large cargoes consisting of a very wide range of consumables, the only ones specific to the Tyne were glass bottles and some grindstones. Ellis, 'The "Black Indies"', pp. 2–12; B. Purdue, 'Ralph Carr', pp. 165–7; Roberts, 'A Newcastle Merchant and the American Colonial Trade', pp. 271–87.

Table 6.8   Newcastle overseas outwards foreign destinations, 1698–99*

Amsterdam 305	Lisbon 3
Drammen 177	Northbergen 3
'The Sound' 64	Stockholm 3
Hamburg 51	Bordeaux 2
Rotterdam 29	Dundee 2
Scotland 22	Island (Ireland) 2
Bremen 12	Newport (America) 2
Danzig 11	Archangel 1
Guernsey 9	Bilboa 1
Narva 9	Boston (America) 1
Emden 7	Bruges 1
Copenhagen 6	Konigsberg 1
Norway 6	Oporto 1
Barbados 5	Ostend 1
Dunkirk 4	Queensboro 1
Gottenburg 3	Virginia (America) 1
Jersey 3	

* 760 outgoing overseas shipments are recorded on the Newcastle upon Tyne 1698-9 Overseas Port Book, however not all of the destination ports were identifiable in the record: 749 had identifiable destinations and 11 destinations were unidentifiable.

Table 6.9   Most common cargoes overseas outwards, 1698–99

Coal
Salt
Glass Bottles
Woolen Goods
Butter
Lead
Rapeseed
Grindstones
Ironmongery
Haberdashery

Table 6.10 Shipments in 1702–03 coastal and 1698–99 overseas inward port books

Month	Coastal	Overseas	Total
January	30	14	44
February	13	17	30
March	10	27	37
April	51	47	98
May	14	52	66
June	12	73	85
July	12	78	90
August	15	68	83
September	9	67	76
October	12	47	59
November	12	47	59
December	16	56	72
Total	206	604	810

difficult to determine. In addition, a significant number of records suggest that duty is being paid on goods being taken out of a Merchant's warehouse where it must have been stored under bond, having arrived as a shipment into the port sometime earlier. Despite these issues, there is a relatively clear picture of the pattern of overseas imports into the Tyne; but the number of identified inward shipments is likely to be an underestimate. The number of these shipments is shown in Table 6.10, along with the coastal inward shipments, giving a picture of the totality of the inward trade, which seems to continue at a steady level throughout the whole year, irrespective of inclement weather in the winter. It is clear that there is a major discrepancy between the inward trade, which is almost exactly one quarter the volume of the outward traffic, suggesting that once again, three quarters of those ships that carried outward cargo must have arrived carrying only ballast.

That a very wide range of overseas inward cargo arrived in the Tyne, from a variety of ports of origin, can be seen in Tables 6.11 and 6.12. Most of the ports from which ships arrived were in the Baltic, once again reflecting the dominance of the Baltic ports in the trade of Newcastle. The most dominant import was timber arriving from ports such as Drammen in exchange for exports mainly of salt and glass bottles.

Table 6.11 Ports of origin of overseas inwards shipments into Newcastle, 1698–99

Rotterdam	Bremen
Hamburg	Konigsberg
Stockholm	Gothenburg
Bordeaux	Narva
Amsterdam	Riga
Scotland	Aalborg
Norway Sound	Northbergen
Emden	Copenhagen
Drammen	

The 1756 port books[36] make an interesting comparison with the 1702–03 port books. Unfortunately, the Overseas port book is in rather poor condition, and, although some individual entries can be read, the legibility is not consistent enough to make a reliable estimate of the shipment numbers. The surviving 1756 Coastal book contains only records for outward shipments and no coastal inwards records. This book is laid out differently from the 1702–3 book, as there are no details of the bondsman and no column to record salt shipments separately; in this book they appear together with other general cargo. The absence of a separate column for salt is partly a reflection of the decline in the salt trade on the Tyne during the first half of the eighteenth century, due to the development of better quality sources.[37] The separate column for coal shipments remains (Table 6.13). Comparing 1702–03 with 1756 (Table 6.14), there appears to have been a very large increase in shipments during the winter months, mostly to London, of all cargoes including coal, with the proportion of coal being carried together with general cargo rising to around 30 per cent. The nature of the general cargo is shown in Table 6.15, and can be seen to have increased dramatically in variety. The range of exported general goods increased, with a larger proportion of manufactured goods both made locally and re-exports of other goods from overseas or brought by overland transport. Part of this increased range was due to the status of Scottish ports as coastal, rather than overseas, since the union – Scotland had been considered an overseas country when the 1698–9 port book was compiled. The widening range of destinations for coastal traffic is shown in Table 6.16.

---

[36] 1756 Coastal Outwards, TNA E/190/256/9; 1756 Overseas Inward and Outward, TNA E/190/257/5.
[37] Ellis, 'The Decline and Fall of the Tyneside Salt Industry', pp. 45–58. Davis, *The Rise of the English Shipping Industry*, p. 350.

Table 6.12 Main commodities imported into the Tyne from overseas, 1698–99

Timber	Food	Cloth
Small Masts	Cheese	German Calico
Oak Board	Herring	Wool
Spars	Brandy	Cambrick
Deals	Strasburg Brandy	Flax
Small Oars	Rye	Candlewick
Balks	Battery Oats	Divers Threads
Staithings	Hopps	Bruges Linen
Roundwood	Middle Malt	Narrow German Linen
Handspokes	Capers	Hankerchieves
Firkin Staves	Almonds	Matts for Rooms
Wainscot Boards	Keggs of Sturgeon	Narrow Hollands
Boat Oars	Rhenish Wine	Dansk Napkins
Boat Knees	Spanish Wine	Thread
Firwood	French Wine	Polonian Linen
Small Balks		Spinning Wool
Carlings		Course Linen
Middle Balks		Hemp

Miscellaneous

Iron	Frying Pans	Kettles
Pantiles	Tar	Pitch
Bags of Shavings	Oyl of Turpentine	Unbound Books
Quicksilver	Cork	Madder
Reams of Coppie Paper	Earthenware Vessels	Fish Oyle
Mull Madder	Chairs	Wooden Bowls
German Iron	Long Steele	Galley Tiles
Iron Staves	Cordage	Twine
Iron Pots	Tow	Gunn Powder
Linseed oil	Nails	Sail Twine
Sheep Skins	Goat Skins	Calf Skins
Shoemakers Thread	Hair	Brimstone
Boxes of Bound Books	Brown Paper	Tree Nails
Platters		

Table 6.13   Coastal outwards port book, 1756

Month	Shipments	London[a]	Coal + cargo[b]	Coal alone[b]	Cargo alone[b]
January	98	55(56%)	37(38%)	57(58%)	4(4%)
February	174	109(63%)	35(20%)	133(76%)	6(3%)
March	126	76(60%)	33(24%)	82(65%)	11(9%)
April	223	126(57%)	56(25%)	154(69%)	13(6%)
May	210	109(54%)	47(23%)	140(70%)	14(7%)
June	296	192(65%)	68(23%)	220(74%)	8(3%)
July	301	176(58%)	73(24%)	213(71%)	11(4%)
August	364	217(60%)	70(19%)	277(76%)	17(5%)
September	302	153(51%)	94(31%)	194(64%)	14(5%)
October	324	181(56%)	84(26%)	230(71%)	10(3%)
November	218	161(74%)	57(26%)	150(69%)	11(5%)
December	202	112(55%)	52(26%)	140(69%)	10(5%)
Totals	2829	1,667(59%)	706(25%)	1,990(70%)	129(5%)

Note: (a) Percentages are proportion of shipments going to London; (b) Percentages are proportion of total shipments of each type of cargo.

Table 6.14   Monthly shipments in coastal outwards port book, 1703 and 1756

Month	1703	1756
January	80 (3.3%)	98 (3.5%)
February	34 (1.3%)	174 (6.2%)
March	183 (8.0%)	126 (4.5%)
April	277 (12.0%)	223 (7.9%)
May	206 (9.0%)	201 (7.1%)
June	185 (8.0%)	296 (10.5%)
July	270 (11.5%)	301 (10.6%)
August	430 (18.5%)	364 (12.8%)
September	299 (13.0%)	302 (10.6%)
October	277 (12.0%)	324 (11.5%)
November	56 (2.4%)	218 (7.7%)
December	25 (1.0%)	202 (7.1%)
Totals	2,280	2,829

Table 6.15   Non-coal commodities coastal outwards, 1756

Iron mongers ware	Paint	Iron pots	Bottled ale	Bellows
Glass bottles	Yarn	Starch	Beeswax	Paper
Manchester wares	Iron nails	Wrought iron	Apples	Alum
Calf skins & hair	Iron	English spirit	Pickled cod	Tar
Casks of ale	Spades	Hearth stones	Porter	White leather
English rape seed	Raisins	Copper	Sheet glass	Dyersware
Green oyl	Salamoniac	Oats	Tallow	Whalebone
Combed wool	Rum	Barley	Brandy	Grass seeds
Powder brimstone	Linen	Candles	Felt hats	Mustard
Spanish wines	Salt	Aqua fortis	Earthenware pots	Corks
Flagstones	Lead	Coffee	Flour	Books
British liquid blue	Cinders	Wheat flour	Charcoal	Whips
English woolens	Grindstones	Deals	Cast iron	Leeds wares
Tanned Leather	Anker chain	Iron hoops	Leather	Chaise & Carriage
Powdered sugar	Butter	Flax	Tobacco stalks	Worsted stuff
English Cordage	Peas	Shovels	Cheese	

Table 6.16   Coastal destinations other than London, 1756

Lynn	Hull	Wells
Stockton	Aberdeen	Boston
Exeter	Blyth	Dover
Leith	Blakeney	Maldon
Berwick	Portsmouth	Ipswich
Whitby	Cowes	Chichester
Newhaven	Southwold	Sunderland
Wisbeach	Montrose	Inverness
Shoreham	Poole	Yarmouth
Perth	Woodbridge	Faversham
Walsham	Harwich	Weymouth
Bridlington	Sandwich	Rochester
Scarboro	Arundel	Kirkwall
Thurso	Plymouth	Dartmouth
Dundee	Dunbar	Alnmouth

There are many areas of illegibility in these records, obscuring the full details of a number of the cargoes, and although it is possible to indicate the wide range of commodities exported to other coastal ports, it is not possible to give a reliable estimate of the exact volumes of each commodity. The most prominent reduction was in the amount of salt exported, which is substantially less than that reported in 1702, due to the increased availability of other sources; the largest volumes of exports continued to be cinders, lead, grindstones and glassware, particularly glass bottles. The increase in shipments out of the Tyne includes shipments to local ports such as Blyth, Sunderland and Scottish ports. These were in ships described as Open Boats, which were likely to have been a boat not dissimilar to a sailing keel, which often took heavier goods like iron and lead that would have been difficult to transport overland.[38]

It is clear that the seventeenth and eighteenth centuries were a period of rapid economic growth in Newcastle upon Tyne, largely as a result of the demand for coal by the growing metropolis of London and the rest of the country. In parallel with the export of coal and other goods there was a flourishing import trade of both foodstuffs and construction materials such as timber from the continent and elsewhere in England. The import of these more utilitarian goods was inevitably accompanied by more luxurious goods, including clothing materials, more exotic foods and wine. Newcastle eventually was supplied directly with a wide variety of consumer goods from the Baltic, the Low Countries and Southern Europe. The consequence of this growth in the local economy was the development of a flourishing community of merchants and tradesmen, who had increasingly high expectations about their prospects for a better quality of life. The evidence from the port books shows very clearly how the demand for household and personal consumables by those of this 'middling sort', to make life at home more comfortable and also embellish their personal appearance, was being fulfilled by the volume and variety of the imports into Newcastle, hopefully improving not just their quality of life, but influencing outside perceptions of their relative status in the community.[39] In addition it was apparent that a large amount of the general cargo exported to coastal ports from Newcastle had not originated there but had been imported from elsewhere, often continental Europe or London. This suggests that the merchants of Newcastle had developed sophisticated

---

[38] Many of these local ports were less than a day's sail to relatively local ports, and would thus require less accommodation for the crew, similar to the local shipping seen on the rivers Thames and Severn; see D. Blomfield, 'Tradesmen of the Thames: Success and Failure Among the Watermen and Lightermen Families of the Upper Tidal Thames 1750–1901' (PhD diss., Kingston University, 2006); Hussey, *Coastal and River Trade*, pp. 21–55; Trinder, *Barges and Bargemen*.

[39] Scammell, 'Was the North East Different from Other Areas?', pp. 12–23; H. Berry, 'Creating Polite Space: The Organisation and Social Function of Newcastle Assembly Rooms', in *Creating and Consuming Culture*, pp. 120–40.

import/export businesses, giving the port many of the characteristics of an entrepôt in its dealings with coastal and overseas trade.

The wide variety of ships that came into Newcastle through the Tyne, seen in the records of the transactions shown in the relevant Newcastle port books, provide an illuminating insight into the nature and volume of coastal and overseas trade into and out of Newcastle during the first half of the eighteenth century. David Hussey has undertaken a similar analysis of the Port Books of Bristol and the ports around the Bristol Channel,[40] and, in many respects, Bristol makes an interesting comparison with Newcastle. Both were sea ports of long standing but with very different backgrounds, Bristol's success being based on a strategic position with good access to the sea with a variety of distant overseas and local coastal trading links, combined with easy access both by river and road to a large area of southern England. Based on this position, a flourishing manufacturing and trading community had developed, enabling Bristol to become one of the largest commercial and trading centres in the country.[41] Newcastle had a similarly long history but, in contrast to Bristol, was based on the exploitation of local natural resources. The large volume and relatively low cost of coal, together with the relative isolation of Newcastle in the North of England, stimulated the development of its thriving port. There is a frequently voiced view that at the end of the seventeenth century Bristol was the most active port after London, with a particularly strong overseas component to its trade.[42] Comparing the numbers of shipments from Newcastle with those described by Hussey for Bristol at about the same time, it is notable that Newcastle had over four times the number of coastal outward shipments and three times the number of overseas outward shipments, although the profile of the respective trading patterns of the towns were significantly different (Table 6.17). Whereas a very large proportion of international trade to and from the Tyne was directed to Northern Europe, and particularly to the Low Countries and the Baltic, there was also an extensive trade with France, Spain and particularly Portugal. Additionally there appeared to have been a number of shipments to North America and the Caribbean with cargoes of general goods rather than coal. However, some of the North American trade from Newcastle was rather different from that of Bristol, in that Newcastle was being used as a convenient and relatively cheap transit and customs clearing point for ships originating in Amsterdam, picking up some relatively low-cost, heavy-ballast cargo on the way. An additional feature accounting for some of

---

[40] D. Hussey, *Coastal and River Trade*.
[41] W.E. Minchinton, 'Bristol – Metropolis of the West in the Eighteenth Century', *Transactions of the Royal Historical Society*, 5th ser., 4 (1954), pp. 69–89.
[42] Willan, *The English Coasting Trade*, p. 171.

the differences in the number of shipments between Bristol and Newcastle is that the Bristol shipments tended to be of relatively high-value-per-unit volume, such as tea and sugar, when compared with the coal, glass and grindstone trade from Newcastle, which was relatively high volume but low value.[43] One might speculate that the consequence of this difference would have been that the local economic impact of the higher value Bristol trade was much more substantial than that of the Newcastle coal trade, even though the latter port appears to have recorded a significantly greater number of individual shipments than the former.

Table 6.17   Comparative levels of shipments to and from Newcastle upon Tyne and Bristol

Newcastle				Bristol			
Coastal (1703)		Overseas (1699)		Coastal (1699)		Overseas	
In	Out	In	Out	In	Out	In(1700)	Out(1688)
206	2280	604	760	920	491	225	240

Source of Bristol figures: Coastal and Overseas trade of Bristol are from D. Hussey, *Coastal and River Trade*, p. 40. The Coastal Outward and Inward data for 1699 are from Hussey himself. The Overseas Outward data for 1688, and the Overseas Inward data for 1700 are from P. McGrath, *Merchants and Merchandise in Seventeenth- Century Bristol* (Bristol: Bristol Record Society, 1955).

Other coastal ports had a major impact upon overseas and coastal trade in England during the seventeenth and eighteenth centuries. Hull, on the east coast, had substantial exports and imports of a more general type of cargo, but of course without the coal. Ralph Davies described the seaborne trade out of Hull and its dependence on communications through the river and canal systems with Yorkshire and the Midlands, including inland ports such as Bawtry. This enhanced its importance as a major port serving the industries of central and northern England enabling it to forge links with the Baltic and the Low Countries, which were very similar to those of Newcastle.[44] On the west coast, Liverpool developed rapidly from a very minor port in the mid seventeenth century to a substantial port that had largely replaced Bristol as the second most important port in England by the end of the eighteenth century. The

---

[43] Ellis, 'The "Black Indies"', p. 2.
[44] R. Davis, *The Trade and Shipping of Hull 1500–1700* (Beverley: East Yorkshire Local History Society, 1964).

transformation was based mainly on the substantial exports of salt and cheese from the surrounding counties, and the rapidly growing transatlantic trade.[45] The most important feature of the coastal and overseas trading out of Tyne was that a significant proportion of ships carried substantial quantities of general cargo in addition to coal to many of its destination ports including London. The large volume of sea trade moving both into and out of Newcastle described in this chapter highlights the very large number of ships using the Tyne, and this in itself may have been one of the reasons underlying why so many ships loaded and unloaded close to the mouth of the river, finding it necessary to use the keel or other boats as a form of intermediary transport. Although Newcastle had a large quay that was frequented by many ships, the town was eight miles up the river from Tynemouth; and although quite big ships could navigate their way up to Newcastle and back to the harbour entrance, this might take some time even with favourable tides and winds. Many ships' masters preferred to stay near the mouth of the river to load their cargo, as this would save time and potential risk of running aground and stranding, particularly if the river became congested with numerous other ships moving both up and down the river. The impact of a cargo ship running aground in the river and being either wrecked or stranded for a considerable period of time could be very serious both in terms of the survival of the ship and its crew. The economic consequences of such events with both the potential losses of cargo and trading time to the owners, would create significant impediments to the flourishing trade of the town.

---

[45] M. Stammers, 'Ships and Port Management at Liverpool before the Opening of the First Dock in 1715', *Transactions of the Historical Society of Lancashire and Cheshire*, 156 (2007), pp. 27–50.

Chapter 7
Ralph Jackson on Tyneside, 1749–1756: A Contemporary Perspective

In an attempt to describe the changes taking place in an urban industrial complex over 200 years ago there can be few better sources than a first-hand account from a participant. This is particularly true of the water-related trades on the River Tyne during the eighteenth century, where the thriving economy was being driven by the demand for coal, particularly from London. A diary written by a young apprentice hostman, Ralph Jackson, between 1749 and 1756 describes in intimate detail his life working in the coal trade along the Tyne. This important contemporary source provides an opportunity to draw together many of the aspects of the water trades on the river Tyne, particularly because Jackson describes in some detail the interrelationships between those working at all levels in the coal trade, allowing them to be seen in the context of the river trade community as a whole. Personal journals and diaries have always been a productive source for historians, as such sources relate the numerous and varying accounts of events to the personal experiences of contemporary observers. Nowhere has this been truer than for students of the seventeenth and eighteenth centuries, where the contribution of diarists to our knowledge has been studied extensively.[1] In the essay at the beginning of his analysis of the Family Life of Ralph Josselin, in which he examines more closely the background to the edition of the Josselin Diaries he published earlier, Alan Macfarlane identifies three main reasons underlying the motives for keeping diaries in the seventeenth and eighteenth centuries. First, many diaries were used as little more than account

---

[1] A. Macfarlane, *The Family Life of Ralph Josselin, A Seventeenth Century Clergyman: an Essay in Historical Anthropology* (Cambridge: Cambridge University Press, 1970), pp. 3–14; M. Masuch, *Origins of the Individualist Self: Autobiography and Self-Identity in England, 1591–1791* (Cambridge: Polity Press, 1997); D. Vaisey, ed. *The Diary of Thomas Turner, 1754–1765* (Oxford: Oxford University Press, 1985); A. Vickery, *The Gentleman's Daughter: Women's Lives in Georgian England* (New Haven: Yale University Press, 1998); H. Berry, 'Sense and Singularity: The Social Experiences of John Marsh and Thomas Stutterd in Late-Georgian England', in *Identity and Agency in England, 1500–1800*, ed. J. Barry and H. French (Basingstoke: Palgrave Macmillan, 2004), pp. 178–99.

books detailing the financial transactions of the diarist. The second apparent reason for writing a diary was that they were an aid to the memory of the diarists, recording what they considered important dates or moments in their lives. The third, and very common motivation was religious, providing an account of the religious life and experiences of the diarist;[2] many of these latter diaries were particularly intense, and appear somewhat self-obsessed.[3]

Ralph Jackson was a North Yorkshire Landowner and Businessman, who lived from 1736 to 1790, about whom a considerable amount is known because he kept his diary for over 40 years, from the age of 13 until his death.[4] The Diary begins in 1749 when he was enrolled as an apprentice to William Jefferson, a Newcastle hostman. Apart from a break of two and a half years from 1753–1756 the diary was kept consistently for over 40 years and amounted to 19 volumes, with only one volume, for 1767–68, missing. Even from the first diary the handwriting is remarkably clear, making them very easy to read.[5] It is also notable that these diaries do not appear to have been studied widely, the only published reference to them being a private publication by the Company of Hostmen of Newcastle upon Tyne to celebrate their four hundredth anniversary.[6] A detailed search of the bibliographies of diarists showed no evidence of the existence of these diaries,[7] although in 1950 William Matthews did note the existence of a

---

[2] Macfarlane, *Family Life of Ralph Josselin*, pp. 3–11; A. Macfarlane, ed., *The Diary of Ralph Josselin* (Oxford: Oxford University Press, 1976).

[3] M. Todd, 'Puritan Self-fashioning: The Diary of Samuel Ward', *Journal of British Studies*, 31 (1992), pp. 236–64.

[4] *The Diaries of Ralph Jackson*, Teeside Archives, U/WJ/1–6.

[5] The Diaries of Ralph Jackson were part of a gift of family documents gifted to Middlesbrough Reference Library by Mr P.W. Ward-Jackson on behalf of the family on 27 March 1961. The collection included diaries from a number of other members of the family between 1749 and 1880. The diaries are all now held in Teeside Archives in the class: *Diaries of Ralph Jackson*, U/WJ/1–6. A full transcription of the diaries together with a family tree and glossary of names has been made available by The Great Ayton History Society on: http://www.greatayton.wikidot.com/ralph-jackson-diaries.

[6] C.E. Thornton, *Bound for the Tyne: Extracts from the Diary of Ralph Jackson, Apprentice Hostman of Newcastle upon Tyne, 1749–56* (Newcastle upon Tyne: Company of Hostmen of Newcastle upon Tyne, 2000); P.D. Wright, 'Water Trades on the Lower River Tyne in the Seventeenth and Eighteenth Centuries' (PhD diss., Newcastle University, 2011), pp. 168–96; The author is indebted to Sir Leonard Fenwick CBE, current Chairman of the Incorporated Companies of the City of Newcastle upon Tyne, who kindly provided a copy of the private publication by Clifford E. Thornton.

[7] Arthur Ponsonby, *English Diaries*, (London, Methuen & Co Ltd 1923); Arthur Ponsonby, *More English Diaries,* (London, Methuen & Co. Ltd.); William Matthews, *British Diaries 1442–1942,* (London, Cambridge University Press 1950).

diary by a Ralph Ward of Guisborough in Yorkshire, kept as a manuscript in the library of Durham University, which was a farming diary kept only from 1754 to 1756. There must be a distinct possibility that this was the same Ralph Ward of Guisborough who was the uncle of Ralph Jackson, and with whom he later worked and whose estates he inherited.[8] Oddly, there is no reference to the Ralph Jackson diary in recent work on eighteenth-century Newcastle.[9] This neglect is unfortunate, since the diary is one of the most detailed that have survived, certainly for the North East, and arguably for the whole country in the eighteenth century. It is difficult to categorize the Ralph Jackson diaries along the lines suggested by Alan Macfarlane, because only a small proportion of the total collection, volumes A to F, which cover the time of his apprenticeship in Newcastle, have been examined in the context of trade on the River Tyne. In addition, a number of features about these sections of the diaries distinguish them from other diaries. Most notably, when he began his diary, during the period we are studying, he was only 13 years old; his main motivation was strong advice from his father when he left his home in Richmond for Newcastle. One of the effects of his youth, was that, although the entries were made daily, they were initially very brief and direct, often just itemizing the activities of the day in the simplest manner. In spite of this, the entries describing his work and that of his master were usually quite clear. Diaries have often provided copious material about the range of friends and social or business contacts made by the author, which have often enabled academics to undertake an analysis of their networks of business and social contacts.[10] Unfortunately, it is difficult, if not impossible, to construct a meaningful network of Ralph's social contacts, mainly because he provided only the forenames of most of the individuals concerned. As a number of his friends shared the same forename, it becomes difficult at times to be certain to which of his friends he is referring. It has been possible, however, to analyse in some detail parts of the network of business contacts of his master William Jefferson, and in particular the ships' captains with whom he was working in the coal trade.

---

[8] W. Matthews, *British Diaries 1442–1942* (London: Cambridge University Press, 1950), 86, refers to the diaries of Ralph Ward of Guisborough kept in Durham University Library, 'Diaries of Ralph Ward' 942.74 WZ.

[9] J. Ellis, 'A Dynamic Society: Social Relations in Newcastle-Upon-Tyne 1660–1760', in *The Transformation of English Provincial Towns 1600–1800*, ed. P. Clark (London: Hutchinson & Co., 1984), pp. 191–227; Ellis, 'The "Black Indies": The Economic Development of Newcastle, c1700–1840', in *Newcastle Upon Tyne: a Modern History*, ed. R. Lancaster and B. Colls (Chichester: Phillimore, 2001), pp. 1–26.

[10] See, for example, Vickery, *The Gentleman's Daughter*, Appendices 4 and 5; Berry, 'Sense and Singularity', pp. 178–99.

Ralph was one of nine children born to a middling and modestly wealthy family in Richmond, Yorkshire. Much of their wealth came from Ralph's mother, Hannah, whose brother was Ralph Ward of Guisborough, a wealthy merchant who has been described as the richest commoner in North Yorkshire.[11] Jackson kept the diary through the initial years of his apprenticeship, but discontinued it in August 1753, not starting again until March 1756. This was the last year of his apprenticeship, which ended on the 4 December 1756. The importance of these diaries is that they are one of the few primary sources that give a direct insight into the working and business relationships of those involved in trade on the Tyne during the eighteenth century; the diary therefore helps to contextualize and amplify the information in the previous chapters of this book. The diaries are particularly revealing because, throughout his apprenticeship, Ralph was resident in his master's house, which appeared to be the centre of the hostman's business. He would frequently mention going into 'the office', although it was never made clear whether this office was in his master's house or close by, but the house was clearly a place where William Jefferson met and entertained his clients.[12] During the early years of the diaries they are less fluent, however, with the passage of time they become more expansive telling us about both Ralph's personal life and also about the business activities of his master, the hostman. As the diaries re-started, in March 1756, Ralph was approaching 20 years old; he was more mature and a 'young man about town'. These later diaries provide much more information about the business processes and the relationships between the various participants in their network, and, as Ralph had almost completed his training, they show him to be carrying out most of the tasks of a hostman. On completion of his seven years of apprenticeship Ralph did not stay in Newcastle and become a hostman, but returned to North Yorkshire to work with his uncle Ralph Ward, whose lands and business he would inherit in 1759.[13]

In 1776 Ralph married Mary Lewin, the daughter of a successful captain in the East India Company. They had four children, three of whom subsequently died, and Mary died in 1781.[14] The surviving son, William Ward Jackson (1778–1842), laid the foundations of the Ward Jackson family which prospered from the industrial development of South Durham and Teeside in the nineteenth century; Ralph Ward Jackson (1806–1880) was the family's most prominent

---

[11] Thornton, *Bound for the Tyne*, p. 3.
[12] F.W. Dendy, *Extracts from the Records of the Company of Hostmen of Newcastle Upon Tyne*, Surtees Society, 105 (Durham, Published for the Society, 1901), p. 193. It was one of the conditions of the apprenticeship that the apprentice was resident with his master.
[13] Thornton, *Bound for the Tyne*, p. 3.
[14] Thornton, *Bound for the Tyne*, p. 3

member.¹⁵ Ralph, the diarist, spent the rest of his life as a businessman and country squire in North Yorkshire, dying in 1790. Ralph was not the most prominent member of his immediate family. His brother George Jackson (1725–1822) gained a knighthood and became Secretary to the Navy before becoming an MP.¹⁶

The diaries describe what the typical career of an apprentice hostman in the mid eighteenth century would have been like. The first series of diaries between 1749 and 1753 begin on the 16 October 1749 as follows:

> My father told me when I began to keep this Journal –
> Let not that Day pass by
> whose low descending Sun,
> Views from thy hand
> No noble action done.¹⁷

The following day he went with his father to visit friends and relatives near to his home, and then, on the 18 October, he went 'to N. Castle & called at Chester of Street, We Din'd at N.Castle & after that We Went To Mr. Jefferson's & Lay'd their'.¹⁸ Having stayed with William Jefferson and his family at their home in Newcastle, while Ralph settled in, his father left to return home to Richmond. Ralph records being bound during these first few days: 'Friday got bound at Peacock, My Father, & My Master, Cousin Jefferson, John Campion, Mr. Simson and Mr. French, being present'.¹⁹ At this meeting, the terms of his apprenticeship were agreed between his father and William Jefferson, in attendance was John Campion who had been Jefferson's apprentice since 1743, who would be required to complete his apprenticeship before Ralph could

---

¹⁵ Thornton, *Bound for the Tyne*, p. 3; P. Waller, 'Jackson, Ralph Ward (1806–1880)', rev. *Oxford Dictionary of National Biography* (Oxford, Oxford University Press, 2004), http://www.oxforddnb.com, accessed 23 March 2014.

¹⁶ Thornton, *Bound for the Tyne*, p. 3; Sir George Jackson (also called Sir George Duckett) was a zealous patron of Captain James Cook whose father had been a dependant of the family and worked as a stable-boy for the Jacksons at Ayton, Yorkshire. In gratitude, Cook named Point Jackson in New Zealand and Port Jackson in New South Wales, Australia (Sydney Harbour), after George Jackson. Michael Duffy, 'Duckett, Sir George, first baronet (1725–1822), *Oxford Dictionary of National Biography* (Oxford: Oxford University Press, 2004), http://www.oxforddnb.com, accessed 23 March 2014.

¹⁷ *Diaries of Ralph Jackson*, Book A: 16 Oct. 1749. Opening page, Teeside Archives, U/WJ/1-6.

¹⁸ *Diaries*, Book A: 18 Oct. 1749.

¹⁹ *Diaries*, Book A: 16 Nov. 1749.

start his.[20] A few days later, on the 24 November, his Indentures took place at Mr French's office, following which 'We Went and Supt at Mrs Hudspeths, it being the first hair [i.e. Hare] that was killed by My Masters bitch, and Played Cards'.[21] Now that Ralph was resident with his master, he became part of the family social circle, and in particular spent much of his free time with Jefferson's nephew Billy Hudspeth and his mother Mrs Hudspeth, who was Jefferson's sister. During the early years of his apprenticeship close attention was paid to Ralph's education, with a number of paid private tutors being employed to improve his skills, particularly in mathematics; these classes were built around the days' tides on the river, which were the limiting feature of the coal trade at that time.[22] His life was not all work and study; there are numerous references to walking in the fields, netting wild birds and attending local horse races with his master and friends.[23]

As would have been normal in an apprenticeship, Ralph became involved in the day-to-day work of a hostman at a very early stage. The diary shows that within a few days of arriving, late in 1749, he was involved with the keels and the keelmen, 'Old George and Me, Went to take an account of the Keel Gear, how they Were in Goodness',[24] Even though it was late in the year and trade was supposed to slowing down for the winter, masters of ships still came to his master's house to do business; in mid December, 'a Master of a Ship Came to our house and I went to seek for My Master, and the Gentleman & My Master Went and sat the evening together'.[25] It became the custom for Ralph to return home over the Christmas and New Year period, so there was no record in the diaries of any business transactions undertaken by William Jefferson during Ralph's absence. It has always been thought that the coal trade stopped over

---

[20] C.E. Thornton, *Bound for the Tyne*, p. 5; Dendy, *Company of Hostmen*, pp. xvlii, 87,103. The Company determined the rules for its apprentices and recorded them in its records, including a published list of enrolled apprentices and officers; see Burn, *The Justice of the Peace and the Parish Officer*, 4 vols (London: Printed by W. Strachan and M. Woodfall for T. Cadell, 1772), pp. 54–92.

[21] *Diaries*, Book A: 24 Nov. 1749.

[22] *Diaries*, Book A: 30 March 1750, 'My Master Turnbull not being well I went down to the shore in both forenoon and afternoon'; *Diaries*, Book A: 18 June 1750, 'In the forenoon walked about the Key, in the afternoon went to school and baithed, came home and my master and billy came in from the Throckley Fell races'; *Diaries*, Book A: 25 Sept. 1750, 'In the afternoon I spoke to Mr Taylor (about) how he could take me at nights, and he told me half a guinea a quarter and a crown entrance'.

[23] *Diaries*, Book A: 12 April 1750, 'In the morning took a walk with Billy to the Forth'. (The Forth was an area of open fields to the West of the City walls); *Diaries*, Book A: 20 Aug. 1750, 'My master and Billy got up early in the morning and went anetting'.

[24] *Diaries*, Book A: 12 Dec. 1749.

[25] *Diaries*, Book A: 15 Dec. 1749.

the winter due to the bad weather for seagoing ships, and the effect of frost in breaking up the coal.[26] However, we see from the diary's evidence that the keelmen were being paid, and by implication still working as late as December and as early as February. In addition, the port books showed conclusively that a significant proportion of the coal export trade did indeed continue throughout the winter, although the Chamberlains' Accounts suggest that not all hostmen were participating.[27] A typical entry in late January emphasizes not only Ralph's participation in working with the keels, but also how his other education was not being neglected:

> In the Morning went to Charlton's landing place, to look at the Workmen mending our Keel, came home to dinner, then went to Mr Ackenheads at the bridge for a cash book but he had none, then I went to Mr. Turnbull's and paid him for My Quarters learning, then retired into My room and got a lesson in My Lattin testament, went down and drank Tea, in the evening sat till My Master smoaked a pipe then retired to bed at Ten.[28]

The diaries illustrate many of the details of the day-to-day work of one of the crucial contributors to the success of the Newcastle coal trade, the hostman. The general principles of the hostman's work have been understood for many years, however the detail given in the diaries amplifies many of these aspects with the immediacy of a first-hand account. The diaries recount that when a ship wishing to load coal arrived at the mouth of the Tyne it moored, usually quite close to the river mouth at North or South Shields.[29] The master of the ship then travelled about seven miles into Newcastle, usually on horseback, where he met one of the hostmen, often dining at his house, and negotiated directly the provision of a cargo of coal for his ship. Many of the ships' masters arrived with a clear idea of how much coal they required and from which colliery. Each hostman usually dealt with a group of collieries, for example Ralph's master, Jefferson, dealt mainly in coal from the Longbenton colliery, which went down to the Tyne at Winkhamlee Staith, together with some coal from Tanfield and

---

[26] E. Hughes, *North Country Life in the Eighteenth Century: the North East, 1700–1750* (Oxford: Oxford University Press, 1952), p. 251; A.W.R. Moller, 'The History of British Coal Mining 1500–1750' (PhD diss., Oxford, University, 1933), p. 552.
[27] Newcastle Chamberlains' Accounts, TWAS MD.NC/FN/1/1/108. See Chapter 6 on the port books.
[28] *Diaries*, Book A: 29 Jan. 1750.
[29] For a full analysis, see Chapter 2, 'The River Tyne, its Navigability and the Problem of Ballast'.

other pits in the Whickham area. Winkhamlee Staith was very important to the business of William Jefferson, as the centre from which much of his coal was distributed, and references to it occur very frequently throughout the diaries. Winckhamlee was situated adjacent to the river in the manor of Low Walker, about one mile downstream from Newcastle. It was clearly a place of some local significance, as there exists in the Bell Collection a copy of the 'Rules for Managing the Gunpowder Magazine at Wincombe-Lee Quay', dated 1771.[30]

When arriving to collect a cargo of coal, the ship's master would deal only with the hostman who could provide the coal they wanted at the right price. If this could not be achieved, he would move on to another hostman, suggesting that a larger volume of trade generated a greater volume of activity. This negotiation could take place only between the ship's master and the hostman himself, and could not be delegated to an apprentice. The process was known as 'fitting' or 'fixing' a ship, hence the alternative description of a hostman as a 'fitter'. Once the order for coal was placed, the hostman's apprentice was sent to organize the necessary number of keels, and to send them to the appropriate staith to load and take the coal down the river to the ship, which was usually moored at North or South Shields. After the loading of the ship was complete, the hostman himself, or occasionally the apprentice, would accompany the master to the Customs House and the Town House to pay the customs duties and the Town taxes following which the master and his ship would be 'cleared' to leave Port. During the processes of negotiation, and of loading and clearing the cargo, the ships' masters often dined at the hostman's house, and frequently stayed there.[31]

An essential feature of the carriage of coal down the river by keel, was that keels carried a specific weight of eight chaldrons, or about 21 tons of coal. This had been defined many years before as a full keel load of coal, and was used as a basis for taxation by the Crown. In an effort to prevent evasion of the taxes by overloading the keels, they were measured at regular intervals to ensure the accuracy of their loading, and a mark was placed on the waterline. In March 1751 Ralph writes 'I got up between five & six o'Clock and lett Jos. out to go and see Ditchburn's Keel Measured wth weights'.[32] When referring to their keels they tended to refer to them using the name of the skipper as an identifier. On this occasion, the keel was measured using weights; these were usually lead weights up to the weight of eight chaldrons at which point the level of the waterline

---

[30] Bell Collection, Vol. 1, NCL/LS, L942.8 T987B.
[31] *Diaries*, Book B: 10 June 1751.
[32] *Diaries*, Book B: 28 March 1751.

of the loaded keel was marked with nails so that the accuracy of subsequent loadings could be confirmed. Many of the taxes paid on coal were for internal trade, from Newcastle to other English ports such as London. About 20 per cent of the coal exported from Newcastle was taken to foreign European ports; internal taxes were not payable for these, and a 'Sufferance' had to be obtained from the Custom House. The process of obtaining these permits and arranging to load a ship was often marked by a series of social exchanges; for example, on 30 May 1751, 'I got up between four and five and went down to Winkhamlee, and I took out a sufferance for Mr. John Jefferson's Ship, the Richard and Ann of Whitby for 200 Chalders of Coals'.[33] Then, on 8 June, 'Mr. John Jefferson dined at our house',[34] and, finally, on 10 June, 'In the forenoon my Master and Billy went down to Shields to dine on Board the Richard & Ann of Whitby, Mr John Jefferson master'.[35]

One of the duties of the apprentice was to keep an account of the hostman's share of the 'Vend', which was the agreed amount of coal that could be sold each week or month. There were close relationships between Jefferson and the other hostmen, and it was quite common for one hostman to borrow coal from another hostman's stocks when he had a higher than usual demand from ships' masters to 'fix' their ships. At the end of each accounting period, the hostman would either pay for the borrowed coal or replace it from his replenished coal stocks. For example, in May 1751 Ralph notes that 'his master sent him to borrow Mrs Hudspeth's and Mr Henry Atkinson's Long Benton coals'.[36] This entry is particularly interesting, as it includes a reference to Jefferson working with one of the few women hostmen, Ann Hudspeth, whose name was included among the hostmen signing a document, dated 1750, listing all of the keelmen they employed.[37] This aspect of the trade became a major part of the bookkeeping needed to keep track of a hostman's accounts, and it became one of Ralph's most important functions in the business. This is revealed in entries in March 1753: 'Thursday ... I went to Mr Ackenhead's & got a Book to copy the Borrowed & Lent Coals into', and the following day, 'went into the Office where I drew out

[33] *Diaries*, Book B: 30 May 1751.
[34] *Diaries*, Book B: 8 June 1751.
[35] *Diaries*, Book B: 10 June 1751.
[36] *Diaries*, Book B: 8 May 1751.
[37] In the Newcastle Chamberlains' Accounts for 1756 (Tyne Wear Archive Service MD.NC/FN/1/1/108) there are frequent references to Mrs Hudspeth completing the clearance of coal-bearing ships. This is almost certainly the same Ann Hudspeth listed as a hostman attached to the list of hostmen (Plate 3.2.), in the Bell Collection, Vol. 1, LS/NCL, L942.8 T987B.

the Fitters Accounts for the last year Borrowed & Lent Coals'.[38] A further entry provides evidence of a ship's master sharing a shipload between two different hostmen, and once again there is clear evidence that at least one of the hostmen was female.[39] Notwithstanding the fact that his master was sometimes critical of his work – 'My Master was angry at me for not finishing the ship Richard & Ann of Whitby'[40] – by May 1752 Ralph was clearly making progress, and his master gave him possession of 'one side of a desk space in the Office and a key'.[41] Before the end of the year he was proudly recounting details of his first personal clearing of a ship.[42]

A key part of the function of the hostman's apprentice was to go to the can-house on a Saturday and pay the keelmen. This payment was based on the number of trips they had made with the tide down to Shields and back to load collier ships with coal. The can-house was what amounted to an alehouse, which was managed by a woman known as the 'can-wife' or 'can-woman'. The can-woman was clearly a person of some importance in the hostman's team, as was shown in 1756 by the response to the death of Jefferson's 72-year-old can-woman, Margaret Bone. Jefferson and a number of other significant people in the town acted as pallbearers at her funeral.[43] The main function of the can-

---

[38] *Diaries*, Book E: 8 March 1753; *Diaries*, Book E: 9 March 1753; Mr Akenhead was a bookseller and publisher who had a shop on the Tyne Bridge and was the source of most of the stationery materials used in the business.

[39] *Diaries*, Book D: 26 Sept. 1752: 'In the morning Jacky Campion came up but did not give the ship on to any Fitter, I waited upon the Key all the forenoon & after dinner when Campion went down I spoke to him about the Loading of L. Benton Coals & he told me that Mrs Atkinson would Load half the Ship if my Master would the other'.

[40] *Diaries*, Book C: 14 Sept. 1751.

[41] *Diaries*, Book D: 11 May 1752.

[42] *Diaries*, Book D: 28 Sept. 1752, 'I got up early in the morning and went down to Winkhamlee, called on board Mr McMillans Ship but he was not on board, ... then Mr McMillan came up to clear and I got Ralph Morton to go along with me for I had never Cleared a Ship before, then I went with him myself to the Town's house and we cleared the Ship there then we came home and I settled with, he gave me £20.2s.0d. in Cash & his promisary Note on demand for 11. 5s. 0d which amounted to £31.7s.0d'.

[43] *Diaries*, Book E: 1 April 1756, 'Margaret Bone my Masters Can-woman died this morning at 4 o'Clock, I went with my Masters service to her Daughter Hannah, to offer anything we had, which might be of service. ... at the request of Mrs Hannah Gothard I was a bidder with William Henderson Carpenter, to her Mothers funeral; my Master being comed in in the evening'; *Ibid.*: 2 April 1756, 'After drinking Tea with my master about five o'Clock I got ready and went to Margaret Bones Funeral, my Master, Mr Aubrey Surtees, Mr William Errington, and Mr Rutter Attorney, being Paul Bearers, and about 14 Mourners followed the Corps, the whole being duly regulated, she was inter'd in the East end of All Saints Churchyard. 72 years old'.

house was to serve as a gathering point for the keelmen, who would wait there to receive their orders and subsequent payment. The payment was in cash per tide, a tide being the time taken for a single round trip for a keel, going down the river on the ebb loaded with coal and returning on the flood tide, having unloaded the coal into a waiting collier brig. The time of day when the trip took place would vary with the times of the high tides on any particular day. Problems were clearly being encountered with coinage that had been tampered with, known as 'Bad Brass', when paying the keelmen: 'in the afternoon I went to the Canhouse with John to pay the Keelmen we had a great deal of Trouble about the bad brass'.[44] For many years part of the wages paid to the keelmen had been in the form of ale, which they drank in the can-house; indeed, in addition to coal Jefferson appeared to keep quite large stocks of malt, much of which was sold on his behalf by his apprentice. It is likely that this malt was used in his own brew-house to produce the beer that was consumed by the keelmen in his can-house, as part of their wages.[45] However, by 1750 this had become a cause of complaint, mainly because the keelmen resented having money deducted from their wages to pay for ale which was provided by their employer in the can-house he also owned. Eventually a statement was circulated:

> Every five shillings of market money we receive, there is 3d stopped from each of us. We are oblig'd to spend more of our money than We Can afford in Waiting at these houses for orders, And if we refuse to Wait or Slow in Drinking we are abus'd and threatened by the Can-house keepers who are all the fitter's servants, to be turned out of our keels, and as this rank of our masters (for we have many degrees of masters) as we are informed have no other wages but the benefit of these Can-houses they make it as Considerable a perquisite as possible, for which reason we have not the same liquor as the other Customers but a Certain Other liquor is brew'd for us which they call Savage Beer, or Beer for Savages, at the same time doing us the Honour to take the Gentleman's price for it.[46]

In addition, they were obliged to take 'two quarts of bad drink' for sixpence out of a shilling allowed by the coal owners to each crew out of every tide they worked, while for casting the coal on board the ships they usually received only

---

[44] *Diaries*, Book C: 7 March 1752.

[45] L. Schwarz, 'Custom, Wages and Workload in England during Industrialization', *Past & Present*, 197 (2007), pp. 143–175.

[46] J.M. Fewster, 'The Keelmen of Tyneside in the Eighteenth Century', *Durham University Journal*, 50 (1957), p. 29, from a MS 'Petition of the Keelmen' in Newcastle City Archives.

an allowance of beer, though if the usual quantity of beer was not given the crew were entitled to 1s 4d.[47]

As was indicated in earlier chapters, the keelmen were an independent-minded group of workers who were not averse to taking industrial action. Throughout the seventeenth and eighteenth centuries there were a series of stoppages and strikes over matters including wages and working conditions.[48] One of the first occasions upon which this was recorded was in 1654, when they had a number of grievances including impressments into the navy and the level of their wages. The keelmen joined together as a group and stopped working, and also prevented others from working. The mayor and magistrates made every effort to satisfy them, but eventually called in troops to quell the disturbance. It would appear that little was done to satisfy their demands, and in 1660 there was a further outbreak of trouble, resulting in the keelmen blocking the river above the Tyne Bridge, once more requiring soldiers to disperse them.[49] This was the beginning of a long history of industrial action by the keelmen, which was highlighted by E.R. Turner in 1916 as one of the first examples of actions by organized labour, preceding that by the Lancashire tailors and wool-combers, which led ultimately to the evolution of trade unionism.[50] The vast majority of these stoppages were related to the keelmen's working conditions and rates of pay. However, the situation was complicated in 1699 when, as a result of an agreement by the keelmen to set aside part of their wages to establish a fund for the relief of their poor and elderly, land was obtained from the town to enable

---

[47] Fewster, 'The Keelmen of Tyneside, p. 30.

[48] Charleton, *Newcastle Town*, 4th ed. (London: Walter Scott, 1885, rep., 1978), p. 325; J.U. Nef, *Rise of the British Coal Industry*, 2 vols (London: George Routledge & Sons, 1932), Vol 2, pp. 178–9; S. Middlebrook, *Newcastle upon Tyne: Its Growth and Achievement* (Newcastle upon Tyne: Newcastle Journal, 1950), p. 123; J. Hatcher, *The History of the British Coal Industry* Vol. 1, *Before 1700: Towards the Age of Coal* (Oxford: Clarendon Press, 1993), p. 468; J.M. Fewster, *The Keelmen of Tyneside: Labour Organisation and Conflict in the North-East Coal Industry, 1600–1830* (Woodbridge: Boydell and Brewer, 2011), pp. 61–108; Fewster, 'The Keelmen of Tyneside', pp. 24–33; Fewster, 'The Last Struggles of the Tyneside Keelmen', *Durham University Journal*, 55 (1963), p. 6; Rowe, 'The Keelmen of Tyneside', *History Today*, 19 (1969), p. 251. Mutinies by the keelmen over their conditions of work and rates of pay occurred on a regular basis, with records of disputes in 1641, 1654, 1660, 1676, 1708, 1710, 1719, 1738, 1740, 1744, 1750, 1771, 1794, 1803, 1809, 1819 and 1822. Rowe, 'The Keelmen of Tyneside', pp. 248–54.

[49] R. Howell, *Newcastle upon Tyne and the Puritan Revolution* (Oxford: Oxford University Press, 1967), pp. 292–3: D. Levine and K. Wrightson, *The Making of an Industrial Society:Whickham 1560–1765* (Oxford: Clarendon Press, 1991), p. 391.

[50] E.R Turner, 'The Keelmen in Newcastle', *The American Historical Review*, 21 (1916), pp. 542–5.

them to build the Keelmen's Hospital, which was completed in 1701. The charitable funds that had been raised were initially managed, at the request of the keelmen, by a board of trustees from the stewards of the Hostmen's Company. However, high levels of distrust between the keelmen and the hostmen over the mismanagement of the charity led to its collapse, the charity being wound up in 1712. This mistrust led to a variety of petitions to parliament in an unsuccessful attempt to re-establish and wrest control of the charity from the hostmen, which led to continuing ill feeling between the keelmen and their employers.[51]

During the very severe winter of 1739–40 the shortage of corn led to riots by both the local pitmen and keelmen, during which the authorities lost control. Grain stores and grain ships were raided at the quayside, and the Guildhall was ransacked. Troops had to be called in to quell the riots, and at the subsequent Assizes six men were condemned to transportation for seven years.[52] Further action occurred four years later, in 1744, when a further dispute concerning working conditions escalated. Once again, troops were sent in when the keelmen struck, because their keels were being overloaded by the coal owners who had been forced to give overmeasure because of price-cutting. The keelmen were not being paid to carry the additional coal, and their lives were being put at risk by carrying excessive loads in their keels in inclement conditions, particularly near the mouth of the river. The dispute was ended when an agreement was signed limiting the load of coal in each keel to eight chaldrons.[53] A further strike, lasting seven weeks in 1750, was similarly caused partially by persistent overloading of the keels, but also by a complaint against the practice of the hostmen paying part of the wages of the keelmen in beer at the can-houses.[54] Again, the military were called in to assist in breaking the strike, however the action persisted, and the hostmen attempted to break the action by publishing a list of over 800 striking keelmen with a notice to others that the striking keelmen were under bond and any person employing them would be liable to legal action.[55] Following this, they made it clear to the keelmen that they would employ other casual workers to man the keels. Alarmed at this, on 4 May 1750 the keelmen manned their keels

---

[51] Ellis, 'A Dynamic Society', p. 211.

[52] Middlebrook, *Newcastle upon Tyne*, p. 123; Fewster, 'The Keelmen of Tyneside', pp. 28, 32; Ellis 'A Dynamic Society', p. 213.

[53] Rowe, 'The Keelmen of Tyneside', p. 251; Fewster, 'The Keelmen of Tyneside', p. 67.

[54] Fewster, 'The Keelmen of Tyneside', p. 29; Ellis, 'A Dynamic Society', pp. 212–13; Levine and Wrightson, *The Making of an Industrial Society*, p. 391; Rowe, 'The Tyneside Keelmen', p. 251.

[55] See Chapter 3, in which this document in the Bell Collection is shown and described in more detail.

and blocked the river, stopping keels that were attempting to work normally and breaking their gear. The military were called to clear the strikers and allow the substitute workers to continue. Seven weeks after the strike began the keelmen were forced to return to work without gaining any substantial concessions other than the re-affirmation of the agreement of 1744. The same problems with overloading continued with further strikes in 1768 and 1770, with the dispute over the can-houses not being finally resolved until 1791.[56]

The often-portrayed picture of the keelmen as a disruptive and troublesome element in the developing industries along the Tyne is not entirely justified. Joyce Ellis comments that:

> Contemporary comment combines an insistence on dire poverty with an equal insistence on reckless spending, but it is perhaps significant that the keelmen could not only sustain protracted strike action but also in a few individual cases build up a moderate amount of real and personal property. Clearly their problem was not so much one of chronically low wages as of the irregular rewards that went with employment in a fluctuating trade.[57]

Ellis also noted that the keelmen were far from an anarchic mob, and that there was little evidence that they were not fully integrated into the community. The most alarming feature for the authorities was that they were able to take direct and very disciplined industrial action, rather than descending into more disorganized protests, and would not hesitate to take well articulated complaints to the coal owners themselves, who had a significant financial interest in the activities of their employing hostmen.[58] Throughout the seventeenth and eighteenth centuries and up to the time when keels stopped being used in the coal trade with the consequent disappearance of the keelmen's occupation in the mid nineteenth century, it is clear that keelmen significantly influenced the trade on the river. They accomplished this through their ability to work together as a cohesive group and attempt to influence the conditions under which they worked in what appears to have been a relatively constructive manner. As Ellis has noted, their ability to work together as a group, organizing disciplined industrial action, and also to achieve such triumphs for the period as the construction of a charitable hospital for their own community, speaks volumes for their relative independence of thinking and sophistication, in contradiction

---

[56] Fewster, 'The Keelmen of Tyneside', p. 74; Fewster, *The Keelmen of Tyneside*, pp. 100–19.
[57] Ellis, 'A Dynamic Society', p. 210.
[58] Ellis, 'A Dynamic Society', p. 212.

to the often published statements about their bad behaviour. These latter views probably originated from those hostmen and town authorities that were their employers at the time.

During the strike or 'stop' of keelmen in 1750, which was against the overloading of keels and also against 'can-money' or the payment of part of the keelmen's wages in beer at the can-house, Ralph records in his diary the effects of this strike and its consequences for some of the keelmen. This provides one of the very few first-hand accounts of a keelmen's strike and its outcome, including what appears to be Ralph's personal involvement, travelling on a loaded keel down to Shields during the strike:

> Monday 19 March 1750. In the Morning went onto the Key and looked at the Keelmen as they Stopped all the Keels that went down the river, and I went to school.[59]

> Tuesday 20 March. Mr Crisp came and Layed at our house that night, we sat and talked about the Keelmen.[60]

> Friday 30 March. My Master had two of our Keelmen to talk with them about this Stop.[61]

> Thursday 12 April. ... in the afternoon the Keelman Stopped a Keel as she was going up River and broke Gear then got the man a Shore and made a great disturbance in the Town.[62]

> Wednesday 25 April. In the Morning went to Towns Court and saw the prisoners carried in.[63]

> Thursday 26 April. In the Morning went to School and took a walk to Sandhill and saw some Skippers carried to Newgate.[64]

---

[59] *Diaries*, Book A: 19 March 1750.
[60] *Diaries*, Book A: 20 March 1750.
[61] *Diaries*, Book A: 30 March 1750.
[62] *Diaries*, Book A: 12 April 1750.
[63] *Diaries*, Book A: 25 April 1750.
[64] *Diaries*, Book A: 26 April 1750; C.E. Thornton, *Bound for the Tyne*, p. 7. Newgate was a prison, which served Newcastle from 1400 to 1823.

> Saturday 28 April. My Master went to meeting of the fitters.[65]
>
> Monday 30 April. In the forenoon took a walk onto the key and saw the Fitters men bring down the Keels from above Bridge.[66]
>
> Tuesday 1 May. In the morning got up early and went down to Winkhamlee and we went on board a loaden Keel and carried her down to Sheels.[67]
>
> Friday 4 May. ... we heard that the Keelmen was risen so we sat still till Supper and then came home.[68]
>
> Wednesday 9 May. Went down to Winkhamlee and saw some of the Fitters men dance, (then) came home.[69]

Following these events surrounding the keelmen's strike, including what appears to be the hostmen and fitters taking keels down the river themselves, the keelmen seem to have returned to work, hence the celebrations of the fitter's men. However, some of the keelmen remained in prison and came to court in August where it appeared that the sentences for the striking keelmen were quite severe, including transportation.

> Saturday 18 August. Got up early in the morning & went to the Towns Court where I saw the Keelmen tried.[70]
>
> Monday 20 August. In the afternoon walked about the Key & saw the prisoners that was to be transported go down to Shields.[71]

Evidence emerges from the diaries of the wide range of other services that were provided by the hostmen to the masters of the ships with whom they dealt, ranging from welfare issues, including attempts to find a doctor to attend a ship's

---

[65] *Diaries*, Book A: 28 April 1750.
[66] *Diaries*, Book A: 30 April 1750.
[67] *Diaries*, Book A: 1 May 1750.
[68] *Diaries*, Book A: 4 May 1750.
[69] *Diaries*, Book A: 9 May 1750.
[70] *Diaries*, Book B: 18 August 1750.
[71] *Diaries*, Book B: 20 August 1750; C.E. Thornton, *Bound for the Tyne*, p. 8. Until the War of Independence in 1776 prisoners were transported to America, thereafter they were transported to Australia after the establishment of a new penal colony in 1788.

master who was ill,[72] to the facilitation of other services required including advertising a ship for sale,[73] negotiating insurance rates for shipments to London[74] and taking out licenses for carrying brandy.[75] In addition, the diaries give much more detail about the day-to-day life and work of the apprentice with the keelmen, and also a number of 'fitter's men' who seemed to be part of the team, although their precise role remains unclear.[76] An entry in June 1753 provides evidence of some of the cargoes other than coal, such as 'soap ashes'[77] that were carried in keels, which also seemed to be managed by Ralph on behalf of his master.[78]

The most important issue affecting trade in Newcastle was the navigability of the Tyne and the limitations that the relative shallowness of parts of the river had upon the ability of larger ships to sail up to the quay at Newcastle. That

[72] *Diaries*, Book C: 11–15 March 1751, Monday 11 March (1751). 'In the Evening I went up to Doctor Askues to desire he would go to see Mr Wm Railston Shipmaster at Sheilds, but he was at Durham'. Tuesday 12 March, 'in the morning I went to see if Doctor Askue could go to Sheilds, but he could not, for he was going to Durham, to see Lau. Rudd was lieing very ill, then went to Dr Lamberts to know if he could go, and he could'. Friday 15 March, 'My Master went down to Mr William Railstone's Funerall'.

[73] *Diaries*, Book E: 23 Feb. 1753, 'I went up to the Printing Offices to tell them to continue the advertisement of Mr Tabor's Brigg, Marigold, lying at the South Shore wch is to be sold by applying to my Master'.

[74] *Diaries*, Book E: 2 March 1753, 'Saml & Jno Campion dined at our house. ... I went to the insurance office to know what they had a hundred for the runn up to London & they told me a Guinea & a half, so I told my Master, for Saml Campion wanted to insure'.

[75] *Diaries*, Book D: 29 May 1752, 'In the morning my Masr. sent me to the Excise Office to take out a Brandy Licence for Mr Railston of Jarrah Key'.

[76] *Diaries*, Book E: 15 March 1753, 'In the morning we heard that Park Coals were to be delivered today so I ordered Alexander down to the Staith and went to order Thompson to Winkhamlee, where I stayed a good while then I went to the Cann house till they drank their Cann then I went down to Winkhamlee in the Keel, was 40 minutes in going down against the Tide wth a strong WesterlyWind, I called at Park as I came from Winkhamlee our business was done, part of Fitter's men came to Geo. Cram's & had something both to eat and drink the names were as follows, Billy Hudspeth, Ra. Simpson, Wm. Carr, Robt. Humble, Thos. Newton, John Simerell, George Blakey & myself, Thos. Hodgson the Offputter was there also'.

[77] The OED defines 'Soap Ashes'as ashes of certain kinds of wood used in forming a lye in soap making.

[78] *Diaries*, Book E: 1 June 1753, 'Went with master Billy to Wm Harpers Keel wch was laying at the other side of the River & was loaded with Soap Ashes, below the Bridge, he told Jno I gave him Leave to take the Tide but when I went he said neither with or against it, but before he took the Tide I told my master I advised him not to take the Tide wch I did do, but did not forbid him to do it, we came across the Water in the same boat we went over in, I walked upon the Key & went to Jno's, to ask him what Keel was ordered to Winkhamlee'.

said, a number of entries in the diary refer to quite large long-distance cargo ships that were indeed able to reach Newcastle quay. These were a subject of considerable curiosity amongst Ralph and his friends.[79] It is of interest to note that Ralph was using boats of other types to travel up and down the River for social and recreational purposes; on 14 July he 'went down to Tinmouth in a Werry, and Bathed, and I dined at Mrs Hudspeth's Lodgings, and came home in a Sculler with Mr & Mrs Haxon'.[80] Ralph found time to pursue his own family business interests, particularly those associated with his uncle Ralph Ward, making reference in May 1753 to enquiries about the cost of kelp, which his uncle used in his North Yorkshire Alum works.[81] In addition, he spent some time assisting his uncle by following up a long-running dispute about sailcloth with the executors of a merchant from Monkwearmouth who had died owing Ward money.[82] No entries appeared in the diary from August 1753 and March 1756, when, fortunately, Ralph started writing his diary again; by this time he was in his last year of his apprenticeship and the entries are those of a much more confident young man, with a variety of interests. The entries now highlight in more detail aspects of the hostman's work encountered in the earlier parts of his diary.

A major influence on coastal trade and the river during 1756 was the impact of the European wars being fought at the time. The Navy was short of volunteers, and the press gangs were very active in Newcastle. The communities along the Tyne had always been a major recruiting area for the Navy, both by voluntary recruitment and from the frequent attention of the press gangs, which had a major impact upon the river trades. Indeed the effect of the press gangs upon the manpower needed to maintain the London coal trade was sufficient to lead to a degree of protection from the press gangs for the crews of colliers and also to some extent for keelmen, and Ralph regularly reported the arrival of the Navy tender coming to collect more pressed men.[83] Many other members

---

[79] *Diaries*, Book E: 14 June 1753, 'I went upon the Key I took a walk as far as the West India Ship which was lying nigh the high Crain. I went on board & saw the curiositys as 2 or 3 Tortesses alive, a Parrott & Parrokett, a Negro Boy, Munkey & pine apples with other curiositys which I was a stranger to'.

[80] *Diaries*, Book C: 14 July 1751.

[81] *Diaries*, Book E: 11 May 1753.

[82] *Diaries*, Book E: 8 March 1756, 'I saw Mr Jonathan Sorsbie's Servt who told me that nothing as yet had been, done as yet about the Effects of Ra: Cook of Monkwearmouth deceas'd, wherein my Uncle Mr Ra: Ward & Thos. Spencer were jointly concern'd, in loss, on the sail cloth Accot' Ralph's uncle, Ralph Ward, and his cousin, Thomas Spencer, jointly owned a sail cloth factory in Guisborough.

[83] Nef, *The Rise of the British Coal Industry*, Vol. 1, pp. 81–2; Middlebrook, *Newcastle upon Tyne*, pp. 164–5.

of the public felt at risk, and Ralph records his master's servant hiding in his room overnight to evade the press gang.[84] Exemptions to the press were negotiated by the Town for keelmen and some collier crews, so that the flow of coal to London could be maintained. One of Ralph's tasks was to collect these dispensations from the Town offices and give them to the keelmen and the masters of colliers.[85] Unfortunately, few documents survive concerning the arrangements made for the protection from the attentions of the press gangs of those in what were regarded as essential services during the seventeenth century. However, a number of documents do survive in the Bell Collection, from 1803, when the press gangs were particularly active during the Napoleonic campaigns. Among these are the handbills inviting both keelmen and shipwrights to attend the Guildhall to obtain protections from the press gangs. It appears that during this period there were adverts inviting not just keelmen and mariners to join the fleet, but 'shipwrights, under 50 years of age who have served an apprenticeship to enter for His Majesty's service in the Royal Dockyards of the Medway and Portsmouth for a period of three months'.[86] It is not unreasonable to suppose that similar pressures were placed on both watermen and shipwrights to enlist into His Majesty's service in 1756.

By this relatively late stage in his apprenticeship, Ralph was now working almost independently, undertaking the vast majority of the hostman's activities other than the fixing of the coal itself which was still the responsibility of his master. Throughout the last section of his diary, from March to December 1756, there are very regular records of masters of colliers coming to agree loading with coal and then being cleared at the Town House for local taxes and the Customs House for excise duties; he took many of these through the clearance process himself, but always in his master's name.[87] In addition, he was now responsible for much of the clerical work and bookkeeping in the office and supervising the work of the keels and keelmen. A good example of the breadth of skills Ralph had developed was his work in organizing the salvaging of keels, which had been damaged on one occasion by a storm, and on another when a keel had run into the Tyne Bridge and sunk. This is a particularly interesting series of diary entries

---

[84] *Diaries*, Book E: 8 March 1756, 'John Dent (my Masters Servant) laid with me this night for fear of the press Gang, who we heard were to go about peoples houses at three or four o'Clock in the Morning and which I hear was accordingly done in Pandon Street'.

[85] *Diaries*, Book F: 2 Oct. 1756, 'I got up early & rode down to Shields upon my Master's Mair & went on board the Mary & Jane, John Galilee, with a Protection'.

[86] Bell Collections, Vol. 2, NCL/LS, L942.8 T987B.

[87] The entries in the Newcastle Chamberlains Accounts always included the name of the hostman, even when, according to the diaries, the actual clearance was done by Ralph.

because they give a unique first-hand account of the salvage process and the relative responsibility of those involved:

> Thursday 7 October 1756. The last night has been the most Windy I ever knew one, a great deal of damage being done both upon the River & Land, the wind blew hard at flat south about Ten till Twelve & then shifted to the West and to the NNW, but no farther. my Master has two loaden Keels sunck at Shields, one of them being moored on board the Diamond Mr Samuel Campion's Ship he expects to be reimburs'd the damage when known, but the other not being moor'd on board any Ship, the Damage falls upon himself, for when a Keel is Moor'd at the Staith and any damage happen her, the Owner of that Staith pays it, but if between the Staith & Ship then the Owner of the Keel, and if moor'd on board of Ship or has been & the Ship People cast her off, then the Owner of the Ship sustains the Loss; a great many other Keels are sunk also at Shields & other Places, & Trees torn up by the Roots.[88]

> Wednesday 13 October. I breakfasted & rode down to Shields I went over the Water and got the Men to work at weighing my Master's Keel, but to no purpose, tho' two of the Water Bailiffs Men came to help.[89]

> Thursday 14 October. We got another lift at the Keel in the morning but the Ebb being strong she canted, however I dined with Mr Wallas, Carpenter at Shields, & got him to assist us, we then got the Keel Swifted & canted bottom down & brought to the shore by Six o'Clock. John Dent came down a little before & brought me a Letter from my Master with a Letter which he had inclosed that the Town Clerk had sent him by order of Sir Walter Blacket, Bart, Mayor & the rest of the Magistrates, containing a Summons to the Court to lay in bail for the Keels being weigh'd, which is first thing of it's kind (for a Keel) ever known.[90]

> Friday 15 October. I rode down to Shields, dined on board the Thomas & Richard & orderd at the Keel every utensil that had been borrow'd for the use of the Keel to be returned to it's proper Owner.[91]

---

[88] *Diaries*, Book F: 7th Oct. 1756.
[89] *Diaries*, Book F: 13 Oct. 1756.
[90] *Diaries*, Book F: 14 Oct. 1756.
[91] *Diaries*, Book F: 15 Oct. 1756.

> Saturday 16 October. I paid the Keelmen £1:15s:4d, & the other Men for assisting at the Weighing of Mr Henderson's Keel Ten Shillings each.[92]

This must have been a period of particularly bad weather, very bad luck or both, because less than a week later Ralph had to organize the rescue of another sunken keel.

> Thursday 21 October 1756. I took a walk wth Billy Hudspeth on board New brigg at St Anthony's, called the Samuel & Martha of Yarm, Mr Tolver being chief owner & Mrs Hudspeth part. John Robinson's Keel was sunk by striking against the Bridge but the Skipper (Robinson) was not in her.[93]

> Saturday 23 October. I got up early & went over the water to Hilgate end where the above Keel is lying, we got a light Keel & took part of the Coals out, I paid the Keelmen £20:8s:7d, got 2 Keels & slung to the sunk Keel which brot her nearer the Shore.[94]

> Sunday 24 October. I found she laid badly having her Stern in the deep, so I got some of the other Skippers & took all the Coals out of her into another Keel, & I stay'd by her wth the Carpenters all the forenoon, and in the afternoon I went to her again.[95]

A feature of the diaries as a whole, and particularly those of 1756, is the wealth of detail that they provide about the ships and their masters who used William Jefferson to provide the coal that they needed. The hostman's trading relationships with the masters were recorded in some depth, and include the names of the ships and their masters and the dates on which they 'fixed' with Jefferson to buy coal, and also the date on which they were cleared to leave (see Appendix). This shows that Jefferson had regular customers. Between March and December 1756, 24 different ships were 'fixed', some of them on five or six occasions, giving a total of 50 shiploads of coal sold during the period. It is interesting to note that the typical time taken between a ship's master fixing with Jefferson to be loaded with coal, and the master and his ship being cleared

---

[92] *Diaries*, Book F: 16 Oct. 1756.
[93] *Diaries*, Book F: 21 Oct. 1756. It is notable that one of the part owners of the new brigg at St Anthony's was Mrs Hudspeth, illustrating a wider spectrum of investment by the woman hostman.
[94] *Diaries*, Book F: 23 Oct. 1756.
[95] *Diaries*, Book F: 24 Oct. 1756.

from the Customs and the Town to depart was four days. In addition, the time taken before the ship returned for another load of coal gives some idea of the time taken to undertake the voyages. Although some ships made only single visits, a significant number were returning at intervals of about four to six weeks for another load of coal. One ship, the John and Mary of Whitby, master John Galilee, made six visits between March and October, and several others made four or five visits.

These records are particularly interesting when compared with the entries in both the coastal port books for Newcastle[96] and the Newcastle Chamberlains' account books,[97] where matching entries can be found for most of the shipments mentioned in Jackson's Diary. Of the 50 shipments recorded in the diaries 46 (92%) could be found in the port books, itself a useful tribute to the comprehensive nature of the source. The vast majority were for coal shipments alone, with only six for shipments of coal together with other articles such as glass bottles, flagstones, grindstones and cinders for East Coast ports such as Lynn and Maldon and lead going to London. It is quite possible that the four shipments mentioned in the diaries that do not appear on the coastal port books, were foreign shipments, which would have been recorded in the overseas port books, which were not sufficiently legible to provide such detail. The Chamberlains' Account Books similarly record 33 (66%) of the shipments noted in the diary. The interpretation of recordings of individual shipments in these accounts is complicated by the fact that on many occasions hostmen include town tax payments for many previous separate shipments by the same ship and her master, the highest number being discovered being 32 dating back over 3 years, all entered under the date of the most recent shipment and tax payment.[98] This probably explains the lower proportion of matching records in the Chamberlains' Accounts, as those shipments that were not recorded contemporaneously, are likely to have been recorded in later volumes of the Chamberlains' Accounts. The effect of this is reflected in the Appendix where the dates of some entries are substantially different from dates in the diary and port book. The Chamberlains' Accounts also record details of the amount of ballast, if carried, and upon which ballast shore it was deposited, together with the charges. In addition a levy was charged on a 'ship's boat' which is assumed to be the ship's tender or dinghy, used for ferrying to and from the shore when at anchor in the river. Four ships were recorded in the Chamberlains' Accounts as

---

[96] Newcastle Port Books 1755–56, Coastal Outwards, TNA E/190/256/9.
[97] TWAM Newcastle Chamberlains' Accounts of Payments and Disbursements 1756, MD.NC/FN/1/1/108.
[98] Chamberlains' Accounts.

having no ballast, implying that they arrived in the port with inward cargo; and six ships recorded in the chamberlains' accounts under Jefferson's name were not found at all in the diaries. The coincidence of data from these different sources does provide a degree of triangulation, which tends to confirm and support the evidence provided in these diaries about the coal trade in Newcastle during the mid eighteenth century. It also confirms that the port books are a relatively reliable source.

As might be expected, the diaries reveal a great deal about Ralph himself. He was clearly very religious, attending the local Anglican churches twice each Sunday,[99] and spending a significant amount of his spare time reading collections of sermons and other religious tracts.[100] During the first years of his apprenticeship, attention was clearly being paid to his general education; he attended classes on a number of subjects including arithmetic.[101] Throughout the period of his apprenticeship Ralph played the German Flute;[102] having taken lessons, he played it almost every day, both on his own and in concert with others. On 10 June 1756 he recorded that he had attended a 'Concert of Musick given by Mr Avison in rooms on the Side'.[103] Much of his working day would be spent either on the Quayside, networking with other hostmen and apprentices, masters of ships and other tradesmen, or at the hostman's house, doing clerical work in the office. In later years Ralph would often travel to Shields or Jarrow staith and meet ships' masters on their ships.[104]

As Ralph matured, he developed an active social life and a wider circle of friends, frequently taking tea with both gentleman and lady friends. He embarked on quite extensive trips, either on foot or on horseback around the local areas of South East Northumberland, watching horseracing on the town moor and occasionally netting game. On occasion, he also embarked with his friends on boat trips on the river. A particularly memorable trip occurred when they hired some keelmen to row a group up the river with the Mayor's Barge to Stella, which was further up the river from Newcastle close to Newburn,

---

[99] *Diaries*, Book F: 12 Sept. 1756.
[100] *Diaries*, Book E: 18 April 1753.
[101] *Diaries*, Book C: 26 February 1751.
[102] *Diaries*, Book C: 17 February 1752.
[103] *Diaries*, Book E: 10 June 1756, ' I walked to Mr Addison's in the Close, who with Mr Dawson Mr Ord & myself went to Mr Avisons private Concert of Musick wch. I thought was very fine'. Charles Avison (1709–1770) was a well-known composer based in Newcastle, whose music is still highly regarded and often played; Bennett Mitchell Zon, 'Avison, Charles (*bap.* 1710, *d.* 1770)', *Oxford Dictionary of National Biography* (Oxford: Oxford University Press, 2004), www.oxford dnb.com. Accessed 23 March 2014.
[104] *Diaries*, Book F: 15 Sept. 1756.

during an annual voyage to mark out the boundaries of the county. It would seem that large quantities of wine were taken and drunk on Ralph's boat, only to be replaced from those stocked on board the Mayor's Barge in even larger quantities. The diary notes that Ralph awoke the next morning suffering from the side effects of this expedition. Ralph clearly enjoyed these trips, as in July 1756 bought himself a part share in a small boat.[105] The nature of his social activities was wide and varied, and during the last year he regularly frequented the local coffee shops, particularly Gray's, to read the London newspapers; he was particularly attentive to the details of the exploits of Admiral Bing in the Mediterranean and their consequences.[106]

Towards the end of his apprenticeship, Ralph went back to Richmond and visited his family, and also his uncle in Guisborough. His uncle suggested that, after he finished his apprenticeship, Ralph should go to work for him in his business, an offer that he appears to have accepted with alacrity.[107] Following this visit, Ralph returned to Newcastle for his final few weeks as a hostman's apprentice. His apprenticeship was due to end on the 23 November,[108] however with the change in the calendar in 1752, and the loss of 11 days, Ralph had to wait until the 4 December to complete his apprenticeship. It appears that he did not apply for entry into freedom of the Hostman's Company, as there is no mention of it in the Diary and no record in the Chamberlains' Accounts or the Hostmen's Records. Following the end of his apprenticeship, he arranged a celebration dinner with several of his friends.[109] After what appears to have been a successful

---

[105] *Diaries*, Book E: 26 July 1756, 'I paid Jno Dawson One Pound, Eight Shillings & 6d, for a quarter part of a New boat wch he calls Mellnion, wherein himself & Mr Wm Addison is part owners'.

[106] *Diaries*, Book E: 29 June 1756, 'I went to the Coffee house where I saw a Letter from Adml Bing (now in the Mediterranean) in the Gazette wherein he's thought to give a poor account of himself'. *Ibid.*: 26 July 1756, I drank Tea at Miss Fairlams and went to Mr Hindmarches Glover in the Flesh market where I saw Admiral Bings Effigy burnt after he'd been carried round the Town for his ill behaviour in the Mediterranian about 3 Months Ago'; *Ibid*.: 27 July 1756, 'I drank Tea at Mrs Forsters, read the London News at the Coffee House and retir'd to bed about Eleven'.

[107] *Diaries*, Book F: 3 Nov. 1756. 'My Uncle told me this morning that he intends me to live with him after I've served my time out, and God grant I may be of Comfort to him, all my Friends & myself, we walked about, as into the Gardens &c &c'.

[108] *Diaries*, Book F: 23 Nov 1756.

[109] *Diaries*, Book F: 4 Dec. 1756, 'This day my Seventh Years Bond expires allowing the Eleven days also, for the alteration of the Stile in 1752, I went with Mr Ord to Mr Winds in Pilgrom street & bespoke a Supper for Seven of my Acquaintances against Monday night'; *Diaries*, Book F: 6 Dec. 1756, 'I got several odd things that I'm desired to carry home, my Master, or Mr Jeferson & I din'd at Mrs Hudspeth's where we had a Pheasant for one Dish, in

evening he packed up all of his belongings, finished off the remaining work in the office and said farewell to all of his friends, leaving Newcastle for the last time on the 9 of December 1756 to begin his new life with his uncle Ralph Ward.[110]

Ralph Jackson's diary has provided a picture of the Newcastle water trades from the perspective of one of the key players, the hostman. The relationships between the various participants in the coal trade were complex, and the patterns of contact between the different participants recorded in the Diary help to clarify the relationships between the respective groups. The most important relationships in Newcastle were essentially the business relationships between those within the trading network, the coal owners, the hostmen and the masters of the coal-carrying ships, and through them the coal importers, mainly in London, whose behaviour would have been influenced by the demands of the merchants and markets where the coal was sold and consumed. Each of these groups would have had their own business infrastructure of employees and apprentices with whatever special skills were necessary. The diary, although it relates only to one small, though important part of this chain, the hostman, provides an overall perspective on all the different aspects of the water trades on the river Tyne and how they related to one another to create the dynamic trading community in Newcastle and along its river. The employees necessary to accomplish the hostman's function included his apprentice, who essentially fulfilled the role of a management trainee who would assist in the management of the other employees. In the case of the hostmen these latter were the skippers and keelmen who worked the keels used to move the hostman's coal; the role of the 'fitter's men' who are often mentioned remains unclear. The hostmen did not necessarily own the keels he used. It would appear that keels were available for rent from shipwrights, and quite probably from other keel owners. The keelmen were often employed on the basis of an annual bond, but paid for work done and the amount of coal carried. A key to the organization of this process was the canhouse, where the keelmen met to await instruction or payment; this institution

---

the evening past five o'Clock, I went to Mr Winds Innkeeper in Pilgrom street, with Seven of my acquaintances, Namely Mr Wm Hudspeth, Thos Ord, Allan Robinson, Alexr Adams, Jno Percival, Wm Addison, & Ra: Morton, where we supt upon a Hair, Veal stakes, & an Apple Pye, we parted a little past Ten, & I retired to bed before Eleven'; *Diaries*, Book F: 7 Dec. 1756, 'I had a very indiferent night last night in the Heart burn, tho' was not in Liquer, I went to Mr Winds & paid him £1:2s:6d for my Treat last night & to the Servant a Shilling. I finish'd all my Master's Books today, Mrs Hudspeth & Misses dined at our House, & I drank Tea there with Mr William only & spent the Evening'.

[110] *Diaries*, Book F: 8 Dec. 1756, 'I Pack'd up all my Cloths & got them to the Carriers'; *Diaries*, Book F: 9 Dec. 1756, 'I took my leave of Newcastle abt Ten accompanied by Mr Thos Ord to Durham'.

was run by a can-woman who appears also to have been an employee of the hostman, and who supplied the beer provided for the keelmen at the can-house. The arrangements as a whole seemed to work very well during the period covered by the diaries, as there are very few mentions in the diaries of difficulties with the keelmen, apart from the 1750 strike over can-money. The dynamics of these business networks and relationships fluctuated throughout the seventeenth and eighteenth centuries, under the influence of extrinsic pressures including the changing demand for coal. However, the diaries provide us with a clearer picture of these structures at an instant in time, which is of value in helping our interpretation of changes with occurred both before and afterwards, and in putting into a clearer perspective those aspects of the water trades along the River Tyne discussed in the previous chapters.

Sadly, the diaries, being those of a very young man learning his trade as an apprentice, reflect only on those contacts in his immediate circle and with whom he dealt personally. The effect of this is to limit our ability to learn more about the wider business network of contacts with whom William Jefferson would have been dealing as part of his business as a hostman. The only networks we have been able to explore in some detail are those related to the internal workings of the business itself, including the keelman and the operation of the can-house system, together with the network of contacts with the various ships' masters with whom Jefferson did business. There were a few brief and rather oblique references to other hostmen, and to contacts with some coal owners or their representatives, illustrated by the references to visits made on his master's business to Mr Featherstone's office.[111] The majority of references in the diary were to contacts with his family and local close friends in which forenames alone were often used making it extremely difficult to establish the details of his social networks outside his family and that of William Jefferson.

Finally, it is possible to speculate about why Ralph came to Newcastle as an apprentice hostman in the first place. In the seventeenth century it was not uncommon for families of some status to arrange apprenticeships, usually for their male children, in professions or occupations not dissimilar to their own.[112] Later in the diaries, there is reference to a John Jefferson, who was a ship owner and master in Staithes in Cleveland, and who was also the brother of William Jefferson, Ralph's master.[113] Although there is no specific mention of any overall

---

[111] *Diaries*, Book F: 23 Sept 1756, 'I paid Mr Ra: Fetherston on my Masrs Accot for Partnership Coals £100, and I walk'd to Elswick to see Mrs Hudspet'.

[112] J. Lane, *Apprenticeship in England, 1600–1914* (London: Routledge, 1996).

[113] A glossary of all the names appears in the published transcription of the Diaries, with notes of the relationships within the family.

plan for Ralph's longer term career, it is possible to speculate that the Ward and Jackson families of Guisborough were acquainted with John Jefferson of Staithes and that Ralph's dispatch to Newcastle as an apprentice to William Jefferson, a hostman, was part of an overall family plan for his future and that of the Ward Jackson family business. This idea gains support from the later sections of the diary, when Ralph has left Newcastle and spends his first few months working with his uncle. During this period it becomes apparent that the Jackson, Ward and Jefferson families were quite close, spending a significant amount of time in each others company during the subsequent months, including meetings during visits from his former Master William Jefferson to his brother John Jefferson in Staithes. This implies the existence of an even wider family and business network extending from Newcastle to North Yorkshire that underpinned the whole episode of Ralph Jackson's apprenticeship in Newcastle.

Chapter 8

Conclusions

This reappraisal of the history of the water trades community in Newcastle and along the lower river Tyne in the seventeenth and eighteenth centuries has provided the opportunity to gain a wider perspective of the true extent of the commercial and shipping activity that existed in Newcastle upon Tyne and its hinterland during this critical period in its history. The picture painted by the various primary sources is of a town with a thriving commercial centre, based around access to the sea through the river. The area was home to a complex water trades community focused on facilitating the intermediate transport of coal and a variety of other exports and imports from the shore to the waiting cargo ships anchored close to the mouth of the river. It is clear that Newcastle at this time, positioned eight miles upstream from the sea, with its trade being confined to a relatively short section of the tidal River Tyne, was different from most of the other significant port towns in England. Many other port towns had the benefit of being strategically positioned either closer to the sea, towards the mouth of a river, or on a major inlet from the sea, such as the Bristol Channel, the Humber estuary or the Thames estuary; such ports usually had the benefit of relatively deep water at most states of the tide enabling loaded ships to come directly to the port. This proximity to deep water meant that there was less need for a form of intermediate transport to convey cargo from ship to shore as was the case in Newcastle. London was an exception; because of the sheer volume of traffic, many ships, and particularly those carrying coal, would anchor in the river, unloading their coal into lighters for transport to the shore. In those ports positioned on a major river that was a significant route for inland trade – including the Thames, Severn and the tributaries of the Humber – smaller ships might reach inland ports such as Bawtry. In addition, a substantial amount of inland trade was conducted by barges and other river craft such as the Thames Lighter, Severn Trow and Humber keel, which further redistributed much of the merchandise entering and leaving a major port.

Examination of the working population of the lower River Tyne between 1600 and 1800, during the period when the community was dominated by the evolving coal trade, confirmed that the coal owners and their agents, the hostmen, controlled the development of the trade and significantly influenced the working lives of all those who worked as water tradesmen during this period. Coal was not the only commodity to be exported, and, as we are now aware, there was a significant import trade, particularly of foodstuffs and other consumables. The shallow and tidal nature of the Tyne meant that much of the cargo for export had to be carried in small boats towards deeper water closer to the mouth of the river for loading onto ships, with the process reversed to a degree for imports, although much non-coal import and export activity occurred at the commodious Newcastle quayside. These activities stimulated the development of a thriving community of water tradesmen whose task was to transport the cargoes on the river. Much has been written about the tradesmen, the most well known of whom were the keelmen. The keelmen have been portrayed by a wide variety of authors as a cohesive group of workers, mainly of Scottish origin, who worked on a seasonal basis on the river, returning to their homes in Scotland in the winter to rejoin their families. They were said to be a tightly knit community, but were always said to be very poor, managing well in the summer when work was plentiful, but experiencing severe deprivation in the winter when the coal trade was said to be reduced due to cold and inclement weather. Various accounts have been given of their numbers but these were largely anecdotal with little documentary evidence to support them. The true characteristics of the community and particularly the extent to which inward migration was a significant contributor are revealed by the evidence obtained from the parish registers and censuses, which confirmed the dominance of the water tradesmen in the riverside parish of All Saints. However, the nature of the population seems to have been more complex, with several recognized indicators of inward migration showing a significant level of population growth from outside the community, including an increase in the number of new surnames, which suggested the arrival of new families in a manner very similar to that found in Whickham by Levine and Wrightson.[1] Like Whickham, All Saints did not show a predominance of Scottish names.

The suggestion that the population of water tradesmen was largely of Scottish origin does appear to be at least partially true, but those that did come usually became settled long-term residents, and they appear to have constituted fewer than half of the population. The issue of the work and the Scottish workers being seasonal and itinerant is not clear. There was little evidence to support the notion, particularly as there was evidence that some keels were undoubtedly used

---

[1] D. Levine and K. Wrightson, *The Making of an Industrial Society: Whickham 1560–1765* (Oxford: Clarendon Press, 1991), pp. 179–80.

to carry coal as well as being employed on other clearance and dredging work during the winter. In addition, there was a number of clusters of three burials of water tradesmen within a day or two during both summer and winter months, indicating the possible deaths of a keel crews at work. The estimates of the size of the keelmen's community from known evidence of coal export volumes appears to give very reasonable comparisons with those figures appearing in the literature, particularly during the eighteenth century. Estimates made of the population of the parish of All Saints, and Newcastle as a whole, were made using both burial and marriage registers, and, as expected, the degree of under-registration associated with religious dissent affected the figures derived from burial registers, with the marriage registers providing the basis for a more reliable estimate. The changing pattern of the different trades in the last 50 years of the eighteenth century was shown in the parish registers. However, throughout this period of accelerating change the water tradesmen remained a significant part of the working community in the parish. Comparison of Newcastle with other port cities in Britain and abroad during the seventeenth and eighteenth centuries is difficult, because there are so few good studies of population dynamics in such cities during this period. Most of the detailed studies relate to the very rapid growth in such cities during the nineteenth and early twentieth centuries, the most detailed account being that of Portsmouth and Gosport between 1650 and 1900, where the population dynamics were complicated by the Admiralty connection.[2] The majority of those cities we now think of as major ports, including Liverpool and Glasgow did not begin to grow substantially until later in the eighteenth century, continuing into the nineteenth and early twentieth century.

It is perhaps more appropriate to compare the water trades communities along the Tyne to other similar riverside communities in England, however the literature concerning communities of water trades people living along rivers in England during the seventeenth and eighteenth centuries is not extensive. One of the most notable contributions is *Fisher Row* by Mary Prior, in which she examines the communities of fishermen, bargemen and canal boatmen in Oxford between 1500 and 1900.[3] The Thames bargemen are the group that bear the closest similarity in work and lifestyle to the most prominent water tradesmen on the Tyne, the keelmen, in that their main function was the

---

[2] B. Stapleton, 'The Admiralty Connection: Port Development and Demographic Change in Portsmouth, 1650–1900', in *Population and Society in Western European Port Cities c. 1650–1939*, ed. R. Lawton and R. Lee (Liverpool: Liverpool University Press, 2002), pp. 212–51.

[3] M. Prior, *Fisher Row: Fishermen, Bargemen, and Canal Boatmen in Oxford, 1500–1900* (Oxford: Clarendon Press, 1982).

transport of heavy loads up and down the Thames in barges, which carried about 70 tons of cargo. However, the upper river Thames near Oxford was a very different environment from the tidal Tyne. By the eighteenth century the Thames was a navigable waterway through to London, which for the majority of its course was not tidal and had relatively few obstructions to water borne traffic. There also appear to be differences in the community lifestyle. Although it was on the banks of the canal in the centre of Oxford, Fisher Row appeared to provide the opportunity for stable family groups of bargemasters to establish dynasties lasting many years, with new recruits to the trade often coming in apprenticeships to young men from families involved in other local trades. In addition, many of the bargemasters were people of some substance in the town of Oxford, some even becoming freemen. In contrast, the water trades community along the Tyne, being part of a growing industrial community, was sustained partly by immigration. Throughout the period under study the keelmen of the Tyne were regarded as relatively socially inferior, were actively prevented from forming their own Company of Keelmen and were certainly never in the position to become freemen of Newcastle.[4] The extent to which trade-related dynasties developed in a manner similar to Fisher Row is unclear; certainly no similar family trees have been uncovered for members of the water trades on the Tyne.

A study of riverside communities based on the Thames by David Blomfield,[5] explored the community of boatmen on the upper tidal Thames between Teddington and Chiswick. Once again, in a manner similar to that described by Mary Prior in *Fisher Row*, the watermen on the lower Thames became tradesmen of some significance with the support of the London Company of Watermen and Lightermen, to which most were apprenticed in the early stages of their career, subsequently becoming members. What was striking about these water tradesmen was that when their business circumstances changed, with the introduction of steam tugs and larger towed barges to replace their manually operated barges and boats, they were able to alter the nature of their trade. The majority continued in a related aspect of their water trade, and on balance they were in a stronger position at the end of the nineteenth century than they had been in 1750. This contrasts starkly with the Tyneside keelmen, whose role in the community as a whole was perceived as much more menial than that of

---

[4] J. Brand, *The History and Antiquities of the Town of Newcastle Upon Tyne*, 2 vols (London, 1789), pp. 261, 361.

[5] D. Blomfield, 'Tradesmen of the Thames: Success and Failure among the Watermen and Lightermen Families of the Upper Tidal Thames 1750–1901' (PhD diss., Kingston University, 2006).

their counterparts on the Thames, and whose trade was effectively abolished by the introduction of steam traction in the mid-nineteenth century.[6] In addition the relative lack of a significant number of surviving records about individual water tradesmen equivalent to those of the London Company of Watermen and Lightermen, makes tracing the detailed history of individual Tyne keelmen and watermen very difficult, although not impossible. Fortunately, the records that do survive did allow some light to be thrown upon those in both the upper and lower strata of those elements of society involved in the river-related trades in Newcastle and along the Tyne.

Water trades communities along other rivers in England have also been examined, including Kings Lynn. Fiona Wood examined the community of boatmen living and working around that port, which appears to have some similarities with the Tyne in terms of the relationships between merchants and boatmen. Like the Tyne keelmen, the boatmen were paid for their work by the voyage, apparently supplemented by cheap beer. However, unlike the keelmen on the Tyne, the Kings Lynn boatmen appeared to be regarded as responsible members of the community, often owning the boats they used; some even became wealthy land owners with wills indicating property amounting to £600.[7] Similarly, Barrie Trinder described in some detail the water trades community along the River Severn, in particular around Bridgnorth, where there was a substantial community associated with the river trade for whom a large amount of information survives, including probate inventories.[8] Trinder describes a community consisting of trading boat owners who owned the main form of river transport, barges, many of which were powered by square sails and were known as Trows.[9] These boat owners were people of some wealth and status in the community, often owning more than one barge. There were also some single-barge owners, who owned and worked their own barges and were

---

[6] J.M. Fewster, 'The Last Struggles of the Tyneside Keelmen', *Durham University Journal*, 55 (1963), pp. 5–15; D.J. Rowe, 'The Decline of the Tyneside Keelmen in the Nineteeth Century', *Northern History*, 4 (1969), pp. 111–31.

[7] Blomfield, 'Tradesmen of the Thames', 37, quoting F.J. Wood, 'Inland Transport and Distribution in the Hinterland of Kings Lynn, 1760–1840' (PhD diss., Cambridge University, 1992).

[8] B. Trinder, *Barges and Bargemen: A Social History of the Upper Severn Navigation 1660–1900* (Chichester: Phillimore, 2005).

[9] M. Stammers, *Sailing Barges of the British Isles* (Stroud: The History Press, 2008), pp. 109–21. The Severn Trow appeared in several forms, including a sailing barge with a square sail on a single-mast that worked on the upper reaches of the Severn, and a more sophisticated version, more like a sailing ship with more than one mast and several sails that worked in the Severn estuary.

much less wealthy; probate records show very modest estates, and they often held leasehold tenements. It would appear that many of the river workers, who included those crewing the trows and those servicing them at the staiths, were poor, and some were active in food riots in 1693.[10] It is clear that until the advent of the railways in the nineteenth century the river was integral to the survival of the community in Bridgnorth, being a main route for transport of both people and cargo to and from the larger towns close to the Severn estuary. In this aspect, it bears many similarities to Newcastle and its dependence on the Tyne for transport and communications, and it is apparent that a complex trading and business network had developed in Bridgenorth involving a wider social and economic spectrum than was apparent in the studies of Oxford and the upper tidal Thames.

The study of the ownership of working boats and ships on the lower River Tyne in the seventeenth and eighteenth centuries provided some new and interesting perspectives on the trading and investment of the time. The results were, of necessity, a reflection of the evidence available from the surviving probate inventories. Notwithstanding these limitations, there was data from sufficient inventories to draw some very clear qualitative conclusions, and provide a basis for a number of legitimate, but cautious quantitative conclusions. Many of the owners of small numbers of working boats were of quite modest means, including some watermen, with the value of their boat contributing the vast majority of their wealth. The owners of shares in ships often had a portfolio of shares in quite a large number of ships, each of quite modest individual value, but in total amounting to quite a large sum; this total sum was however often much less than half of the total estate. The results of the examination of the distribution of boat and ship ownership did yield some surprises. While it was no surprise to find that Merchants and Hostmen featured prominently in the list of those who owned both working boats and ships, the unexpected finding of the study was that among the major contributors, and significant owners of keels, were the shipwrights who built them. The large numbers owned were more than would be anticipated if their only role was as makers of keels, and it is now apparent that they derived an income by hiring keels to those who used them. Many of the shipwrights additionally had significant ownership of shares in ships, apparently maintaining a financial interest in the ownership and performance of the ships they had built. This contribution of shipwrights to these trading networks has not been described before, and this study demonstrates the extent of their participation in the wider business and trading networks that existed on the

---

[10] Trinder, *Barges and Bargemen*, p. 51.

River Tyne. The wide discrepancies between the estate sizes of those who owned boats or ships and those who did not, in all of the occupational groups studied, may be indicative of a social and economic hierarchy within each of the different occupational groups. It would be helpful to compare the patterns of working boat and ship ownership with that which must have occurred in other port cities. Unfortunately, there is very little published work examining ship and boat ownership before The Registration Act of 1786. Ville, in particular, has explored ship ownership, noting how the Act appeared to stimulate an era of professional ship ownership using the Henley family in London as an example.[11] Prior to The Registration Act details of ship ownership were not well recorded, making study very difficult. The use of probate inventories as a source has given us some insight into the diversity of ship ownership, but due to the limited survival of this resource will never give us a complete picture. Studies of ship ownership in other ports in England before The Registration Act, including London, Bristol and Liverpool, give a similarly limited picture, although Minchinton suggested that Bristol citizens were more concerned with overseas and especially transoceanic shipping, and as a result never owned more than 30 coastal ships.[12]

The rapid growth in the local economy of Newcastle and its hinterland resulted in the development of a flourishing middle class of merchants and tradesmen. This in turn created a demand for household and personal consumables that might both make life at home more comfortable and embellish personal appearance, in turn improving perceptions of their relative status in the community.[13] This demand for consumables, which stimulated the import and export trade into the river Tyne, was revealed by the wide range of commodities shown in the transactions that were discovered in the Newcastle Port Books. These port books provided an illuminating insight into the nature and volume of coastal and overseas trade out of Newcastle during the first half of the eighteenth

---

[11] S.P. Ville, *English Shipowning During the Industrial Revolution: Michael Henly and Son, London Shipowners 1770–1830* (Manchester: Manchester University Press, 1987).

[12] S.P. Ville, 'Patterns of Shipping Investment in the Port of Newcastle Upon Tyne, 1750–1850', *Northern History*, 25 (1989), pp. 205–21; W.E. Minchinton, 'Bristol – Metropolis of the West in the Eighteenth Century', *Transactions of the Royal Historical Society*, 5th ser., 4 (1954), pp. 69–89. M. Stammers, 'Ships and Port Management at Liverpool before the Opening of the First Dock in 1715', Transactions of the Historical Society of Lancashire and Cheshire, 156 (2007), pp. 27–50.

[13] L. Scammell, 'Was the North East Different from Other Areas? The Property of Everyday Consumption in the Late Seventeenth and Early Eighteenth Centuries', in *Creating and Consuming Culture in North-East England, 1660–1830*, ed. H. Berry and J. Gregory (Aldershot: Ashgate, 1996), pp. 12–23; Berry, 'Creating Polite Space: The Organisation and Social Function of Newcastle Assembly Rooms', in *ibid.*, pp. 120–40.

century. The analysis by Hussey of the Port Books of Bristol and the other ports around the Bristol Channel made an interesting comparison with Newcastle.[14] Both were seaports of long standing but with very different backgrounds. Bristol's success was based on a strategic position with good access to the sea with a variety of distant overseas and local coastal trading links, combined with easy access by both river and road to the natural resources of a large area of southern England. Based on this position a flourishing manufacturing and trading community had developed, enabling Bristol to become one of the largest commercial and trading centres in the country.[15] Newcastle had a similarly long history, but, in contrast to Bristol, its establishment was based solely on the exploitation of local natural resources. The large volume and relatively low cost of coal, together with the relative isolation of Newcastle in the North of England, stimulated the development of its thriving port, the evidence of the port books indicating that Newcastle had over four times the number of coastal outward shipments as Bristol and three times the number of overseas outward shipments. The profile of the respective trading patterns of the towns were significantly different, however; the main differences were that the Bristol shipments tended to be of relatively high value per-unit volume, such as tea and sugar, when compared with the coal, glass and grindstone trade from Newcastle, which was relatively high volume but low value.[16] The consequence of this difference was that the local economic impact of the higher-value Bristol trade was much more substantial than that of the Newcastle coal trade. A further interesting contrast between Newcastle and other port cities in England during the seventeenth and eighteenth centuries is that Newcastle, uniquely, was dependent for its trading success largely upon a local resource – coal – whereas other ports, such as Hull, London, Bristol and Liverpool, were each at the centre of extensive inland communications networks of rivers, canals and roads that directed commodities to and from the ports from a much wider hinterland.[17]

The extraordinary detail contained in the diary of Ralph Jackson has given us the opportunity to gain a contemporary perspective of life at the centre of the

[14] D. Hussey, *Coastal and River Trade in Pre-Industrial England: Bristol and Its Region 1680–1730* (Exeter: Exeter University Press, 2000).

[15] Minchinton, 'Bristol – Metropolis of the West', pp. 69–89; T.S. Willan, *The English Coasting Trade, 1600–1750* (Manchester: Manchester University Press, 1938), p. 171.

[16] J. Ellis, 'The "Black Indies": The Economic Development of Newcastle, c. 1700–1840', in *Newcastle Upon Tyne: a Modern History*, ed. R. Lancaster and B. Colls (Chichester: Phillimore, 2001)', p. 2.

[17] R. Davis, *The Trade and Shipping of Hull, 1500–1700* (Beverley: East Yorkshire Local History Society, 1964); Stammers, 'Ships and Port Management at Liverpool'; Minchinton, 'Bristol – Metropolis of the West'.

trading community in Newcastle in the middle of the eighteenth century. This diary, although it related only to one small, if important, part of this chain, the hostman, provides an overall view of all the different aspects of the water trades on the river Tyne, and, in some respects, summarizes the complex relationships between the river itself, the river-related trades and the community who lived and worked there. Ralph's accounts of the daily work of the hostman have been shown to relate very closely to the other sources of information, particularly the Port Books and the Chamberlains' Accounts, emphasizing the concordance between these different sources in producing a picture of the workings of this aspect of the coal trade in the eighteenth century. In addition, the diary highlighted the detailed workings of the trade and showed the dynamics of some of those business networks and relationships that fluctuated throughout the seventeenth and eighteenth centuries under the influence of the changing demand for coal.

A feature of the coastal trading out of Tyne was the significant proportion of ships that carried substantial quantities of general cargo in addition to coal to and from many of its destination ports including London. This has not been described in such detail in other accounts of the history of Newcastle and the Tyne, but does have significant implications for the way the river traffic worked and the functions it was intended to perform. In particular, a key reason colliers loaded coal close to the mouth of the Tyne was that the river was said to be too shallow and tortuous to allow the larger ships to come up the river to load. If this was indeed the case, it seems implausible that those ships carrying general cargo would be loaded with that cargo higher up the river, then moved to the mouth of the river to load the coal on top of the general cargo. It is more likely that the general cargo was loaded after the relatively dirty bulk coal at the same anchorage, implying that a keel or other working boat brought the cargo to the ship for loading. This implies a broader spectrum of activity by the keels and those who worked and managed them; indeed we have already seen that some keels were involved in the shipment of ballast to the ballast shores. In the Ralph Jackson diaries there are some references to the hostman helping ships' captains arrange other more general cargoes which were transported to the ships by keel, which may be yet another reflection of the wide range of shipping and trading activity that appears in the port books. Although we know that Newcastle had what has been described as a large and commodious quay, which was frequented by many ships, we also know that the quay was eight miles up the river from the mouth of the Tyne; although quite large ships could navigate their way up to Newcastle, this might take some time, even with favourable tides and winds. It is reasonable to assume that many ships' masters preferred to stay near the mouth of the river to load their cargo, as this would save time and potential risk of stranding while sailing up and down the river, particularly if the river became congested with numerous other ships trying to navigate the waterway.

The fundamental importance of the free movement of coal and other commodities up and down the river Tyne to the economy of the region cannot be underestimated. It was a particular feature of trade on the Tyne, and essential to the development of Newcastle in the seventeenth and eighteenth centuries, as the major coal-exporting centre that supplied the growing demands for energy from London and much the rest of the country. This would not have been possible without the skill and flexibility of the local river tradesmen who were essential to the handling of so much of the flow of material to and from the waiting ships, thus enabling the whole process to succeed. The evidence arising from the additional primary sources does indicate that the range of trade and its related activities in Newcastle and along the River Tyne was much more extensive than has sometimes been suggested. Indeed the magnitude of the import and re-export of overseas and coastal general cargo other than coal, suggests that the merchants of Newcastle had succeeded in expanding the breadth of their trade to make the port an entrepôt of some significance. The water trades community itself has been shown to be more complex than previously thought, and rather than being a purely seasonal and itinerant community, it became a growing and stable community supported by inward migration, both from Scotland and locally, consistent with patterns found in other growing urban and industrial societies. One of the challenges of any historical reappraisal is collating the vast amount of information contained in primary sources such as probate inventories and Port Books. This is sometimes limited either due to loss of documents, or if surviving, to their physical frailty, which may in many cases lead to serious difficulty in interpretation such that, in many cases, it may be possible to make only a qualitative rather than a quantitative evaluation. As technologies improve it is to be hoped that many more of these sources will become more easily available and readable, potentially leading to a wider understanding of this important area of trade in early modern England.

The lessons to be learned from this reappraisal of the historiography of Newcastle upon Tyne during the seventeenth and eighteenth centuries include the value of incorporating the widest range of primary sources into such an investigation. The previous historiographies of Newcastle depended very heavily on a single primary source originating from a relatively small, though important, group within the community. This initial approach provided a very colourful picture of the town at this critical period in its development, but there is the risk that such a restricted perspective may not provide the full story. This view is confirmed by the way in which the detail contained in the additional primary sources used in this reappraisal has not only served to clarify and expand our understanding of many aspects of the development of the town itself during this critical period, but has also enabled a clearer understanding of the place of Newcastle relative to other towns and ports elsewhere in Britain and abroad. The persistent failure of the Burgesses of the town of Newcastle to improve the state of the River Tyne continued until the middle of the nineteenth century, when, because of competition from other ports, it became such a threat to the local economy that a number of Tyne Improvement Acts were passed from the mid nineteenth century onwards. These enabled the dredging and straightening of the river, and the building of piers at Tynemouth and South Shields, which shaped the river as we know it today.

Appendix

Ships 'Fixed' by Newcastle Hostman Jefferson between March and December 1756 as described in the Ralph Jackson Diaries

Ship	Ship's Master	Diary[a]	Port Book[b]	Chamberlains' Accounts[c]
John & Mary of Whitby	John Galilee	1/3	4/3, London 114	1/3, Ball.Will. 40, Cl 110
		9/4	13/4. London, 114	17/5, Ball. Anth 24 Cl 110
				7/5, B Will. 30. Cl 110
				16/6 Ball. Burd. 50,Cl 112
		8/7	8/7 London 116	8/7 Ball. Will. 52, Cl 112
		3/8	2/8 London 115	2/8 Ball. Will. 50, Cl 112
		1/9	1/9 London 112	1/9 Ball. Will. 50, Cl 112
		28/9	28/9 London 119	
Samuel of London	Joseph Aust	2/3	2/3 London 118	2/3 Ball. Will. 60, Cl 118
Warren of London	Joseph Martin	4/3	13/3 London 105	
Myrtilla	Josiah Martin	17/3		
Old Fortune of Whitby	Fergus Foster	5/4	7/4 London 85	
		8/9	8/9 London 88	
William & Mary of London	James Tippell	9/4	12/4 London 24	12/4 Ball. Will. 14, Cl 24
		5/6	8/6 Maldon 27	5/6 Ball. Will. 14, Cl 28

Ship	Ship's Master	Diary[a]	Port Book[b]	Chamberlains' Accounts[c]
		2/7	14/7 Maldon 27 +Flagstones & Bottles	14/7 Ball. Will. 16, Cl 28
				21/8 No Ballast, Cl 27
		27/9	1/10 Maldon 27 + 600 doz bottles	1/10 Ball. Anth. 14, Cl 24
		16/11		22/11, No Ballast, Cl 26
Elizabeth of Scarboro	William Smith	15/4	24/4 London 110 + 36 fothers of lead	3/6 Ball. B'ling. 30, Cl 108
Two Brothers of Newcastle	Thomas Lammas	3/5	3/5 Yarmouth 36	
		15/9		
		17/10	20/10 Yarmouth 36	
Brilliant Star	Nicholas Frampton	10/5	15/5 Portsmouth 60	15/5 Ball. Jarr. 76, Cl 60
		23/7	23/7 Poole 60	22/7 Ball. Jarr. 60. Cl 60
Good Intent	Edward Dillon	10/5	18/5 Falmouth 80	
Betsy of Pool	Robert Rickarby	2/6	9/6 Poole 67	7/6 Ball. Will. 50, Cl 64
		29/7	4/8 Poole 64	
		27/9		
Contents Increase	Peter Jackson	2/7	6/7 London 169	6/7 Ball. Burd. 54, Cl 160
Joseph & Samuel	Samuel Brown	8/7	8/7 Lynn 36 + 1 Grindstones	8/7 Ball. Jarr. 24, Cl 36
				23/8 Ball. Jarr. 24, Cl 36
Samuel and Robert of Yarmouth	William Sargeant	27/10	28/10 London 156	
Molly of Ipswich	John Cuffley	9/7	13/7 Ipswich 64	
		16/8	19/8 Ipswich 64	
Fortune of Yarmouth	William Hillam	29/7	2/8 Harwich 64	2/8 Ball. Anth. 20, Cl 52
		26/8	30/8 London 52	30/8, Ball. Will. 26, C 50

Appendix

Ship	Ship's Master	Diary[a]	Port Book[b]	Chamberlains' Accounts[c]
		27/9	1/10 London 50	1/10, Ball. Will. 20, Cl 50
		15/11	15/11 Yarmouth 52	15/11, Ball. Will. 30, Cl 48
Triton of Whitby	Richard Knaggs	29/7	4/8 London 164	6/10, Ball. Will. 60, Cl164
		5/10	5/10 London 96	6/10, Ball. Jarr 80, Cl 144
Luke & Nelly	John Clifton	10/8	13/8 Lynn 32 + 24 Cinders	13/8 No Ballast, Cl 32
		5/9	18/9 Lynn 42 + 4 Cinders	18/9 No Ballast, Cl 40
Joseph & Samuel of Bridport	James Brown	23/8	23/8 Lynn 36	
Diamond	Samuel Campion	24/8	27/8 London 94	
		11/10		
		18/11	23/11 London 88	
Hannah of Whitby	William Galillee	17/9	17/9 London 76	
		20/10	20/10 Harwich 76	
William of Whitby	William Richardson	18/9	18/9 London 72	18/9, Ball. Jarr. 30, Cl 68
Thomas & Rachel of Whitby	Nathaniel Campion	17/10	30/10 London 218	
York of York	John Edmonds	20/10	20/10 London 97	
Edward of Scarboro	Thomas Russell	11/11	9/11 London 209	10/11, Ball. Will. 64, L'ming. 40, Cl 208
Total Entries		50	46	33

Note: (a) The dates in the Table represent the dates in the diaries when the ships and masters were identified. There were a number of entries in the Chamberlains' Accounts where ships 'fixed' by Jefferson were not mentioned in the diaries. (b) The Port Book entries show the date of the entry, which was not always the same as the diary entry, and the destination together with the amount of coal carried in Newcastle chaldrons. Any other cargo also identified. (c) The Chamberlains' Account entries show the date of the shipment, those entries which were retrospective show the date of the entry in brackets; Ballast =Ball., The Ballast shores were; Will.= Willington, Jarr. = Jarrow, Anth. = St Anthony's, B'ling = Brandling, Burdo. = Burdons, L'ming = Laming. The coal was described in Newcastle Chaldrons = Cl, and in some cases the amounts shown were slightly less than those shown for the same shipment recorded in the port books.

Bibliography

Archival Sources

The Borthwick Institute, University of York:
    The Prerogative Court of York (PCY) Probate Inventories
The British Library (BL):
    Burney Collection of Newspapers
    Newcastle Courant, 1725, 1756
Durham University Library, (DUL):
    Durham Probate Records, GB 033 DPRI. 1600–1750
    Durham Probate Inventories in DPRI/1. 1600–1750
Eighteenth Century Collections Online:
    The Case of the Poor Keelmen of Newcastle upon Tyne (London, ?1712)
    A Farther Case of the Poor Keelmen of Newcastle upon Tyne (London, ?1712)
Newcastle Libraries and Information Service, Local Studies Section (NCL/LS):
    The Bell Collection:
        John Bell, Collections Relative to the River Tyne its Trade and the Conservancy, Vols 1 and 2. L942.8, T987B
    Parish Registers (Transcriptions), L929 3/N536:
        Gateshead
        Jarrow/ Heworth
        Longbenton
        Newburn
        Newcastle All Saints
        Newcastle St Andrews
        Newcastle St Johns
        Newcastle St Nicholas
        South Shields
        Tynemouth
        Wallsend
        Whickham

Local Newspapers:
    Newcastle Courant, 1725, 1756
Newcastle University, Robinson Library, Special Collections:
    Port of Newcastle upon Tyne, *Rules and Regulations to be Observed by the Water Bailiff's Boatmen, by the Messengers Employed on Board of Ballast Keels, by the Masters of Ships and by Ballast Keelmen, and Others Employed in the Delivery of Ballast in the River Tyne* (Newcastle upon Tyne: Port of Newcastle, 1830), Friends 57
The National Archive (TNA):
    The Prerogative Court of Canterbury (PCC), Newcastle and District Probate Inventories 1600– 1750 PROB 3, 4, 5, 16, 31 and 32
    Exchequer Kings Remembrancer, E/190:
        Newcastle Port Books: 1698–99. TNA: E/190/207/4
        Newcastle Port Books: 1702–03 TNA: E/190/209/1
        Newcastle Port Books: 1755–56.
        —, Coastal Outwards: TNA: E/190/256/9
        —, Overseas Inward and Outward. TNA: E/190/257/5
Teeside Archives:
    Diaries of Ralph Jackson, U/WJ/1–6
Tyne Wear Archives and Museums (TWAM):
    Papers Relating to Ralph Gardner
    Keelmen's Papers, GU. 394 (Part MF). 1160
    Newcastle Chamberlains' Accounts of Payments and Disbursements, MD.NC/FN/1/1/65, MD.NC/FN/1/1/68,MD.NC/FN/1/1/108
    Newcastle Common Council Books, 589, 4–16
    Newcastle Quarter Sessions Papers, QS.NC, Part MF
    H. Moll Map of River Tyne 1650, dx275.4
    Greenvile Collins Chart of the Tyne 1693, d.ncp.5.1
    Map of the Tyne 1700–1750, d.ncp.5.2
    Map of the Tyne 1765, d.ncp.5.3
    Corbridge, Plan of Newcastle, 1723, 825
    Bielby map of Newcastle 1788, d.ncp.2.8
    Records of Ballast Hills Burial Ground, MF
    Records of the Company of Hostmen of Newcastle upon Tyne. GU.HO.298
    Records of the Company of Shipwrights of Newcastle upon Tyne. GU.SH (Part Microfilm (MF))
    Records of the Company of Merchant Venturers of Newcastle upon Tyne,

GU.MA.298:
All Saints Parish Settlement Records, MF.356.
All Saints Parish Overseers Accounts, MF.349.

Printed Primary Sources

Akenhead, D., *The Picture of Newcastle Upon Tyne*, Facsimile Reprint (London: E & W Books, 1969; original, 1807).
Anon., *The Case of the Poor Skippers and Keelmen of Newcastle, Truly Stated: With Some Remarks on a Printed Paper Call'd and Pretended to Be Their Case* (London, 1712), in Eighteenth Century Collections Online
—, *A Farther Case Relatif to the Poor Keelmen of Newcastle* (London, 1712), in Eighteenth Century Collections Online
—, *Port of Newcastle Upon Tyne: Rules and Regulations 1830* (Newcastle upon Tyne: Clayton Town Clerk, 1830).
—, *The Shipowner's Manual; or a Seagoing Man's Assistant* (Newcastle upon Tyne: D. Akenhead, 1795).
Baillie, J., *An Impartial History of the Town and County of Newcastle upon Tyne and Its Vicinity* (Newcastle upon Tyne: Vint and Anderson, 1801).
Bourne, H., *The History of Newcastle Upon Tyne* (Newcastle upon Tyne: John White, 1736; rep., Newcastle upon Tyne: Frank Graham, 1980).
Brand, J., *The History and Antiquities of the Town of Newcastle Upon Tyne*, 2 vols (London, 1789).
Burn, R., *The Justice of the Peace, and Parish Officer*, 4 vols (London: Printed by W. Strachan and M. Woodfall for T. Cadell, 1772).
Campbell, R., *The London Tradesman*, Vol. 1 (London: T. Gardener, 1747; Reprint, Newton Abbot: David and Charles, 1969).
Charleton, R.J., *Newcastle Town*, 4th ed. (London: Walter Scott, 1885; rep., 1978).
Defoe, D., *A Tour Thro' the Whole Island of Great Britain*, Vol. 2 (London, 1726; reprint London: Frank Cass & Co., 1927, 1968).
Graunt, J., *Natural and Political Observations on the Bills of Mortality* (London, 1662; 3rd ed., 1665).
Gray, W.G., *Chorographia, or a Survey of Newcastle Upon Tyne* (Newcastle upon Tyne: Andrew Reid, 1883; orig. pubd Newcastle upon Tyne, 1649; Rep., Frank Graham 1970).

Hinde, J.H., 'On the Original Site and Progressive Extension of Newcastle Upon Tyne, with an Estimate of Its Population at Various Periods', *Archaeologia Aeliana*, 2nd ser., 3 (1859), pp. 53–64.
Holmes, J.H.H., *A Treatise on the Coal Mines of Durham and Northumberland* (London: Baldwin, Cradock and Joy, 1816).
Mackenzie, E., *Descriptive and Historical Account of the Town and County of Newcastle upon Tyne* (Newcastle upon Tyne: Mackenzie and Dent, 1827).
Taylor, T.J., 'The Archaeology of the Coal Trade', *Proceedings of the Archaeological Institute of Great Britain and Ireland at Newcastle* (1852).

Secondary Sources

Albert, W., *The Turnpike Road System in England 1663–1840* (Cambridge: Cambridge University Press, 1972).
Aldcroft, D. and M. Freeman, *Transport in the Industrial Revolution* (Manchester: Manchester University Press, 1983).
Aldridge, D., 'English East Coast Trade with the Baltic in the Closing Years of the Great Northern War 1714–1721', in *Britain and the Baltic*, ed. P. Salmon and T. Barrow (Sunderland: Sunderland University Press, 2003), pp. 119–30.
Arkell, T., 'Interpreting Probate Inventories', in *When Death Do Us Part*, ed. T. Arkell, N. Evans and N. Goose (Oxford: Leopard's Head Press, 2000), pp. 72–102.
—, 'Multiplying factors for estimating population totals from the hearth tax', *Local Population Studies*, 28 (1982), pp. 51–7.
—, 'The Probate Process', in *When Death Do Us Part*, ed. T. Arkell, N. Evans and N. Goose (Oxford: Leopard's Head Press, 2000), pp. 3–13.
—, N. Evans and N. Goose, eds, *When Death Do Us Part* (Oxford: Leopard's Head Press, 2000).
Ashton, T.S. and J. Sykes, *The Coal Industry in the Eighteenth Century* (Manchester: Manchester University Press, 1929).
Barke, M., 'The People of Newcastle: A Demographic History', in *Newcastle Upon Tyne, a Modern History*, ed. R. Colls and B. Lancaster (Chichester: Phillimore, 2001), pp. 133–66.
—, 'The Pre-Civil Registration Population of Newcastle Upon Tyne: Estimating Vital Events', *Northumbria University, Division of Geography and Environmental Management, Occasional Papers*, 37 (2000).
Barker, T.C. and D. Gerhold, *The Rise and Rise of Road Transport*, Economic History Society Series (Basingstoke: Macmillan, 1993).

Barrow, T., 'Corn, Carriers and Coastal Shipping: The Shipping Trade of Berwick and the Borders 1730–1830', *Journal of Transport History*, 21 (2000), pp. 6–27.

—, *The Whaling Trade of North-East England 1750–1850* (Sunderland: Sunderland University Press, 2001).

Beier, A.L. and R. Finlay, *The Making of the Metropolis: London 1500–1700* (London: Longman, 1986).

Berry H., 'Creating Polite Space: The Organisation and Social Function of Newcastle Assembly Rooms', in *Creating and Consuming Culture in North-East England, 1660–1830*, ed. H. Berry, and J. Gregory (Aldershot: Ashgate, 2004), pp. 120–40.

—, 'Sense and Singularity: The Social Experiences of John Marsh and Thomas Stutterd in Late-Georgian England', in *Identity and Agency in England, 1500–1800*, ed. J. Barry and H. French (Basingstoke: Palgrave, 2004).

— and J. Gregory, eds, *Creating and Consuming Culture in North-East England, 1660–1830* (Aldershot: Ashgate, 2004).

Beveridge, W., *Prices and Wages in England from the Twelfth to the Nineteenth Century* (London: Longmans, Green & Co., 1939).

Bond, M,. 'Materials for Transport History amongst the Records of Parliament', *Journal of Transport History*, 4, no. 1 (1959), pp. 37–52.

Bradley, L., 'An Enquiry into Seasonality in Baptisms, Marriages and Burials', *Population Studies from Parish Registers*, ed. Michael Drake (Matlock: Local Population Studies, 1982).

Brewer, J. and A. Bermingham, *The Consumption of Culture, 1600–1800: Image, Object, Text* (London: Routledge, 1995).

Brewer, J. and R. Porter, *Consumption and the World of Goods* (London: Routledge, 1993).

Buckatzsch, E.J., 'Places of Origin of a Group of Immigrants into Sheffield 1624–1799', *Economic History Review*, 2nd ser., 2 (1950), pp. 303–6.

Chalklin, C.W., *The Provincial Towns of Georgian England* (London: Edward Arnold, 1974).

Chartres, J.A., *Internal Trade in England 1500–1700* (London: Macmillan, 1977).

—, 'Spirits in the North East? Gin and Other Vices in the Long Eighteenth Century', in *Creating and Consuming Culture in North-East England, 1660–1830*, ed. H. Berry and J. Gregory (Aldershot: Ashgate, 2004), pp. 37–56.

Clark, P., *The Early Modern Town: a Reader* (London: Longman, 1976).

—, 'The "Mother Gin" Controversy in the Early Eighteenth *Century*', *Transactions of the Royal Historical Society*, 5th ser., 38 (1988), pp. 63–84.

—, *The Cambridge Urban History of Britain*, Vol. 2, *1540–1840* (Cambridge: Cambridge University Press, 2000)

Corfield, P., 'A Provincial Capital in the Late Seventeenth Century: the Case of Norwich', in *Crisis and Order in English Towns 1500–1700*, ed. P. Clark and P. Slack (London: Routledge, 1972), pp. 233–72.

—, 'Urban Development in England and Wales in the Sixteenth and Seventeenth Centuries', in *The Tudor and Stuart Town, 1530–1688: A Reader in English Urban History*, ed. J. Barry (London: Longman, 1990), pp. 35–62.

Cox J. and N. Cox, 'Probate 1500–1800: a System in Transition', in *When Death Do Us Part*, ed. T. Arkell, N. Evans and N Goose (Oxford: Leopard's Head Press,), pp. 14–37.

Crafts, N.F.R., *British Economic Growth During the Industrial Revolution* (Oxford: Clarendon Press, 1985).

Cromar, P., 'The Coal Industry on Tyneside 1715–1760', *Northern History*, 14 (1978), pp. 193–207.

D'Cruze, S., 'The Middling Sort in Eighteenth Century Colchester: Independance, Social Relations and the Community Broker', *The Middling Sort of People*, ed. J. Barry and C. Brooks (London: Palgrave, 1994), pp. 181–207.

Davies, J.C., 'Shipping and Trade in Newcastle Upon Tyne, 1294–1296', *Archaeologia Aeliana*, 4th ser., 31 (1953), pp. 175–204.

Davis, R., *The Rise of the English Shipping Industry in the Seventeenth and Eighteenth Centuries* (London: Macmillan, 1962).

—, *The Trade and Shipping of Hull, 1500–1700* (Beverley: East Yorkshire Local History Society, 1964).

—, *English Overseas Trade 1500–1700* (London: Macmillan, 1973).

Dear, I.C.B. and P. Kemp, eds, *The Oxford Companion to Ships and the Sea*, second edition (Oxford: Oxford University Press, 2005).

Dendy, F.W., *Extracts from the Records of the Merchant Adventurers of Newcastle upon Tyne*, Vols I–II, Surtees Society, 93, 101 (Durham: Andrews & Co., 1894–99).

—, *Extracts from the Records of the Company of Hostmen of Newcastle Upon Tyne*, Surtees Society, 105 (Durham: Published for the Society, 1901).

Dietz, B., *The Port and Trade of Early Elizabethan London: Documents* (London: London Record Society, 1972).

—, 'The North-East Coal Trade, 1550–1750: Measures, Markets and the Metropolis', *Northern History*, 22 (1986), pp. 280–94.

—, 'Overseas Trade and Metropolitan Growth', in *London 1500–1700: The Making of the Metropolis*, ed. A.L. Beier and R. Finlay (London: Longman 1986), pp. 114–40.

Drake, M., *Population Studies from Parish Registers* (Matlock: Local Population Studies, 1982).
—, *Time, Family and Community* (Oxford: Open University Press, 1994).
Dyos, H.J., 'Transport History in University Theses', *Journal of Transport History*, 4, no. 3 (1960), pp. 161–73.
—, 'Transport History in University Theses, 1959–63', *Journal of Transport History*, 7, no. 1 (1965), pp. 54–6.
— and D.H. Aldcroft, *British Transport* (Leicester: Leicester University Press, 1969).
Earle, Peter. *The Making of the English Middle Class: Business, Society and Family Life in London 1660–1730* (London: Methuen, 1989).
Ellis, J., 'The Decline and Fall of the Tyneside Salt Industry, 1660–1790: A Re-Examination', *Economic History Review*, 2nd ser., 33 (1980), pp. 45–58.
—, 'A Bold Adventurer: The Business Fortunes of William Cotesworth, c. 1668–1726', *Northern History*, 17 (1981), pp. 117–32.
—, *A Study of the Business Fortunes of William Cotesworth, c1668–1726*, (New York: Arno Press, 1981).
—, 'A Dynamic Society: Social Relations in Newcastle-Upon-Tyne 1660–1760', in *The Transformation of English Provincial Towns 1600–1800*, ed. P. Clark (London: Hutchinson & Co., 1984), pp. 191–227.
—, 'Cartels in the Coal Industry on Tyneside 1699–1750', *Northern History*, 34 (1998), pp. 134–48.
'The "Black Indies": The Economic Development of Newcastle, c. 1700–1840', in *Newcastle Upon Tyne: a Modern History*, ed. R. Lancaster and B. Colls (Chichester: Phillimore, 2001), pp. 1–26.
—, *The Georgian Town 1680–1840* (New York: Palgrave, 2001).
Engerman, S.L. and P.K. O'Brien, 'The Industrial Revolution in Global Perspective', *The Cambridge Economic History of Modern Britain.*, ed. R. Floud and P. Johnson (Cambridge: Cambridge University Press, 2004), pp. 451–64.
Fewster, J.M., 'The Keelmen of Tyneside in the Eighteenth Century', *Durham University Journal*, 50 (1957), Pt.1 pp. 24–33, Pt.2 pp. 66–75, Pt.3 pp. 111–23.
—, 'The Last Struggles of the Tyneside Keelmen', *Durham University Journal*, 55 (1963), pp. 5–15.
—, *The Keelmen of Tyneside: Labour Organisation and Conflict in the North-East Coal Industry, 1600–1830* (Woodbridge: Boydell & Brewer, 2011).
Finch, R., *Coals from Newcastle* (Lavenham: Terence Dalton, 1973).
Flinn, M.W., *The History of the British Coal Industry*, Vol. 2, *1700–1830: The Industrial Revolution* (Oxford: Oxford University Press, 1984).

Forster, E., *The Keelmen* (Newcastle upon Tyne: Frank Graham, 1970).
Fraser, C.M.,'Medieval Trading Restrictions in the North East', *Archaeologia Aeliana*, 4th ser., 39 (1961), pp. 135–50.
—, 'The Early Hostmen of Newcastle upon Tyne', *Archaeologia Aeliana*, 5th ser., 12 (1984), pp. 169–79.
—, 'The Masters and Mariners of Newcastle upon Tyne in the Late Seventeenth Century', *Archaeologia Aeliana*, 5th ser., 33 (2004), pp. 161–73.
— and K. Emsley, 'Newcastle Merchant Venturers from West Yorkshire', *Archaeologia Aeliana*, 5th ser., 6 (1978), pp. 117–29.
Freeman, M., R. Pearson and J. Taylor, 'Technological Change and Governance of Joint-Stock Enterprise in the Early Nineteenth Century: The Case of Coastal Shipping', *Business History*, 49 (2007), pp. 573–94.
Gibb, A., 'Industrialisation and Demographic Change: A Case Study of Glasgow, 1801–1914', in *Population and Society in Western European Port Cities, c. 1650–1939*, ed. R. Lawton and R. Lee (Liverpool: Liverpool University Press 2002), pp. 37–73.
Grassby, R., 'English Merchant Capitalism in the Late Seventeenth Century: The Composition of Business Fortunes', *Past & Present*, 46 (1970), pp. 87–107.
—, *The Business Community of Seventeenth-Century England* (Cambridge: Cambridge University Press, 1995).
Greenwell, W., *Wills and Inventories from the Registry of Durham, Part II*, Surtees Society, 38 (London: Surtees Society, 1860).
Griffiths, B., *Fishing and Folk, Life and Dialect on the North Sea Coast* (Newcastle upon Tyne: Northumbria University Press, 2008).
Grigg, D.B., 'E.G. Ravenstein and the "Laws of Migration"', *Journal of Historical Geography*, 2 (1977), pp. 41–51.
Guthrie, J., *The River Tyne, its History and Resources* (Newcastle upon Tyne: Andrew Reid, 1880).
Halcrow, E.M., 'Chamberlain's Accounts, Newcastle upon Tyne', *Journal of the Society of Archivists*, Vol. 1, Issue 10 (1955), pp. 289–91.
Harding, V., *The Dead and the Living in Paris and London, 1500–1670* (Cambridge: Cambridge University Press, 2002).
Hatcher, J., *The History of the British Coal Industry*, Vol. 1, *Before 1700: Towards the Age of Coal* (Oxford: Clarendon Press, 1993).
Hausman, W.J., 'Size and Profitability of English Colliers in the Eighteenth Century', *Business History Review*, 51 (1977), pp. 460–73.
—, 'Market Power in the London Coal Trade: The Limitation of the Vend, 1770–1845', *Explorations in Economic History*, 21 (1984), pp. 383–405.

—, 'Profitability of English Colliers in the Eighteenth Century, Reply to a Reappraisal', *Business History Review*, 58 (1984) pp. 121–5

Hewitt, F.S., 'Value to Economic Historians of the Buddle Papers', *Mining Engineer*, 25, 36 (1962), pp. 406–12.

Hey, D., *Packmen, Carriers and Packhorse Roads* (Leicester: Leicester University Press, 1980).

Hodgson, J., *Wills and inventories from the registry at Durham, Part III* Surtees Society, 112 (Durham: Surtees Society, 1906).

Hoon, E.E., *The Organization of the English Customs System* (Newton Abbot: David & Charles, 1968 [orig. pubd. 1938]).

Houston, R.A., *The Population History of Britain and Ireland 1500–1750* (Basingstoke: Macmillan, 1992).

Howell, R., *Newcastle Upon Tyne and the Puritan Revolution* (Oxford: Oxford University Press, 1967).

—, ed., *Monopoly on the Tyne, 1650–58: Papers Relating to Ralph Gardner* (Newcastle upon Tyne: Society of Antiquaries of Newcastle upon Tyne, 1978).

—, 'Newcastle and the Nation: The Seventeenth Century Experience', in *The Tudor and Stuart Town, 1530–1688: A Reader in English Urban History*, ed. J. Barry (London: Longman, 1990), pp. 274–96.

Hughes, E., *North Country Life in the Eighteenth Century: the North East, 1700–1750* (Oxford: Oxford University Press, 1952).

Humphrey-Smith, C.R., ed., *The Phillimore Atlas and Index of Parish Registers* (Chichester: Phillimore, 1984).

Hussey, D., *Coastal and River Trade in Pre-Industrial England: Bristol and Its Region 1680–1730* (Exeter: Exeter University Press, 2000).

Hyde, R., 'Seven Manuscript Thames Charts by Greenville Collins', *Journal of the Society of Archivists*, 5 (1974), pp. 38–40.

Jackman, W.T., *The Development of Transportation in Modern England* (London: Frank Cass & Co., 1962).

Jarvis, R.C., 'Sources for the History of Ports', *Journal of Transport History*, 3, no. 2 (1957), pp. 76–93.

—, 'The Appointment of Ports', *Economic History Review*, 2nd ser., 11 (1958), pp. 455–66.

—, 'Critical Historical Introduction', in E.E. Hoon, *The Organization of the English Customs System, 1696–1786* (Newton Abbot: David & Charles, 1968 [orig. publ. 1938]), pp. vii–xxvii.

Kitch, M.J., 'Capital and Kingdom: Migration to Later Stuart London', in *London 1500–1700: The Making of the Metropolis*, ed. A.L. Beier and R. Finlay (London: Longman, 1986.), pp. 224–51.

Kung, E., 'English Commercial Activity in Narva During the Second Half of the Seventeenth Century', in *Britain and the Baltic*, ed. P. Salmon and T. Barrow (Sunderland: Sunderland University Press, 2003), pp. 77–109.

Kussmaul, A., *A General View of the Rural Economy of England, 1538–1840* (Cambridge: Cambridge University Press, 1990).

Landau, N., 'The Regulation of Immigration: Economic Structures and Definitions of the Poor in Eighteenth-Century England', *The Historical Journal*, 33 (1990), pp. 541–72.

—, 'Who was subjected to the Laws of Settlement? Procedure under the Settlement Laws in Eighteenth-Century England', *Agricultural History Review*, 43 (1995), pp. 139–59.

Lane, J., *Apprenticeship in England, 1600–1914* (London: Routledge, 1996).

Langton, J., 'Residential Patterns in Pre-Industrial Cities: Some Case Studies from Seventeenth-Century Britain', *Transactions of the Institute of British Geographers*, 65 (1975), pp. 1–27; reprinted in . *The Tudor and Stuart Town, 1530–1688: A Reader in English Urban History*, ed. J. Barry (London: Longman, 1990), pp. 166–205.

Lasker, G.W. and D.F. Roberts, 'Secular Trends in Relationship as Estimated by Surnames: a Study of a Tyneside Parish', *Annals of Human Biology*, 9 (1982), pp. 299–307.

Laslett, P., 'Mean Household Size in England Since the Sixteenth Century', in *Household and Family in Past Times*, ed. P. Laslett and R. Wall (Cambridge: Cambridge University Press, 1972), pp. 125–58

Lawton, R., 'The Components of Demographic Change in a Rapidly Growing Port-City: The Case of Liverpool in the Nineteenth Century', in *Population and Society in Western European Port Cities, c. 1650–1939*, ed. R. Lawton and R. Lee (Liverpool: Liverpool University Press, 2002), pp. 91–123.

Lee, R. and R. Lawton, 'Port Development and the Demographic Dynamics of European Urbanization', in *Population and Society in Western European Port Cities, c. 1650–1939*, ed. R. Lawton and R. Lee (Liverpool: Liverpool University Press 2002), pp. 1–36

Levine, D. and K. Wrightson, *The Making of an Industrial Society: Whickham 1560–1765* (Oxford: Clarendon Press, 1991).

McCord, N., *North East England: the Region's Development, 1760–1960* (London: Batsford Academic, 1979).

—, *Strikes* (New York: St Martin's Press, 1980).

McGrath, P., *Merchants and Merchandise in Seventeenth-Century Bristol*, Bristol Record Society's Publications, xix (Bristol: Bristol Record Society, 1955)

McKendrick, N., J. Brewer and J.H. Plumb, *The Birth of the Consumer Society: The Commercialisation of Eighteenth-Century England* (London: Europa, 1982).

Macfarlane, A., *The Family Life of Ralph Josselin, a Seventeenth-Century Clergyman: an Essay in Historical Anthropology* (Cambridge: Cambridge University Press, 1970).

—, *The Diary of Ralph Josselin* (London: Oxford University Press, 1976).

Mascuch, M., *Origins of the Individualist Self: Autobiography and Self-Identity in England, 1591–1791* (Cambridge: Polity Press, 1997).

Matthews, W., *British Diaries 1442–1942* (London: Cambridge University Press, 1950).

Middlebrook, S., *Newcastle Upon Tyne: Its Growth and Achievement* (Newcastle upon Tyne: Newcastle Journal, 1950).

—, *Picture of Tyneside, or Life and Scenery on the River Tyne Circa 1830* (Newcastle upon Tyne: Oriel Press Ltd, 1969).

Minchinton, W.E., 'Bristol – Metropolis of the West in the Eighteenth Century', *Transactions of the Royal Historical Society*, 5th ser., 4 (1954), pp. 69–89.

Mitcalfe, W.S., 'The History of the Keelmen and Their Strike in 1822', *Archaeologia Aeliana*, 4th ser., 14 (1937), pp. 1–17.

Mokyr, J. 'Accounting for the Industrial Revolution', *The Cambridge Economic History of Modern Britain*, ed. R. Floud and P. Johnson (Cambridge: Cambridge University Press, 2004), pp. 1–27.

Morgan, G. and P. Rushton, *Rogues, Thieves and the Rule of Law: the Problem of Law Enforcement in North East England, 1718–1800* (London: University College London Press, 1998).

Muller, L., 'Britain and Sweden: The Changing Pattern of Commodity Exchange 1650–1680', in *Britain and the Baltic*, ed. P. Salmon and T. Barrow (Sunderland: Sunderland University Press, 2003), pp. 61–76.

Nef, J.U., *The Rise of the British Coal Industry*, 2 vols (London: George Routledge & Sons, 1932).

O'Brien, J.B., 'Population, Society and Politics in Cork from the Late-Eighteenth Century to 1900', in *Population and Society in Western European Port Cities, c. 1650–1939*, ed. R. Lawton and R. Lee (Liverpool: Liverpool University Press, 2002), pp. 326–46.

Osler, A.G., 'Newcastle's Last Mayoral Barge', *Archaeologia Aeliana*, 5th ser., 16 (1988), pp. 239–43.

—, 'Aspects of the Tyne's Overseas Trade as Evidenced by the Customs Bills of Entry, 1861–1880', *Archaeologia Aeliana*, 5th ser. 36 (2007), pp. 325–39.

— and A. Barrow, *Tall Ships, Two Rivers: Six Centuries of Sail on the Rivers Tyne and Wear* (Newcastle upon Tyne: Keepdate Publishing, 1993).

Overton, M., 'Prices from Probate Inventories', in *When Death Do Us Part*, ed. T. Arkell, N. Evans and N. Goose (Oxford: Leopard's Head Press, 2000), pp. 121–41.

—, J. Whittle, D. Dean and A. Hann, *Production and Consumption in English Households, 1600–1750* (London: Routledge, 2004).

Petty,W., 'Another Essay in Political Arithmetick Concerning the Growth of the City of London, 1682', *The Economic Writings of Sir William Petty*, ed. C.H. Hull (Cambridge: Cambridge University Press, 1899).

Phelps Brown, H. and S.V. Hopkins, *A Perspective of Wages and Prices* (London: Methuen & Co., 1981).

Ponsonby, A., *More English Diaries* (London: Methuen & Co., 1927).

—, *English Diaries* (London: Methuen & Co., 1925).

Pratt, E.A., *History of Inland Transport and Communication in England* (London: Kegan Paul, Trench, Truber & Co., 1912).

Prior, M., *Fisher Row: Fishermen, Bargemen, and Canal Boatmen in Oxford, 1500–1900* (Oxford: Clarendon Press, 1982).

Purdue, A.W., *Merchants and Gentry in North East England, 1650–1830* (Sunderland: Sunderland University Press, 1999).

Purdue, B., 'Ralph Carr: A Newcastle Merchant and the Baltic Trade in the Mid Eighteenth Century', in *Britain and the Baltic*, ed. P. Salmon and T. Barrow (Sunderland: Sunderland University Press, 2003), pp. 157–68.

Ridley, U., 'The History of Glass Making on the Tyne and Wear', *Archaeologia Aeliana*, 4th ser., 40 (1962), pp. 145–62.

Rimmer, W.G., 'The Evolution of Leeds', *Thoresby Society Transactions*, 50 (1967): pp. 91–2, 107–29.

Roberts, W.I., 'A Newcastle Merchant and the American Colonial Trade', *Business History Review*, 42 (1968), pp. 271–87.

Robinson, A.H.W., *Marine Cartography in Britain: a History of the Sea Chart to 1855* (Leicester: Leicester University Press, 1962).

Rowe, D.J., 'The Decline of the Tyneside Keelmen in the Nineteenth Century', *Northern History*, 4 (1969), pp. 111–31.

—, 'The Keelmen of Tyneside', *History Today*, 19 (1969), pp. 248–54.

—, *The Records of the Company of Shipwrights of Newcastle Upon Tyne 1622–1967*, Surtees Society, 181 (Gateshead: Northumberland Press for the Society, 1970).

Salmon, P. and T. Barrow, eds, *Britain and the Baltic* (Sunderland: Sunderland University Press, 2003).

Scammell, L., 'Was the North East Different from Other Areas? The Property of Everyday Consumption in the Late Seventeenth and Early Eighteenth

Centuries', in *Creating and Consuming Culture in North-East England, 1660–1830*, ed. H. Berry and J. Gregory (Aldershot: Ashgate, 1996), pp. 12–23.

Schwarz, L., 'Custom, Wages and Workload in England During Industrialization', *Past & Present*, 197 (2007), pp. 143–75.

Smith, R. *Sea-Coal for London* (London: Longmans, 1961).

Snell, K.D.M., 'Pauper Settlement and the Right to Poor Relief in England and Wales', *Continuity and Change*, 6 (1991), pp. 375–415.

Souden, D. 'Migrants and the Population Structure of Later Seventeenth-Century Provincial Cities and Market Towns', *The Transformation of English Provincial Towns 1600–1800*, ed. P. Clark (London: Hutchinson & Co., 1984).

Speck, W.A., *A Concise History of Britain* (Cambridge: Cambridge University Press, 1993).

Spufford, M. *Small Books and Pleasant Histories* (London: Methuen & Co., 1981).

—, *The Geat Reclothing of Rural England: Petty Chapmen and Their Wares in the Seventeenth Century* (London: The Hambledon Press, 1984).

Stammers, M., 'Ships and Port Management at Liverpool before the Opening of the First Dock in 1715', *Transactions of the Historical Society of Lancashire and Cheshire*, 156 (2007), pp. 27–50.

—, *Sailing Barges of the British Isles* (Stroud: The History Press, 2008).

Stapleton, B., 'The Admiralty Connection: Port Development and Demographic Change in Portsmouth, 1650–1900', in *Population and Society in Western European Port Cities, c. 1650–1939*, ed. R. Lawton and R. Lee (Liverpool: Liverpool University Press, 2002), pp. 212–51

Taylor, P. and A. Williams, 'The Newburn Wherries: Remnants of the River Tyne's Industrial Past', *Archaeologia Aeliana*, 5th ser., 39 (2010), pp. 401–25.

Taylor, T.J., 'Archaeology of the Coal Trade', *Proceedings of the Archaeological Institite of Newcastle upon Tyne* (1852), pp. 159–173.

Thornton, C.E., *Bound for the Tyne: Extracts from the Diary of Ralph Jackson, Apprentice Hostman of Newcastle Upon Tyne, 1749–1756* (Newcastle upon Tyne: Company of Hostmen of Newcastle upon Tyne, 2000).

Todd, M., 'Puritan Self-Fashioning: The Diary of Samuel Ward', *Journal of British Studies*, 31 (1992), pp. 236–64.

Trinder, B., *Barges and Bargemen: A Social History of the Upper Severn Navigation 1660–1900* (Chichester: Phillimore, 2005).

Turner, E.R., 'The Keelmen of Newcastle', *American Historical Review*, 21 (1916), pp. 542–5.

Vaisey, D., ed., *The Diary of Thomas Turner, 1754–1765* (Oxford: Oxford University Press, 1985).

Viall, H.R., 'Tyne Keels', *Mariner's Mirror*, 28 (1942), pp. 160–62.

Vickery, A., *The Gentleman's Daughter: Women's Lives in Georgian England* (New Haven: Yale University Press, 1998).

Ville, S.P. 'Size and Profitability of English Colliers in the Eighteenth Century, A Re-appraisal', *Business History Review*, 58 (1984), pp. 103–20.

—, *English Shipowning During the Industrial Revolution: Michael Henly and Son, London Shipowners 1770–1830* (Manchester: Manchester University Press, 1987).

—, 'Shipping in the Port of Newcastle 1780–1800', *Journal of Transport History*, 9 (1988), pp. 60–77.

—, 'Patterns of Shipping Investment in the Port of Newcastle Upon Tyne, 1750–1850', *Northern History*, 25 (1989), pp. 205–21.

Wade, J.F., 'The Overseas Trade of Newcastle Upon Tyne in the Late Middle Ages', *Archaeologia Aeliana*, 5th ser., 30 (1994), pp. 31–48.

Weatherill, L., *Consumer Behaviour and Material Culture in Britain, 1660–1760*, 2nd edition (London and New York: Routledge, 1996).

Welford, R., *History of Newcastle and Gateshead*, 5 vols (London: Walter Scott, 1885).

—, 'Newcastle Householders in 1665; Assessment of Hearth or Chimney Tax', *Archaeologia Aeliana*, 3rd ser., 7 (1911), pp. 49–76.

Whiting, W.R.G., 'The Newcastle Galley', *Archaeologia Aeliana*, 4th Series, 13 (1936), pp. 95–116.

Willan, T.S., *The English Coasting Trade, 1600–1750* (Manchester: Manchester University Press, 1938).

—, *Studies in Elizabethan Foreign Trade* (Manchester: Manchester University Press, 1959).

—, *River Navigation in England 1600–1750* (London: Frank Cass & Co., 1964).

—, *The Inland Trade* (Manchester: Manchester Universty Press, 1976).

Wood, H.M., *Wills and Inventories from the Registry at Durham, Part IV*, Surtees Society, 142 (Durham: Andrews for the Society, 1929).

Woodward, D., 'Sources for Maritime History (III): The Port Books of England and Wales', *Maritime History*, 3 (1973), pp. 147–65.

Wrightson, K., *English Society 1580–1680* (London: Hutchinson, 1982).

—, *Earthly Necessities: Economic Lives in Early Moderm Britain* (London: Yale University Press, 2000).

— and D. Levine, 'Death in Whickham', in *Famine, Disease and the Social Order in Early Modern Society*, ed. J. Walter and R. Schofield (Cambridge: Cambridge University Press, 1989), pp. 129–65.

—, *Poverty and Piety in an English Village, Terling, 1525–1700* (Oxford: Clarendon Press, 1995).

Wrigley, E.A., 'A Simple Model of London's Importance in Changing English Society and Economy, 1650–1750', *Past & Present*, 37 (1967), pp. 44–70.
—, 'Urban Growth and Agricultural Change: England and the Continent in the Early Modern Period', *Journal of Interdisciplinary History*, 15 (1985), pp. 683–728.
—, 'Country and Town: The Primary, Secondary and Tertiary Peopling of England in the Early Modern Period', *The Peopling of Britain, the Shaping of a Human Landscape*, eds P. Slack and R. Ward (Oxford: Oxford University Press, 2002), pp. 216–54.
—, 'British Population During the Long Eighteenth Century', *The Cambridge Economic History of Modern Britain*, ed. R. Floud and P. Johnson (Cambridge: Cambridge University Press, 2004), pp. 57–95.
—, 'English County Populations in the Later Eighteenth Century', *Economic History Review*, 2nd ser., 60 (2007), pp. 35–69.
—, 'Rickman Revisited: The Population Growth Rates of English Counties in the Early Modern Period', *Economic History Review*, 2nd ser. 62 (2009), pp. 711–35.
—, R.S. Davies, J.E. Oeppen and R.S. Schofield, *English Population History from Family Reconstituion, 1580–1837* (Cambridge: Cambridge University Press, 1997).
— and R.S. Schofield, *The Population History of England 1541–1871, a Reconstruction* (London: Edward Arnold, 1981).

Unpublished Theses

Basten, S., 'Registration Practices in Anglican Parishes and Dissenting Groups in Northern England 1770–1840', PhD diss., Cambridge University, 2008.
Blomfield, D., 'Tradesmen of the Thames: Success and Failure Among the Watermen and Lightermen Families of the Upper Tidal Thames 1750–1901', PhD diss., Kingston University, 2006.
D'Sena, P.A.M., 'Perquisites and Pilfering in the London Docks, 1700–1795', M.Phil. Thesis, Open University, 1986.
Elliott, N.R., 'Tyneside, a Study in the Development of an Industrial Seaport', PhD diss., Durham University, 1955.
Moller, A.W.R., 'The History of British Coal Mining 1500–1750', PhD diss., Oxford University, 1933.
Osler, A.G., 'Responding to Change: Shipping Deployments in the Baltic Trade of the Tyne 1860–1880', PhD diss., University of Hull, 2006.

Wood, F.J., 'Inland Transport and Distribution in the Hinterland of Kings Lynn, 1760–1840', PhD diss., Cambridge University, 1992.

Wright, P.D. 'Water Trades on the Lower River Tyne in the Seventeenth and Eighteenth Centuries', PhD diss., Newcastle University, 2011.

Electronic Resources

Baigent, E., 'Collins, Greenvile (d. 1694)', *Oxford Dictionary of National Biography* (Oxford: Oxford University Press, 2004; online edn, Sept 2010), www.oxforddnb.com.

Borthwick Institute for Archives. University of York, http://york.ac.uk/inst/bihr/.

Duffy, M., 'Duckett, Sir George, first baronet (1725–1822)', Oxford Dictionary of National Biography (Oxford: Oxford University Press, 2004, online edn Jan 2008), www.oxforddnb.com.

Eighteenth Century Collections Online, Gale Group, http://find.galegroup.com.

Essex, University of. 'Histpop – the Online Historical Population Reports Website', http://www.histpop.org/ohpr/servlet/.

Hyde, R., 'Buck, Nathaniel (1724–1759)', *Oxford Dictionary of National Biography* (Oxford: Oxford University Press, 2004), www.oxforddnb.com.

Hyde, R., 'Buck, Samuel (1696–1779)', *Oxford Dictionary of National Biography* (Oxford: Oxford University Press, 2004), www.oxforddnb.com.

The National Archives, http://nationalarchives.gov.uk.

Ralph Jackson's Diaries, Great Ayton History Society, www.greatayton.wikidot.com/ralph-jackson-diaries.

Reinhartz, D., 'Moll, Herman (1654?–1732)', *Oxford Dictionary of National Biography* (Oxford, Oxford University Press, 2004; online edn, 2008), www.oxforddnb.com.

Waller, P., 'Jackson, Ralph Ward (1806–1880)', *Oxford Dictionary of National Biography* (Oxford, Oxford University Press, 2004), www.oxforddnb.com.

Zon, B.M., 'Avison, Charles (bap. 1710–1770)', *Oxford Dictionary of National Biography*, (Oxford: Oxford University Press, 2004), http://www.oxforddnb.com.

Index

References to illustrations are in **bold**.

Aldridge, D. 122
All Saints parish
   burials, unregistered 68
   census data 77
   family groups, identification 76
   map **64**
   marriages 69, 70
      registers 69–70
   migration 69–73, 74, 76
   occupational profiles 77
   parish registers, limitations 63, 65
   pauper records 76
   population 67–8, 69, 70, 71, 74
   settlement records 75
   water trades 70, 71, 74, 76, 162
      occupations 66–7, 77
Amsterdam 109, 110, 121, 123, 125, 130
Anderson, Henry 16

Baillie, J. 50
ballast, definition xi
   see also Tyne, ballast
Ballast Assessor, duties 39–40
Ballast Office 39
Baltic trade
   Newcastle 107, 109, 124
   Ralph Carr 109–10
Barke, Michael 47, 74
barque
   cat 27
   definition xi
Basten, Stuart 63, 65
Bawtry, inland port 11
Bell Collection 37, 50, 58, 140, 151
Berry, Helen, and Gregory, Jeremy 107, 121
Blomfield, David 164

boatmen 67
Bourne, Henry 23, 37, 57, 58
   The History of Newcastle upon Tyne 35
Brandling, Lady 39
Bridgnorth, trading boat owners 165–6
Bristol
   Newcastle, shipments, comparison 131, 168
   population (1600–1801) 8
   port books 112, 130, 168
Britain
   Industrial Revolution 8, 9
   infrastructure 9
   population (1680–1801) 8
   see also England
British Linen Company 109
Buck, Samuel & Nathaniel
   Keels off Newcastle Quay 87, **88**
   The South East Prospect of Newcastle upon Tyne 33, **34**
Burgesses of Newcastle 4, 15, 23, 113
   Church, conflict 17
   monopoly of Tyne trade 17

can-house 142
   definition xi
   function 143–4, 157–8
can-money, complaints about 143, 158
can-woman 142, 158
   definition xi
Carr, Ralph, merchant 111
   American trade 110
   Baltic trade 109–10
chalder boat 89
   definition xi
chaldron (chalder) 89, 140

definition xi
Charles I, King of England 17
Charles II, King of England 17
Charleton, R.J. 50, 57
Chartres, J.A. 10, 11, 108
Clayton, Nathaniel 19
Cliffe, Thomas 4
coal boat 88, 89, 96
    definition xii
coal owners 2, 4
    cartels 20
coal trade 1
    early references 53–4
    and freemen 15
    and hostmen 14, 54–5
coastal transport, increase 11
collier brigs 1
Collins, Greenvile, Capt 24
    Tyne map 28, **29**
consumables
    demand for 107, 167
    in probate inventories 108
consumption, North East, boom 107, 111
conveyors 39
Corfield, P. 71
Cotesworth, William 60
Court of Probate Act (1857) 82
Customs House Shipping Records 81

Davies, Ralph 131
Defoe, Daniel, on Newcastle 7, 12
Dendy, F.W. 14, 15, 18, 49, 75
diaries, motives for keeping 133–4
    see also Jackson, Ralph, diaries

Elizabeth I, Queen of England 16
Ellis, Joyce 5, 20, 72, 114, 146
Endeavour, James Cook's ship 27
England
    transport patterns, development 9–10
    urban population (1600–1801) 8
Exchequer Port Books 5, 6, 111, 114, 115
    see also port books
Exeter, population (1600–1801) 8

Fewster, J.M. 4, 75

fittage 54, 81
    definition xii
fitters 18–19, 140, 143, 148, 157
    definition xii
Fitters Accounts 142

Gardner, Ralph 4
Gateshead 16
glass manufacturing, River Tyne 20, 38, 113–14
glossary xi–xv
Grassby, R. 102
Graunt, J. 67
Gray, William, *Chorographia, or a Survey of Newcastle Upon Tyne* 3, 15, 19
Great North Road 10
Guthrie, J. 23

Harding, Vanessa 67
Hatcher, John 2, 12, 55, 56
Hearth Tax returns 67
    Newcastle 45, 53
Hey, David 10
hostman 2, 4, 18, 73, 162
    and coal trade 14, 54–5
    day-to-day work 139–40, 169
    definition xii
    female 141, 142
    keelmen, conflict 145–6
    listing **59**, 60
    prestige position 100
    probate inventories 100
    regulations 19
    ship and boat ownership 100–101
    ships masters
        negotiations 140, 153
        services to 148–9
    workrate 54
Hostmen's Company 3, 18, 86, 100
    incorporation 16–17
    Orders and Minutes of 49
    records 4, 14
Howell, Roger 16
Hudspeth, Ann, female hostman 141
Hudspeth, Billy 138
Hull, seaborne trade 131

Hussey, D. 112, 114, 130, 168

Jackson, George 137
Jackson, Ralph 60
    apprenticeship 136, 137–8
        completion 156–7
    day-to-day work 149
    diaries 6, 133, 134
        excerpts 137, 138, 140, 141–2, 147–8, 152–3
        importance of 135, 136, 168–9
        ships 'fixed' by William Jefferson, list 173–5
    education 138, 155
    family 136
    keelmen, payment of 142, 143
    keels, work with 138–9, 140, 151–3
    musicianship 155
    religious character 155
    skills 151
    sociability 155–6
Jackson, Ralph Ward 136–7
Jackson, William Ward 136
Jefferson, John 158, 159
Jefferson, William 60, 135, 136, 138, 153, 158, 159
    ships 'fixed' by (1756) 173–5

keelmen (watermen) 1, 23, 39, 66, 67
    deaths 163
    definition xiii
    demise of occupation 146
    grain riots 145
    hostmen, conflict 145–6
    House of Commons, petition to 49–50
    industrial action 144, 145–6, 147–8
    numbers of 50, 57, 58, 73, 162, 163
        handbill listing 58, **59**, 60
    origins 73, 162
    payment of 142
        stoppages 143
    as proto-trades unionists 3
    religious dissenters 66
    Thames bargemen, comparison 163–5
    working conditions 50–51
        bond 51, **52**, 53

Keelmen's Hospital 76, 145
keels 1, 14, 24, 36, 54, 56
    annual overhaul 48
    annual rental, profit 98–9
    coal, weight limit 140, 145
    definition xii–xiii
    description of 86–7
    engraving **88**
    measurement of 86
    numbers of 57, 57–8, 60
    ownership 81
        merchants 104, 166
        shipwrights 104, 166
    pann 2
        definition xiii
        Ralph Jackson's work with 138–9, 140, 151–3
    regulation of 60–61
    rental 104–5
    salvaging of 151–3
    valuations 91
Kings Lynn
    boatmen, study 165
    population (1600–1801) 8
Kitch, M.J. 71

Landau, Norma 74
Lasker, G.W., and Roberts, D.F. 46, 72
Lawton, Richard, and Lee, Robert 43
Levine, David, and Wrightson, Keith 46, 71, 74, 78, 162
    The Making of an Industrial Society: Whickham 1560–1765 5
lighters 2, 51, 91fn26, 161
Liverpool, seaborne trade 131–2
London, population (1600–1801) 8
London Company of Watermen and Lightermen 164, 165

Macfarlane, Alan 133, 135
Maddison family 101, 103
Maddison, Henry
    mayor of Newcastle 101
    ships and boats 102
    wealth 101
Maddison, Lionel 101, 103

Maddison, Thomas 103
Magistrates, Common Council of the 4
Marriage Act (1754) 65, 69
Matthews, William 134–5
merchants
    keel ownership 104, 166
    ownership, ships and boats 99–100
Minchinton, W.E. 167
Mokyr, Joel 9
Moll, Herman 24, 26, 28
Moller, A.W.R. 48

Navigation Act (1786), registration of
    vessels 81–2, 167
Nef, J.U. 56, 81
    Rise of the British Coal Industry 12
Newburn 1, 90
Newcastle Chaldron 14, 55, 56
    definition xi
    variations 54
Newcastle Chamberlains' Account books
    38, 40, 41, 60, 115, 121, 139, 154
Newcastle Colliers 27
Newcastle Common Council 3, 4
    Minute Books 38
Newcastle Company of Merchant Venturers
    16
Newcastle Inwards Overseas book 122
Newcastle Overseas Inwards and Outwards
    Port Book (1698–9) 121
Newcastle Port Books 56, 121, 154
    studies of 112–13, 114–15
Newcastle upon Tyne
    Baltic trade 107, 109, 124
    Bristol, shipments, comparison 131, 168
    butter exports 20
    cargo shipments 116, 169
    coal shipments (1600–1800) 13
    coal shipments (1702–03) 116
    coal trade 1, 113
        characteristics 16
        exports, Europe 12, 141
        predominance 11–12, 168, 170
    coal-mining 20
    Coastal Inwards port book 115
    Coastal Outwards port book 115

Defoe on 7, 12
expansion 43–4
exports 12, 113
    table 122
Head Port 111
Hearth Tax returns 45, 53
hinterland 12
historiography, reappraisal 170–71
imports 113, 126
    cloth 126
    food 126
    main commodities, table 126
    timber 126
Improvement Acts, nineteenth century
    171
industries 20
map (1736) 33, **35**, 36
population
    1560-1831: 44
    1600-1801: 8
    1700-1840, changing 47
    1750: 69
    evidence for 45–6
Register of Freemen 45
salt shipments (1702–03) 116
sea traffic, high volumes 113
shipments (1698–99)
    inward
        overseas 123, 124
            ports of origin 123, 124, 125
    outwards
        coastal 122
        overseas 122
            foreign ports 121, 123
            most common cargoes 123
shipments (1702–03)
    inwards coastal 119, 124
        ports of origin 120
    London imports 120
    non-coal commodities 118
    non-London destinations 119
    outwards
        coastal 116
        overseas 122
shipments (1703), outwards, coastal 127
shipments (1756)

outwards
    coastal 127
    non-coal commodities 128
    non-London destinations 128
  spirits, imports of 108
  timber imports 124
  see also Burgesses of Newcastle
North East, consumption, boom 107, 111
Norwich, population (1600–1801) 8

Overton, M. 90
Oxford, Fisher Row 164
  study 163

parish burial registers, under registration 67
Parish Registers 53
Pearson, Robin 92
Petty, William 67
Plymouth, population (1600–1801) 8
port books 111–12
  Bristol 112, 130, 168
  Bristol Channel, ports in 114, 130
  limitations 112
  see also Exchequer Port Books; Newcastle Port Books
Prior, Mary, *Fisher Row* 163, 164
probate inventories 82, 83, 165, 166
  accuracy of 103–4
  consumables in 108
  examples 95, 96, 96–7
  hostmen 100
  ship and boat ownership 83–4
property, ownership, sources of evidence 82

Register of Shipping 92
Riddell, Lady 39
river transport 11
roads, turnpike toll finance 10
Robinson, A.W.H. 24

St Andrew parish 63, **64**
St John parish 63, **64**
St Nicholas parish 63, **64**
Salisbury, population (1600–1801) 8
salt-making, Tyne 20
  decline 114

salt-trade 113
Sandgate 45, 63, 76
  population 53
Scammell, Lorna 108
Selby, William 16
Seller, John, *The English Pilot* 24
settlement laws 74–5
Severn, River, water trades 165
ship masters, hostmen
  negotiations 140, 153
  services from 148–9
ships and boats
  cargo 92
  longevity 92
  ownership 81, 94
    by decade **85**, **93**
    by parish 84
    Henry Maddison 102
    hostmen 100–101
    merchants 99–100
    occupations 94–6
    patterns 105–6
    shipwrights 97–9
    studies 167
  registration of 81–2
  on the Tyne (1600–1750) **86**
  valuations 83–4, 90–91, 92, 93, 94
  see also keels
shipwrights
  Company of 4
    Minutes and Order Book 98
  definition xiii
  keel ownership 104, 166
  ownership, ships and boats 97–9
  trading networks, contribution to 166–7
skippers 66, 67
  definition xiii
South Shields 33, 171
spirits, imports, Newcastle 108
Sunderland 23
Sutton, Thomas 16

Thames, River
  bargemen
    Newcastle keelmen, comparison 163–5

see also Oxford, Fisher Row
  navigability 164
timber, imports, Newcastle upon Tyne 124
Trinder, Barrie 165
Trows 165
Turner, E.R. 144
Tyne, River
  All Saints parish see All Saints parish
  Anglican parishes, map **64**
  ballast
    deposition of 23, 37–8, 113
    hills (shores) 37, 38
      1702 and 1756 41, 42
    management of 38–40, 41, 42
    quantities 41
  Bill Quay 28
  coal exports 55–8, 61
  communities 27
  Dents Hole 28
  depths 26–7, 30, 32–3
  docks 33
  engraving, *South East Prospect of Newcastle upon Tyne* 33, **34**
  Fallenshore (mod.Felling) 28
  food exports 61
  Fryers Goose 28
  glass manufacturing 20, 38, 113–14
  Glasshouse Bridge 27
  Howdon 28, 33
  industries 89
  Jarrow 28, 33
  maps
    1650: 24, **25**, 26–7, 30
    1693: 28, **29**, 30
    1700–1750: **31**, 32
    1736: 26, **35**, 36
    1765: 32
  navigability 23, 37, 149–50, 169–70
  navigation hazards 30
  Navy recruitment 150–51
  North Shields 10, 33
  Ouseburn 56
  Petershore (mod.St Peters) 27
  salt making 20
    decline 114
  salt-pans 28

  sandbanks 26
  Sandgate 45, 63, 76
    population 53
  ships
    number using 27
    types 27
  South Shields 33, 171
  tidal range 1, 30, 161, 162
  water-borne trade 20
  Woolington Ballast Quay (mod. Willington Quay) 28, 32
  wrecks, clearing of 48–9
Tyne and Wear Archives 73
Tynemouth 171
Tynemouth Priory 17

urban population, England (1600–1801), table 8

vend 18, 19, 141
  definition xiv
Viall, H.R. 86–7
Ville, S.P. 167

wagons, wheel-based 10–11
Wallis, Robert 117
War of Spanish Succession, outbreak (1702) 114
Ward, Ralph 135, 136, 150, 157
Water Serjeant 39
water trades
  All Saints parish 70, 71, 74, 76, 162
  community 161
  numbers 62
  occupations 66–7
  population estimates 48
  sources 5–6, 53
watermen 66, 67
  definition xv
wherrymen 66, 67
wherrys 2
  construction 89
  definition xv
  size 89–90
  surviving examples 90
Whickham

community study 5, 16, 162
migration 46–7, 72
Willan, T.S. 11, 20, 113
   Studies in Elizabethan Foreign Trade 112
   The English Coasting Trade 1600–1750 112
wills, proving of 82–3

Winkhamlee Staith 139–40
Wood, Fiona 165
Woodward, D. 112
Wrigley, E.A., and Schofield, R.S. 65
Wylam 1

York, population (1600-1801) 8